Also by Linda Chavez

Out of the Barrio (1991)

An Unli
Conserv

An Unlikely Conservative

THE TRANSFORMATION OF AN EX-LIBERAL

[Or, How I Became the Most Hated Hispanic in America]

LINDA CHAVEZ

BASIC
BOOKS

A Member of the
Perseus Books Group

Copyright © 2002 by Linda Chavez
Published by Basic Books,
A Member of the Perseus Books Group

Designed by Janice Tapia

Library of Congress Cataloging-in-Publication Data
Chavez, Linda
  An unlikely conservative : the transformation of an ex-liberal, or, how I became the most hated Hispanic in America / Linda Chavez.
    p. cm.
  Includes bibliographical references and index.
    ISBN 0-465-08903-8
  1. Chavez, Linda. 2. Women politicians—United States—Biography. 3. Hispanic American politicians—United States—Biography. 4. Hispanic American women—United States—Biography. 5. Politicians—United States—Biography. 6. Conservatism—United States. 7. United States—Politics and government—1945–1998. 8. United States—Politics and government—1989–. I. Title.
  E840.8.C435 A3 2002
  973.92'092—dc21

                                          2002006058

First Edition
02 03 04 05 / 10 9 8 7 6 5 4 3 2 1

For my husband, Chris,
the love of my life

And my mother, Velma,
for all her sacrifices on my behalf

Contents

Acknowledgments

DESPITE HAVING LED A PUBLIC LIFE for some two decades, I am, by nature, a very private person. The decision to write this book was a difficult one. I could not have done it without the encouragement of my husband, Chris, who has stood by my side through bad times and good. I also wish to thank my children—David, Pablo, and Rudy—who have been the joy of my life. If it were not for the love and understanding of my family over the years, I would never have accomplished anything. They are my inspiration and my refuge. To my mother, who may find some of what I have written painful, I express my deepest love and gratitude for her strength and endurance.

My agent, Eric Simonoff, and my editor, Jo Ann Miller, helped nurture this project with patience and insight. I am indebted to Jennifer Swearingen for her careful copyediting, which helped polish this manuscript, and to Candace Taylor for her work in preparing the manuscript. I was also aided by the advice of several readers of early drafts of individual chapters, including John J. Miller, Roger Clegg, Tom Klingenstein, and Max Green—thank you. Thanks also to Nancy Barnes, my informal archivist, for saving so many important documents, notes, and photographs, which made my research so much easier. I am also indebted to John Garcia and Paul Horvat, who assisted me in tracing my family history in New Mexico, and to Mark Hellweg, who tracked down references for me at the Library of Congress. The Earhart Foundation in Ann Arbor, Michigan, provided a small grant for research related to this book, for which I am grateful.

Prologue: On Top of the World

Heav'n from all creatures hides the book of Fate

—Alexander Pope, *Essay on Man*

THE CALL INVITING ME TO AUSTIN came on New Year's Eve 2000. Clay Johnson, the head of president-elect George W. Bush's transition office, reached me at my Washington office, where I was dutifully filling out reams of paperwork I'd been asked to complete in the event that the president-elect nominated me to become his secretary of labor. Johnson, a no-nonsense Texas businessman, seemed surprised that I was spending the holidays at work. "The president-elect will be impressed when I tell him," he said. "He wants to meet with you one more time. Can you come to Austin tomorrow evening?"

I was thrilled. Johnson wasn't exactly telling me I'd been picked for the post, but I couldn't imagine that the president-elect would send for me on a holiday just to ask a few more questions. Bush had already spent an hour interviewing me a few days earlier at the Madison Hotel in Washington, and his parting words were, "I'm going to think about this over the weekend. We'll be in touch."

I first met George W. Bush in the Texas governor's office in June 1998. Bush had not yet announced his presidential candidacy, but even two years out, he was already viewed as the odds-on favorite to capture the Republican nomination. A friend had suggested that I meet with Bush on one of my frequent visits to Texas and had called Karl Rove, Bush's longtime political strategist, to arrange it.

I went into the first meeting with Governor Bush with low expectations. I imagined him to be a moderate in the mold of his father, President George Bush, whom I admired for his personal qualities but whose policies had been a disappointment to me. We talked for nearly an hour, with Bush's press secretary, Karen Hughes, and Rove the only others present. Bush listened as much as he spoke, asking questions, venturing opinions with an easy, open manner, much like his mother, Barbara. Governor Bush mentioned having been greatly influenced by the book *The Dream and the Nightmare: The Sixties' Legacy to the Underclass* by Myron Magnet. I knew the book well, since both Magnet and I had worked at the Manhattan Institute, a libertarian-leaning New York think tank, in the early 1990s. The book's central thesis—that the counterculture values of the sixties had helped to create and perpetuate the underclass—was one widely shared by neoconservatives, like me, who had come of age during that period and had crossed the political Rubicon from Left to Right during the Reagan era.

I came into the meeting with Governor Bush expecting to meet an affable politician. Instead I encountered someone who could talk seriously about ideas. He discussed with passion the plight of the black family in America and the problem of rising out-of-wedlock birthrates among all racial groups, voicing concern about the growing number of births to Hispanic teenagers as well. He also spoke of the power of the bully pulpit, the need for clear moral direction, and the failure of leadership from Washington during the Clinton years. We talked briefly about his political ambitions, too. He told me that he hadn't decided whether to run for president and that he worried about what a presidential campaign would mean for his twin teenage daughters. "They'll be entering college, and that's a very special time for any young person." I left the meeting impressed not only with the future presidential candidate but with the man. Waiting for a taxi outside the state capitol, I called my husband, Chris Gersten, from my cell phone. "We've found our candidate," I announced.

Some months later, Indianapolis mayor Steven Goldsmith called and asked me to head a task force on immigration issues for the Bush campaign. Goldsmith—a brainy, innovative two-term mayor—had been assigned the role of issues coordinator for the campaign. My function would be informal and sporadic, answering specific questions on policy as they arose and flagging hot-button issues that the candidate might be expected to address on the campaign trail. I pulled together a group of like-minded immigration experts, all of whom were on record favoring generous immigration levels and opposing the onerous restrictions popular among some conservatives.

Certainly nothing in my relationship with Governor Bush during the next two years suggested that I might have a shot at a high-level political appointment if he were elected. I provided advice to the campaign, attended the Republican Convention in Philadelphia at the Bush campaign's request, and made a few campaign appearances on television and around the country, describing Bush's virtues and Al Gore's failings. Like most Americans, I found the long delay in determining the outcome of the election maddening—and I blamed Gore entirely. Gore's behavior had been objectionable during the election—inciting class hatred, race-baiting, and scaring seniors into thinking that Bush would take away Social Security. But it seemed more dangerous in the weeks the Florida debacle dragged on. Gore's legal challenges were a pure power grab meant to delegitimate a Bush presidency—if not usurp it altogether.

It wasn't just Gore and the Democratic Party that infuriated me, however. I also became enraged at the AFL-CIO's role in the Florida mess. I had once been a labor union official, but the labor movement had veered toward the Left since then—and sharply so when John Sweeney became president of the AFL-CIO in 1995. Under Sweeney's helm, organized labor had become more immersed in partisan politics than ever before. In the 2000 campaign, labor unions contributed $75 million in direct contributions to political candidates—almost all of them Democrats—plus additional millions in so-called soft money donations. By one estimate, unions spent $800 million in support of Democrats, much of it hidden, with Al Gore's campaign the chief beneficiary.[1]

Sweeney also dispensed hundreds of union staffers to Florida to monitor the recount and generate guerrilla street theater. The AFL-CIO troops joined forces with civil rights leaders, including Jesse Jackson, who accused Republicans of trying to disenfranchise black and elderly voters. "It seems that in West Palm Beach, the African Americans and the Jewish senior citizens were targeted," Jackson claimed, with nothing to back it up. Sweeney himself joined Jesse Jackson for a massive protest in Tallahassee the day after the U.S. Supreme Court stopped the Florida recount, which effectively ended the election haggle in Bush's favor. The Left went ballistic. "He will be president legally. But he does not have moral authority, because his crown did not come from the people. It came from the judges," Jackson declared, with Sweeney at his side.

Sweeney's actions infuriated me, but my anger was personal as well as partisan. Many Americans know me from my years in the Reagan administration, as director of the U.S. Commission on Civil Rights and then director of the White House public liaison office. Before joining the Reagan administration, however, I had worked in the labor movement for nine years. For most of that time, I was editor of the quarterly magazine of the American Federation of Teachers, *American Educator*, where I had been given almost free rein by AFT president Albert Shanker to produce a journal of ideas. Many of my views, most notably on affirmative action and bilingual education, were formed during that period and were profoundly influenced by Shanker, whom I regarded as a mentor. Shanker was not afraid to take principled but unorthodox stands on a variety of issues. In 1968, he led a strike in the Ocean Hill–Brownsville neighborhood of Brooklyn, which lasted fifty-five days and landed him in jail. The strike was prompted not by the usual demand for better wages or working conditions but by a racial power play. A group of black nationalists, funded by the liberal Ford Foundation, had taken over the local school board and fired the white, mostly Jewish teachers, prompting the walkout. Shanker's refusal to back down at a time when university presidents and others were capitulating to the often racist demands of black radicals earned Shanker a national reputation as a staunch opponent of race-based hiring.

With Shanker's blessing, the magazine took on a decidedly neoconservative point of view under my editorship. From 1977 to 1983, I published articles calling for moral education in the schools, decrying the breakdown of the American family, and criticizing bilingual education and race-based preferences in college admissions—written by a host of conservative authors, many of whom were not well known at the time, including William J. Bennett, Robert Bork, Jeane J. Kirkpatrick, and Thomas Sowell. With Shanker's death in 1997 and the labor movement's leftward lurch in recent years, no union would publish such fare today.

As I watched events unfold in Florida, I became convinced that Republicans needed to take on the labor unions if they were to have any hope of winning future presidential elections or retaining control of Congress. I was equally sure that the party was not prepared to do so. Although a handful of Republican congressmen had ties to local unions, virtually no one in the Republican Party had come out of the labor movement or, I believed, truly understood how unions operate in the political arena. Past Republican presidents had had some support from organized labor—both Ronald Reagan and Richard Nixon had won the endorsement of the International Brotherhood of Teamsters—and had received a fair share of union members' votes as well (Reagan won an estimated 47 percent of union households in 1984[2]). But much had changed in the labor movement in the years since. What George W. Bush and the Republican Party needed was someone who could do two things: work to build ties to those unions, mostly in the construction trades, whose members are conservative, relatively affluent, and more likely to vote Republican; and block unions from using their members' dues for illegal political activities. I believed I was that person. And what better position existed to accomplish these objectives than secretary of labor? I combined a tough-minded, free-market attitude on labor issues with an insider's understanding of how unions operate. Now, my only problem was convincing Bush that he needed me.

The delay in determining the outcome of the election made it difficult to launch a campaign for a cabinet appointment. Bush was nervous about appearing to move too quickly to vet candidates, especially after the media criticized him for behaving, briefly, as president-elect, although two official recounts had given him Florida. Nonetheless, I decided to consult a few close friends and some political allies, soliciting their advice. One of the first people I called was Kate O'Beirne, the Washington editor of *National Review* magazine. Kate and I were old friends, and I knew her as someone with excellent political instincts, as well as good relationships on the Hill. She was eager to help and called Dave Hoppe, Senate Majority Leader Trent Lott's chief of staff. The timing couldn't have been better. Hoppe, Lott, and a group of other Republican congressional leaders were on their way to Bush's ranch to meet with the president-to-be. I later learned that someone—Lott or Hoppe—mentioned my name for labor secretary in the meeting. Bush's response, as reported back to me, was surprising: "What will the AFL-CIO think?" The Associated Press carried the first story naming me in a list of candidates for labor secretary, and the story bore a Texas dateline, suggesting that it had been leaked either by someone in the Bush campaign or by one of Bush's recent congressional guests. My candidacy was suddenly real, if still a long shot.

I decided it was time to place a few calls to former colleagues and friends in the labor movement. With my name all over the papers, I had no trouble getting phone calls returned. In typical Washington fashion, people who wouldn't have given me the time of day a few weeks earlier were now ready to declare me their long-lost bosom buddy. I expected that I would have no trouble garnering support among a handful of union presidents who would be eager for access to the new administration. With Republicans in control of Congress and likely to be moving into the White House, union influence in Washington was about to plummet. However, many of the union officials I called were hedging their bets until the outcome of the election was determined by the legal battle taking place in the U.S. Supreme Court. Most weren't ready to commit support until Bush was declared the winner in Florida. Nonetheless, it was clear from several conversations that some officials welcomed my candidacy; at least their phone calls would be returned if I ended up in office. On December 12, the U.S. Supreme Court overturned the Florida Supreme Court ruling that had dragged the Florida recount on for more than five weeks after Election Day, and Al Gore conceded defeat the following day. Now a number of union presidents wanted to be helpful, and none was more solicitous than Sandra Feldman, president of the American Federation of Teachers.

Feldman and I had worked together nearly two decades earlier, when I was editor of AFT publications and she sat on the AFT's executive council as president of the union's most powerful local union, New York City's United Federation of Teachers. We had a cordial relationship, though not a close one. Feldman was Al Shanker's protégé, dating to the Ocean Hill–Brownsville strike, and she was his hand-picked successor as UFT president and his clear choice to succeed him as AFT president. But her politics were not identical to Shanker's on all issues, and nowhere did they differ more than on race. Shanker, like me, was an outspoken critic of racial quotas and skeptical of many affirmative action programs. Feldman, who is married to the former president of the New York City Urban Coalition, was regarded as "soft" on affirmative action by those inside the AFT who shared Shanker's hard-line views. I knew when I called Sandy that my position on affirmative action might make her unlikely to assist me. I was pleasantly surprised when she seemed ready to help.

"Who would have ever imagined we'd be having this conversation when we got to be grown-ups?" she laughed, when I reached her at her Washington apartment. I told her that I expected opposition to my nomination from some of the civil rights leaders, mentioning Jesse Jackson in particular, but that I hoped I would get a fair hearing from the AFL-CIO. She offered to talk to AFL-CIO president John Sweeney, whom she'd be meeting with in a few days. She also said that although the AFT usually hewed to the AFL's position on nominations, it wasn't inconceivable that the AFT might take its own position or remain neutral if the AFL-CIO decided to oppose me.

A week later, Sandy called me from the Washington–New York Metroliner on her way home to New York for the holidays to report on her conversation with Sweeney. "You've got more opposition there than I thought," she said, but she still held out hope that the AFT would take, at worst, a neutral position. She also mentioned that Sweeney was miffed that the president-elect had not called him. "That's not right, Linda. It makes Sweeney look bad in front of his own executive council," she said, noting that Sweeney had reported to the fifty-member council that he had placed a call to congratulate Bush, which had not been returned. I wondered, silently, whether Sweeney had placed the call before or after he had stood by Jesse Jackson's side to declare the Bush presidency illegitimate.

Over the next few days, I continued to talk to labor union officials, including the presidents of the bricklayers and operating engineers unions, who were more receptive to my views on affirmative action and other social issues, if not on economic issues. I also met with some key senators and congressmen to press my candidacy. Oklahoma Senator Don Nickles, the Republican assistant majority leader, was supportive but pessimistic. "We might get a filibuster over your nomination. Maybe we could win a cloture vote," he offered, none too reassuringly. One of the more conservative members of the Senate, Nickles understood well that I would be a lightning rod for liberal groups if nominated. I also met with Representative Rob Portman of Ohio, who was not only a close adviser to the Bush transition team but also an old friend from our days serving on a United Nations subcommission in Geneva in the early 1990s.

"Have you talked to anyone in Austin or at the transition office?" Portman asked when I told him I was interested in joining the administration. I admitted that despite numerous media accounts that I was under consideration for the labor post, no one had yet contacted me. With the nightly television news programs showing potential cabinet members going in and out of the new Bush-Cheney transition office in the Virginia suburbs, I interpreted the lack of contact as an ominous sign. "Maybe I should just call Karl Rove," I said. Portman suggested that I e-mail him instead and gave me Rove's private e-mail address. I went back to my office and sent Rove a brief note. Within hours he wrote back: "Some folks have raised questions about things you've written, and I've answered them as best I could. But it would be helpful if you'd send me copies of all your articles." I spent the rest of the afternoon copying hundreds of newspaper and magazine articles I'd written over the previous decade.

On the following Monday, December 18, I flew to San Francisco for a board of directors meeting for ABM Industries, where I serve as a director. As I walked through the terminal, I heard my name paged over the intercom. I called my office from my cell phone. "You've got to get back here right away," my assistant, Amanda Butler, told me. "Clay Johnson's office called. You're scheduled to be interviewed tomorrow afternoon. I've already booked your return." Apparently the e-mail to Rove had worked. I was now officially a candidate for secretary of labor.

The trip back to Washington proved more complicated than expected. My seventy-nine-year-old mother was due to arrive on December 19 from Albuquerque, flying into Baltimore–Washington International Airport, about an hour-and-a-half drive from my farm in Loudoun County, Virginia. My husband was supposed to pick her up, while I flew into Dulles Airport about the same time and drove myself to the interview. Before leaving for the San Francisco Airport that morning, I turned on the television to check the weather: A big snowstorm was predicted to hit the Washington area that afternoon. Even a few inches of snow can virtually shut down the city, so I knew my meeting with

Johnson could be jeopardized. I called my office and home every hour or so from the plane to monitor the storm on the ground. By midafternoon, a foot of snow had already accumulated at my farm, trapping my husband. I had taken our only four-wheel-drive vehicle, a Dodge Dakota pickup, to the airport. Now he had no way to get my mother in Baltimore.

"It's not a problem. I'm meeting with Johnson at five o'clock, and she's not due in until nine. I'll just drive to BWI after my interview," I told him.

Snow was coming down heavily when I landed. The flight was late getting in, and the drive from Dulles to the transition office in McLean was torturously slow. Road conditions were so bad that it took all my concentration to keep from losing control of my unwieldy truck, with no time to think about my impending interview. I pulled into the parking lot of the nondescript suburban office building around six-thirty—an hour and a half late for my appointment. Television satellite dishes surrounded the building, as journalists tried to get a glimpse of who was coming and going. I was worried that someone would recognize me, but the snow must have driven away most of the veteran reporters, and I sneaked in undetected. Johnson was busy on his daily conference call with Karl Rove and other staffers in Austin, so I waited about half an hour before his secretary, Brooke Vosburgh, who had worked with me in the Reagan White House, ushered me in.

Johnson looked exhausted. He had clearly been putting in sixteen-hour days, seven days a week. His temporary office was sparsely furnished with the standard government-issue Formica desk and table and dark, metal blinds. We sat opposite each other in plastic chairs. He told me a little about himself, that he had known George Bush since their days at Andover, that he had come out of the business world, that he had handled political appointments when Bush first became governor. "I'm the guy who decides if the candidates are qualified to do the job. I'm here to look at merit," he said. His deep voice fit his six-foot-three-inch frame and gave away his Texas roots. I handed him a folder containing my resumé and a few columns I'd written.

"Tell me about yourself," he said, "your family, where you come from." I outlined a brief history, trying to include relevant facts without overloading him with details he probably didn't want to hear. He took notes on a yellow legal pad as I talked, saying almost nothing. Then, flipping to a blank page, he turned the notepad to me.

"This is what I know about the labor department," he said. "I'd like you to help me fill in the blanks. This isn't some kind of test. I just don't know what the department does, and I expect you do," he insisted.

I proceeded to describe the various functions of the department and map out the challenges, including how the department could be used as both a carrot and a stick to deal with the troublesome labor movement.

We talked for nearly an hour, and I grew nervous thinking about my mother getting off the plane at BWI with no one to greet her. I looked at my watch.

"I've got to pick up my mother in Baltimore," I apologized.

"You go ahead. But this is the process—if we proceed to the next step. The president-elect will want to meet with you personally, either here or in Austin. And we've got Fred Fielding handling the sensitive stuff. I guess you probably know Fred from the Reagan White House."

Indeed I did. Fielding's office was right next to mine on the second floor of the West Wing when I was President Reagan's director of public liaison. Now an attorney in private practice, Fielding is one of Washington's premier power brokers.

"Fred will ask you whether there's anything in your background that might embarrass the president. And if there is, we'll deal with it. But if you keep anything back and it comes out, you're on your own."

I took it all in casually, but Johnson's words were later to come back to haunt me as I replayed the mental tape of our conversation over and over again in the weeks to come.

As with everything else that day, I arrived late to pick up my mother. Her plane came in a little early, despite the snow, and by the time I got to the gate, the passengers had all deplaned. I looked around but didn't see her anywhere. I asked the lone agent at the desk whether the wheelchair passengers were off the plane yet.

"Are you the lady coming in from San Francisco?" she asked. My mother, in her usual fashion, had probably told the agent my life story while she was explaining her situation. "She's over there," she said motioning to my mother sitting in a wheelchair, hidden behind a huge, orange pillar. Each time I had seen my mother in recent years, I had been shocked by how little and frail she appeared. The glamorous blond with china-blue eyes and porcelain skin was now a tiny, white-haired waif of a figure, and she had become even more so since her bout with breast cancer three years earlier. Still, she was beaming, and her skin looked, as always, smooth and flawless, with hardly a wrinkle to show for her nearly eight decades.

"Well, how'd it go?" she asked, eager to hear about the interview. I told her everything as I wheeled her through the terminal to the baggage claim. "I don't know why you want this job," she said, expressing her often-voiced fear about my going back into public life. "But if it's what you really want, I'm glad to hear it went well." She both relished the notoriety and hated the criticism I frequently provoked with my controversial stands on public policy issues.

We arrived home after a harrowing drive through western Maryland, with the snow blowing so hard that I drove my pickup off the road without realizing it. Thankfully, few vehicles were on the highway that night. But the ones that had ventured out were all fifty-three-foot tractor trailers that seemed to navigate the road by radar, blasting past me at sixty miles an hour, throwing brown slush against my already obscured windshield. I was so exhausted when I finally got home, I fell into bed immediately. But I couldn't sleep.

"I think I may have a problem," I told my husband, Chris, as we lay awake talking about my conversation with Clay Johnson. "If I tell them about Marta, they're not likely to pick me. If I don't tell them, they're likely to find out anyway," I said.

Marta was a Guatemalan woman who had lived with us for about a year nearly a decade earlier. A friend and professional colleague, Peter Skerry, had asked me whether I might give her a place to live temporarily. At the time, Marta was living with a woman who worked for Peter and his wife, but the situation was becoming untenable. I agreed to take her in, as I had several other people over the years. I had given Vietnamese refugees, out-of-work friends and relatives, and neglected children a place to live, sometimes for several weeks or months, much as I had been helped by friends and relatives as a child. But, unlike the others I'd helped, Marta was an illegal alien. At the time she moved into my house, the furor over illegal aliens was becoming a hot political issue. A majority of Americans—65 percent according to public opinion polls at the time— were skeptical of legal immigration in the early 1990s and were overwhelmingly opposed to illegal immigration. By 1993, when Zoe Baird, President Clinton's first nominee for attorney general, revealed that she employed an illegal alien couple as a nanny and driver, the anti-immigrant backlash had reached fever pitch, and the revelation doomed her nomination.[3] In the wake of "Nannygate," the question of who vacuumed a nominee's house or babysat the children was as likely to derail a nominee's approval as suspicious ties to foreign governments or financial conflicts of interest. I was worried that my relationship with an illegal alien would cause similar problems if I became a nominee, even if the circumstances were different.

"You worry too much," Chris said.

"You're probably right," I answered, not fully believing my own words.

The following day, my youngest son, Rudy, graduated from the University of Maryland. With my mother in town and Christmas just days away, I had little time even to think about my candidacy. The whole family—including my two other, married sons, David and Pablo—attended Rudy's commencement ceremony at Cole Field House that evening. After dinner in College Park, it was too late to drive home, so Chris and I stayed at a motel near the campus. For the second night in a row, my sleep was fitful. I awoke early the next morning, anxious. I needed more information before I could decide whether my relationship with Marta would sabotage my chances of becoming secretary of labor. I couldn't even remember what year she had lived with us and had no idea how to find her now. Although she had returned to Guatemala after living with me, I knew she was back in the United States because she had come by to visit a few years later, with her new baby boy. She was now married to an American citizen and, as far as I knew, was a legal U.S. resident, but I'd lost track of her again when she changed phone numbers.

There was one person, however, who might at least be able to provide me with a clue to when Marta lived in my house: my former neighbor, Margaret Zwisler, for whom Marta had worked when she was living with me. I knew Peggy and her husband, Carl, only casually. A pretty, petite woman about my age, Peggy lived in the same cul-de-sac in Bethesda where I had lived for fourteen years. I saw her occasionally at neighbors' parties, where she struck me as typical of the hard-charging and tightly wound attorneys that define much of the Washington social scene. What I did not know was that Peggy was a partner in the same law firm as W. Neil Eggleston, Bill Clinton's former White House lawyer, or that her brother was Terry Moran, White House correspondent for ABC News.

I called Peggy's home first, where her maid gave me her direct line at work. Peggy seemed surprised to hear my voice.

"I'm not sure whether you've seen the news stories yet, but I may be a candidate to become secretary of labor," I told her, after exchanging brief pleasantries.

"No, I haven't seen them, but that's great. Congratulations," she said.

"There may be one problem, and I have to decide whether to pursue the job or not. You remember Marta?" I asked.

"Gee, I forgot we shared Marta," she said.

I thought that was an odd way of putting it. It sounded almost as if she considered Marta a commodity, but I went on anyway. "If you felt it necessary to go public about Marta, I probably won't pursue the job."

"Look, if you're asking me what I thought about Zoe Baird," Peggy responded, "I think she got screwed. And I think Kimba Woods got screwed even worse," she said, referring to Clinton's second nominee for attorney general, who withdrew her name after allegations she also employed an illegal alien.

Peggy was right, of course. I was a frequent and vocal critic of the Immigration Reform and Control Act, which brought down Baird and Woods, writing in 1993 that the law "succeeded only in penalizing employers like Zoe Baird while having no discernible impact on reducing illegal immigration."[4] Nonetheless, in my mind the Baird-Woods situations were not analogous to mine. I hadn't gone out looking to hire a nanny or housekeeper. Marta had come to me needing a place to live, and I'd obliged, assuming it would be for a short time. But the weeks turned into months, and I became increasingly involved in her life, typing up advertisements for her to hand out in the neighborhood so that she could find work, helping her enroll in English classes, giving her clothes, books, and occasionally, money. I did all the household cooking, but she chipped in to help around the house, as any long-term guest would, especially when I went out of town. She spent most of her time in her room, depressed and unhappy, often crying for the daughters she left behind in Guatemala. Although I tried to befriend her as best I could, with my poor Spanish and her trouble with English, communication was difficult. But I managed to learn enough to know that her life had been very hard in Guatemala and that she was hopeful that one day she could bring her daughters to America.

"I don't know how much you knew about Marta's situation when I took her in, but she was escaping a violent relationship and was in desperate shape. She had no place else to go," I said.

"Yeah, I remember she got beat up pretty badly that one time." Peggy was referring to an incident that had occurred while Marta lived with me. One day, Marta came home after being away for a few days, with her eyes blackened and her lips horribly swollen and split open. She looked as if she'd been in a car accident, and I asked her if she needed to go to the doctor. Then she told me what had happened. She'd been at a party and one of the men, an American, had assaulted her. I persuaded her to let me call the police on her behalf, and they interviewed her in my living room, with me at her side. But in the end, she wouldn't press charges against the man who had beat her.

"Do you remember what year she worked for you?" I asked, hoping Peggy could fill in the blanks in my own memory. I knew it was the early nineties but couldn't remember the exact year.

"No. If only I could remember which baby I had at the time," she said.

"I think it was your little girl," I replied.

"Well then it must have been '95."

"It was earlier than that, I'm sure."

Suddenly, Peggy's voice sounded agitated. "You know it wasn't against the law to hire illegal aliens back then," she said. I didn't contradict her, though I knew full well that the law barring employers from hiring illegal aliens dated to 1986. The Immigration Reform and Control Act made it illegal to hire undocumented aliens, forcing all employers to determine whether prospective employees were born in the United States or have the proper work permits, called "green cards," to work here. The law places exactly the same administrative burden on individuals employing one person to clean their house or care for their children—even part-time or for a few months—as it does on corporations employing thousands of employees, with full-service human resources departments to handle the paperwork. Despite the sweeping and punitive nature of the law, it has been largely ineffective. Today, more than a decade and a half after the law was enacted, the number of illegal aliens in the United States has increased exponentially to an estimated ten million.

"You just had to pay the taxes on them. And I paid taxes on Marta," Peggy asserted.

I didn't argue with her, although I knew Marta had no Social Security number at the time, so it would have been difficult to pay taxes on her wages.

"Why would anybody ask me about Marta?" she asked, now with a slight edge in her voice. I had clearly touched a raw nerve.

"I don't know that anyone will, but the liberal interest groups will be trying to dig up anything they can about me. I'm not their favorite person. This is the kind of issue they often use to derail a nomination. And the FBI will do a background check. They usually talk to the neighbors. Of course, if they ask you about Marta, you'll have to tell them the truth," I added, though I hardly needed to remind an attorney of her obligation to be truthful to the FBI.

"Well, I don't have to volunteer anything. I can't imagine it will come up. But I'll let you know what happens," she added.

Perhaps alarm bells should have sounded when Peggy became defensive about her hiring an illegal alien, but none did. With Peggy's assurances that she didn't intend to make an issue of Marta's stay in my home, I put the issue out of my mind.

For the next few days, I spent time shopping for Christmas gifts and entertaining my mother—who was content to stay at home watching game shows and doing crossword puzzles. Meanwhile president-elect Bush was announcing cabinet and White House appointments every other day. But I had done what I could to promote my candidacy—getting senators to make calls, strategizing with business lobbyists, soliciting a few union presidents to weigh in on my behalf. Now I had to wait patiently.

It was easier than I had expected. I felt a kind of equanimity about the job. I wanted it—but not that badly. I had a great life. I enjoyed what I did, running my own organization, writing my weekly syndicated column, giving paid speeches around the country. I had time for my two granddaughters—Phoebe, 4, and Abby, 1—seeing them several times a week. I loved living in the country, far away from the bustle and noise, something I was loathe to give up if I did become secretary of labor, although I knew I would have to since the fifty-mile commute to Washington would be too long to make every day. Besides, what was I going to do with my dogs if I had to take an apartment in the city? It was a standing joke in my family that my three dogs controlled all our lives. Sam, a fourteen-year-old white standard poodle, was on her last legs, almost blind, largely toothless. But she still dragged her decrepit old body to the door, wagging her tail when I came home from every trip, and I couldn't imagine putting her down.

I didn't expect that anything would happen the week between Christmas and New Year's, but I knew from the nightly news that Bush was scheduled to come to Washington at the end of the week. There were only a handful of cabinet selections still to be announced, among them secretary of labor. Nonetheless, I didn't hear anything all week. As I was cooking dinner Thursday evening, the phone rang.

"Linda, this is Kathleen Shanahan, vice president-elect Cheney's assistant. Your meeting with the president-elect and vice president-elect tomorrow morning has to be pushed back to nine o'clock. We want to pick you up and drive you to the Madison Hotel. We've got a way to whisk folks into the garage and up the service entrance so the press doesn't get a look at who's coming in. Where will you be at eight-thirty? And will that give us enough time?" Her breakneck speed took my breath away. No one had called me about any meeting, but I decided not to let on that I had no idea what she was talking about.

"I can be at my downtown office by eight-thirty. I'm just a couple of blocks from the Madison," I told her.

"Let's make it eight-fifteen, just in case. Do you have a cell phone we can reach you on?" We exchanged cell numbers so we could be in touch with each other if the need arose. I hung up and told my husband and mother, who were standing in the kitchen, that I was going to meet with Bush and Cheney in the morning.

"What are you going to wear?" my mother asked. Leave it to my mother to put things in proper perspective. I owned three good suits, and they had seen more than their fair share of use in recent days. I hoped at least one of them was clean.

The next morning, decked out in my best periwinkle-blue knit, I headed for Washington, with my son David driving my Dodge Dakota. I loved my pick-up, with its dirt-encrusted truck bed looking the worse for the daily mile-long drive along the gravel path that led to my log cabin. It was the first new vehi-cle I'd ever owned, and I knew it didn't fit my image, which made it that much more appealing. There was no traffic on the Dulles toll road or on I-66, the main arteries into Washington from the far-flung Virginia suburbs, and the D.C. streets were nearly deserted on this Friday before the long New Year's weekend. As we stopped at a traffic light at Connecticut and H Streets, just a couple of blocks from the White House, Bill Bennett crossed the intersection, looking older and heavier than the last time I'd seen him.

"Hey, Bill," I yelled, sticking my head out the window. He waved, no doubt thinking I was one of his many fans. Then he realized it was me.

"Out awfully early aren't you, Linda?" It was only about seven-thirty.

"You, too," I smiled, wondering if he was headed to the Madison himself or perhaps had been there already. I hadn't heard his name mentioned for a cab-inet position, and certainly his endorsement of John McCain in the primaries hadn't helped his cause. But Bennett was one of the most ambitious men I'd ever known—and one of the most talented. I wouldn't have been surprised to hear that he was headed back into the new Republican administration in some capacity.

At eight-fifteen precisely, the phone in my office rang. I was to proceed to the front of my building where a black SUV was waiting to drive me to the Madison. The temperature had remained cold all week, and it was drizzling outside, so I donned my heavy, black sheepskin coat, turning up the collar to conceal my face. I put on a blue cowboy hat to complete my disguise, figur-ing if anyone did see me, they'd think I was some big-haired Texas matron in the president-to-be's entourage. The young man who drove me was a volun-teer out of the Texas campaign headquarters. He had just come back from Florida, where he worked around the clock in the recount fight. Now he was part of the driving pool, hoping to end up in the administration come January 20.

We pulled into the underground parking lot next to the hotel, where a Central American garage attendant motioned us down the ramp. Another young man with a walkie-talkie pointed to an empty lane, where the driver parked the car, leaving the engine running. When we got out of the vehicle, other young men, who looked like Secret Service agents, directed us up a service elevator, past food trolleys loaded with dirty dishes and large laundry bins filled with soiled pink tablecloths.

"Sorry, ma'am, you'll have to walk up the last flight. We've blocked off the president-elect's floor," my escort informed me. Great, I thought. My coat weighed at least ten pounds. I fretted that I'd arrive for my meeting with Bush panting and sweating. Thankfully, I was ushered into a small holding room, really just a regular hotel room with a couch in place of a bed, where I could catch my breath. A large console with trays of half-eaten fruit, croissants, and coffee sat against one wall of the room. The television was tuned to one of the morning shows.

"Good morning," Clay Johnson greeted me, as he strode into the small room. "It's cold out there."

"Where's your overcoat?" I asked. He seemed startled at the question. Perhaps I was being a bit too familiar.

"My coat? It's on its way here from Texas in a box, along with the rest of my entire household." His tone softened.

"Well, maybe you better take an hour or two off and buy another one. It could get nasty." Why was I playing housemother to this man my own age who showed no interest in small talk? I was more nervous than I realized. Thankfully, a group of military personnel crowded into the room before I could say something even more inane. They had obviously just completed Bush's daily national security briefing. One of the men introduced himself, reminding me that we had met before. I drew a complete blank, but I covered my memory loss well.

"You ready?" Johnson, still standing, asked.

"As ready as I'll ever be."

We entered the larger, crowded room next door while Bush and half a dozen others were pouring themselves coffee. A Mexican American man about my age said hello on his way out the door. He looked like a Secret Service agent, probably on detail from the Texas office. Just as Bill Clinton and Al Gore, two Southerners, had made conscious efforts to include black agents in their personal retinues, I thought Bush, a Texan, would likely make a similar statement by including Hispanics.

"Morning, Linda." Bush reached out and gave me a quick hug and peck on the cheek. I was struck again by how much better looking he was in person than on television, a trait he shared with his father, who is both more handsome and bigger than he appears on camera. He acted as if we were old friends, though I had met him only a few times and had spoken with him at any length just once. "Want some coffee?"

"Always," I beamed.

He signaled one of the other men in the room to pour me a cup as we wove our way through the maze of chairs and oversized banquet tables blocking our way. He took a seat in a large, upholstered chair facing the hotel windows overlooking 15th Street and the *Washington Post* building. I sat to Bush's left in a similar chair situated at a right angle to his. Cheney and Johnson sat at some distance from Bush, with their backs to the windows, while Andy Card, Bush's newly announced White House chief of staff, sat on the couch opposite my chair and to Bush's right. The elliptical configuration would make it difficult to include everyone in the conversation—exactly what Bush intended. He and I could talk, while he could monitor the others' reactions and I could not. Such things don't happen by accident in Washington. Staffers probably spent considerable time rearranging the furniture until they got it right.

"How's your daughter doing?" I asked. Jenna, one of the Bushes' eighteen-year-old twins, had undergone an emergency appendectomy on Christmas and was recuperating in Texas. The incident caused some snide press attention when Bush decided not to cancel a short Florida fishing vacation with his parents and brother Jeb, leaving Laura Bush to stay home with their daughter.

We chatted about family, mostly his, for several minutes before Bush launched into the matter at hand. His first questions were general, similar to Johnson's. But unlike Clay, Bush interrupted my answers to ask rapid-fire additional questions. This was not the dim-witted Bush of *Saturday Night Live* caricatures.

"What do you think we ought to do about the H-1B program?" he asked, referring to a program that allows some 100,000 immigrants with specialized skills to obtain temporary visas through their employers.

"How about H-2As, is that a labor department program?"

He had me stumped. I knew the program provided visas for agricultural workers, but I wasn't sure which department administered it. He moved on to more questions, now turning to the politics of appointments.

"So who's your likely opposition, and what will they say about you?"

I explained my adversaries were likely to come from civil rights groups that didn't like my position on racial preferences. The labor department runs the biggest federal affirmative action program—administered by the Office of Federal Contract Compliance Programs or OFCCP—and my appointment would be viewed as a huge threat.

"What about the unions?" he asked. I expected the question, knowing he'd raised the same issue when my name first came up at the meeting with Trent Lott in Texas a few weeks earlier.

"I have some support—the Operating Engineers Union, the Bricklayers, and I think the AFT will be okay—and I expect I can get some more support from the building trades, maybe the Carpenters Union and a few others. You know, their members are pretty conservative."

"Yeah, the vice president-elect used to belong to one of those unions, as I recall," Bush smiled.

For the first time, I shifted in my chair to look at Cheney, who joined the banter.

"I put myself through college as an IBEW lineman. Held a union card for years," Cheney noted.

"They're not going to like what you've said on minimum wage," Bush said, bringing the conversation back to me. Like most conservatives, I was skeptical of the benefits of minimum wage laws, believing that they were more likely to lead to fewer entry-level jobs, and had written several columns to that effect. He flipped through some papers in a manila folder, no doubt a briefing memo on my most controversial stands on labor issues.

"By the way, we tracked down that Sweeney call," he added. I had complained to both Clay Johnson and Karl Rove that Sweeney was offended when Bush didn't return his phone call a few weeks earlier. "You're going to fight labor on policy; there's no point ticking them off over some perceived personal slight," I had told them both. But no one in the transition office could find a record of the call, so I got Sandy Feldman's assistant to give me the date, which I passed on to Rove.

"Turns out I returned the wrong John Sweeney's call. I called the guy from New York," Bush laughed, referring to the Republican congressman from the Twenty-Second District in upstate New York.

"Yeah, Congressman Sweeney got two calls from us. He sure wasn't about to 'fess up that he hadn't placed the call," Andy Card piped in for the first time, his Massachusetts accent sounding oddly out of place in this room full of Westerners.

"Why don't you get Sweeney on the phone right now?" Bush directed. Card left the room to place the call, returning quickly to inform Bush that Sweeney was in a meeting but would call back shortly. When Sweeney called back a few minutes later, the conversation was brief but congenial, at least on Bush's end. I was struck most by Bush's modesty. You could tell he was speaking to someone older. His tone of voice was more respectful than friendly. He called the labor leader "Mr. Sweeney"—a nice touch, I thought, though it was probably wasted on Sweeney, who was implacably hostile to Republicans.

I had spent about forty-five minutes thus far with Bush, and we had covered most of the territory I expected: my ideas for transforming the department, my positions on various labor issues, some controversial columns I'd written over the years. Then Bush threw out a totally unexpected question.

"You haven't done any gay bashing in your column, have you?"

"I don't think so," I said, trying to remember what, if anything, I'd said over the years on gay issues—a topic I'd mostly avoided.

"I don't favor including gays under the federal civil rights laws, but not because I have any problems with hiring gays," I added. "In fact, one of my longtime employees is a gay man with AIDS, who also happens to be a staunch conservative, and he agrees with me on the issue." Bush's question seemed a little out of left field, but perhaps with the civil rights, feminist, and labor lobbies against me, he figured he didn't need yet another interest group riled up to oppose me.

Bush signaled that the interview was over by telling me he was going to appoint three additional cabinet members in a few hours: Wisconsin Governor Tommy Thompson as secretary of health and human services, Houston school superintendent Rod Paige as secretary of education, and Gale Norton, former attorney general of Colorado, to be secretary of the interior. I was genuinely surprised at the Norton nomination. Gale was an old friend—and very conservative. I noticed that Bush's cabinet announcements were following a pattern. Whenever he announced a genuinely conservative pick for one department, he coupled it with the announcement of a moderate to head another agency, for example naming Senator John Ashcroft to be attorney general on the same day he announced Governor Christine Todd Whitman to head the Environmental Protection Agency. By grouping nominees in this way, he gave the press less ammunition to pigeonhole him as a right-winger. But with Whitman, his most prominent moderate, now onboard, and only three cabinet nominations left to make—energy, transportation, and labor—it might be harder to fit me into the mix.

I decided not to stick around my deserted office, which was closed for the holidays. I was on my way back to Virginia when the phone in my truck rang. It was Chris. Clay Johnson was trying to reach me. I returned the call immediately.

"It's time to move to the next step," he said. "Give Fred Fielding a call. He's got a packet of forms waiting for you to fill out. We need you to do this as quickly as possible."

I thanked him and called Fielding's office. They were ready and waiting for me. My son David dropped me off at Fielding's K Street law firm and waited at Border's Books nearby.

I had not seen Fielding in years, but he looked remarkably the same, pink-cheeked and jolly. He had the kind of avuncular persona that perfectly suited his line of work, inspiring instant trust from perfect strangers who would have to pour out their guts to him. His office was filled with old toys, brightly colored antique cars and trucks that gave the room a festive air. After giving me a big bear hug, he handed me a three-inch-thick black binder. In it was a letter informing me that I was under consideration for a cabinet post and requesting that I complete the enclosed forms within five days.

Fielding and I chatted about the old days in the Reagan White House, recalling mutual friends, including some who were now headed back into the new administration, such as Mitch Daniels, tapped to be the new Office of Management and Budget director. Then Fred got down to the tough questions.

"You've been through this drill before," he said, as I had in 1983 and 1986 when my positions in the Reagan administration required FBI full field investigations. "Anything in your background that might embarrass the president?" he asked.

I mentioned a student loan I'd paid back late and a few other minor issues, none of which was likely to cause any problems. When Fielding asked me directly about any "nanny problems," I explained that my oldest son, born in 1968, didn't have a nanny. My husband and I took turns caring for him while we were in school, and he attended private preschool after we moved to Washington. The woman who took care of my two younger boys for most of their childhood was a Salvadoran immigrant legally in the country. She became a U.S. citizen while she worked for me, and I paid Social Security taxes on her wages, as I did on the dozen or so other women who worked for me doing part-time housework off and on over the years.

But I didn't bring up Marta. She certainly didn't fit the category of nanny. My younger sons were teenagers when Marta began living with us, and I worked exclusively at home at the time, so I had no need of a nanny. I had given Marta a place to live, periodically gave her money to send home to her children in Guatemala, and helped pay for her airfare when she decided to return home, but none of this constituted a violation of the law. Nonetheless, allowing an illegal alien to live in my home was a potential political problem. And my failure to raise the issue with Fielding would later prove my undoing.

I will never know whether Bush would have nominated me had I told Fielding about Marta. Bush had already nominated Christine Todd Whitman for a cabinet-level position, despite her having hired and failed to pay taxes on two illegal aliens in the early 1990s, about the same time Marta was living with me.[5] Whitman's offense sparked barely a casual mention during her nomination process, even after my relationship with Marta earned front-page coverage in every newspaper in the country. But, then, Whitman was a moderate with no serious opposition, whereas I was a conservative with lots of interest groups gunning for me.

I left Fielding's office a little uneasy about my lack of candor but quickly put it out of my mind. Two days later, I was on a flight headed for Austin to meet with the president-elect. I checked into the Omni Hotel in Austin and spent most of the evening rereading my own newspaper columns. If anything could foil my nomination, surely it was hidden somewhere in the hundreds of articles I'd written over the past decade and a half. Why was I so acerbic? Why did I have to take on so many controversial topics? Why hadn't I pulled my punches, at least occasionally? I was going to have a lot of explaining to do when the Senate took up my nomination. But I was getting ahead of myself. Bush hadn't even offered me the job yet.

At nine-thirty the following morning, January 2, I went downstairs to meet the driver who would take me to the governor's mansion. Although Bush had formally resigned as Texas governor, he continued to use a portion of the mansion as his base of operations. At the elevator, I ran into Spence Abraham, who had lost his Michigan Senate seat and was rumored to be Bush's choice to head the transportation department.

"I can't say I'm surprised to see you," I grinned. "So you got transportation?"

"No, actually, energy," Abraham beamed back.

"Gee, that's great. So who got transportation? Elaine Chao?" I asked. Chao's name had been mentioned frequently, and she had served as deputy secretary of the department in the first Bush administration.

"Don't know," Abraham answered, none too convincingly. He wished me well, and I headed out to the van waiting to take me to the mansion. A television crew waited in the lobby, but, again, I eluded them. The van drove onto the mansion driveway through a side entrance and under a plastic canopy that kept nosy camera crews at bay. I got out and waited in the cold for several minutes before someone led me into the mansion. Bush was walking down the hall with Albert Hawkins, his Texas comptroller, whom he introduced to me. "This guy's a genius with numbers," he told me after Hawkins left. "There were some old-timers around here who didn't think a black man could do the job. Albert showed 'em differently," he added. Bush was clearly genuine in his efforts to break down barriers, a trait that he carried over to his new job as president.

"I'd like you to be my secretary of labor," Bush said, wasting no time. "I'm going to announce three more appointments this afternoon. In addition to labor, I'm naming Spence Abraham as secretary of energy and Norm Mineta to head transportation." An Arab American, a Japanese American, and a

Mexican American. Two men and one woman. Two staunch conservatives and a moderate Democrat. You couldn't get much more diverse than that.

"I can't tell you how honored I am, Mr. President-elect," the title sounded awkward.

"Does that mean you accept?" he interrupted before I could get out the rest of my thanks.

"Yes, sir, it does. I'm thrilled!" And indeed I was.

"This isn't going to be easy. They're going to come after you with everything they've got. I know that people think Ashcroft and Norton are going to have the toughest time," he said, referring to his picks for attorney general and sec-retary of interior. "But I think you're going to be the hard one. I want you to know, I'm going to stick with you. I'm going to fight for you."

"And I promise not to give up, no matter how hard it gets," I answered, feel-ing emotion welling up inside me.

Within a week, we would both break our promises. I would be forced to withdraw my nomination, and my reputation would be shattered. But for the moment, I was on top of the world.

1

Skeletons in the Closet

All which a man has belongs to those who gave him birth and brought him up.

— Plato, *Laws*

I WAS BORN AT 6:50 P.M. on June 17, 1947, at St. Joseph's Hospital in Albuquerque, New Mexico. My mother, Velma McKenna, was twenty-five years old, a blue-eyed natural blonde with skin the color of alabaster. I was her third child. Her first two boys, Dickie and Michael, were six and four years old when I was born and lived with their paternal grandmother and aunt in Casper, Wyoming. I saw my half-brothers only twice during my childhood. They were beautiful boys. Michael had my mother's fair coloring, and Dickey had dark, curly hair like his father, a bandleader whom my mother had married soon after she graduated from high school in Sheridan, Wyoming, and divorced right after the end of World War II.

For years I wondered why my mother had given up her boys, but I never asked her about it. I doubt that I would have got a straight answer. She would have treated it as she did all unpleasant or unusual facts of family history, as if it were the most natural thing in the world to let someone else raise your children. It was hard to blame her for feeling that way because her mother had given her up too, when she was barely a toddler. My maternal grandfather, Clement McKenna, the fifth of eight children of a devout Irish Catholic family, had walked out on his wife, Eva, and their four young children when my mother was only two. He later turned up in Alaska, where he died in 1956, never having seen his wife or children again. Unable to raise the children alone, Eva sent the two oldest, John and Mary, to live with Clement's family in Sioux City, Iowa. She gave my mother to her sister Velma, my mother's namesake, who lived just down the street in Sheridan with her husband, Glenn Speed. Eva kept only the youngest child, Milton, who was a baby when my grandfather disappeared.

After the war, my mother, newly divorced, moved to Albuquerque, where she met and fell in love with my father, Rudy Chavez, a tall, handsome man with his own family demons. I grew up hearing my father's childhood tales, absorbing them as if they were my own. When my father was six years old, his father, Ambrose, went to prison for bootlegging whiskey. My father often talked of being humiliated as he watched federal agents march his dad to the train station in handcuffs on his way to prison. Ambrose spent eleven years in jail, most of it served at Leavenworth Federal Penitentiary in Kansas. His prison records describe Ambrose as a "suave, self-confident, well-poised man . . . a very cheerful sort of person, who is well adjusted temperamentally, does not seem to be disturbed by his present situation." But the description defies credulity. Ambrose's imprisonment thrust the family deeply into poverty, and he was helpless to do anything about it. My grandmother Petra, who had little formal education, was left to care for five young children on her own through much of the Great Depression. As a result, my father assumed the burden of providing for his brothers and sisters when he was barely more than a child himself.

The family often went without decent food and clothing while Ambrose was in prison. Every Thanksgiving while I was growing up, my father told the story of his own holiday memories when there was barely enough money to buy a few slices of bologna for Thanksgiving. He recalled the pain of standing in the butcher's shop, embarrassed to order the lunch meat for his mother and four siblings, while those around him bought plump turkeys, yams, and cranberries. He told me that he saved the butcher's string for use as laces for his school shoes, stuffing cardboard inside to cover the gaping holes in the soles. The story always left me feeling guilty for what I had when my father had had so little. In the tenth grade, my father left school permanently. Ashamed of his situation and eager to earn money so that his younger sister Irene could stay in school, he joined the Civilian Conservation Corps and left home for California. Irene, a real beauty, was a schoolmate of Pete Domenici, who years later would become the Republican senator from New Mexico.

But my father's family history was also full of contradictions. For although my father and his siblings lived in desperate poverty through much of his childhood, the family had at one time been very prosperous. The stories of the family's gloried past were as much a part of the family lore as my father's reminiscences of want and deprivation. Both my grandfather and my grandmother, Petra Armijo, came from old, politically powerful colonial families who helped settle New Mexico in the early seventeenth and eighteenth centuries. Like many Spanish families in New Mexico intent on preserving racial "purity" and forging economic alliances, the Chavez and Armijo families intermarried generation after generation, so that the two families were intertwined over two centuries. (My grandparents were actually third cousins, once removed.) Ambrose's father, Eduardo Chavez, was a wool broker from Valencia County, south of Albuquerque. Ambrose described his father in an interview while he was in prison as a "college graduate, wool broker by occupation . . . a man of good health, strict disciplinarian, moderate drinker, law-abiding person," who died at the age of fifty-seven "from heart trouble when [Ambrose] was twenty-seven."

As a child, I used to love to look at Eduardo's wedding portrait, which my grandfather gave me when I was about five. The sepia-colored photograph shows a handsome, mustachioed man with dark, deep-set eyes dressed in a three-piece pinstriped suit. A large diamond stud secures a gold fob chain and pocket watch. His bride, Excelsa Armijo, is dressed in an elaborate silk gown with a train, a flower-encrusted bonnet and veil framing her pleasant but plain face, the very image of Victorian respectability. I would study the photograph intently, imagining that the family still lived in the beautiful house with the heavy drapes and elaborately carved furniture so unlike the often dreary surroundings in which we often lived.

Both Ambrose's mother, Excelsa, and his wife, Petra, were from the same Armijo family of successful merchants, among the wealthiest in New Mexico, who traded along the Santa Fe Trail from St. Louis, Missouri, to Chihuahua, Mexico, before and after the territory became part of the United States in 1848. The Armijos owned much of the land that now encompasses modern-day Albuquerque, and their ancestral home—Casa Armijo, now La Placita restaurant—still stands on the corner of the Old Town Albuquerque plaza, with a plaque commemorating the family history. The house was once owned by General Manuel Armijo, the last Mexican governor of New Mexico (1838–1844). Manuel (born in 1792) was the younger brother of both my great-great-great-great grandfather Jose Francisco Armijo (born in 1780) on Ambrose's side and my great-great-great grandfather Santiago Armijo (born in 1773) on Petra's side. Irredentist Mexican Americans still revile Armijo for surrendering the New Mexican territory to General Stephen W. Kearny's American forces without a shot being fired. But I've always been proud of his role in New Mexico history, without which I might not be an American today.

Once out of prison, Ambrose started a successful real estate business, but he continued to sell bootleg liquor out of his home as well. As a child of four or five in the early 1950s, I remember him unloading cases of whiskey and beer into his kitchen to be sold after-hours and on Sunday to cash customers. On particularly lucrative weekends, I would sit in my grandparents' dining room while Petra's radio played her favorite polka music and Ambrose counted up the piles of money spread out across the table. He wore a rubber thimble on his thumb to keep the bills from sticking as he counted them one by one, stacking them in their proper denominations on the lace tablecloth that covered their big maple table.

My father did not get along with his father, perhaps because Ambrose was absent through much of Rudy's childhood, which was haunted by the poverty and humiliation brought on by Ambrose's time in jail. But I adored my grandfather, whom I remember as a stern businessman in a gray Stetson hat who doted on me and took me everywhere with him. Even though he sold whiskey out of his house, he rarely drank liquor himself, unlike my father, preferring Seven-Up to alcohol of any kind. He ran his real estate business out of an office next door to his home, and I enjoyed long days at his side while he worked at his large oak roll-top desk or took me with him on client calls in his black Studebaker. My grandfather gave us the only house we ever owned, a one-room, flat-roofed adobe with a huge yard on Dolores Drive, atop the mesa on Albuquerque's west side. My father added two additional rooms and a patio and planted grass on the front lawn—a novelty in Albuquerque's vast brown, desert-like neighborhoods—carefully tending it all summer until it was lush and green. We lived there only a year or so before we were forced to sell the property when one of my father's drinking episodes left him seriously injured in a car accident.

In 1952, my younger sister Wendy was born. But that was also the year I lost my half-sister, Pamela, my father's daughter by his first wife, Cecily Little, an Australian woman whom he had married during World War II. Pamela and I spent much of our early childhood together, sharing the same babysitters while our mothers worked, even living together for a short while when we were infants. But about the time Wendy was born, Cecily decided to give Pamela up for adoption, which required my father's permission. On the day he was to sign the papers, Cecily had to track him down at a bar, where he'd gone to drown his guilt. My parents told me that Pamela would be going away to live with a nice family in Clovis, New Mexico, because Cecily was unable to take care of her on her own. But I wondered why Pamela couldn't just live with us. Unlike my half-brothers whom I barely knew, Pamela was my best friend, and losing her was devastating. We were like mirror images of each other, one blond and blue-eyed and the other dark, chubby-cheeked with the same thick curls always dangling over our eyes. At a time when divorce was rare and "blended" families even more rare, my family seemed a strange hybrid of partial connections and incomplete bonds, with children sent away on a whim. But the loss of Pamela turned out to be only the first of many such wrenching episodes in

my childhood, which left me perpetually terrified that I would lose those closest to me and might someday be sent away myself.

In 1955, my mother's oldest child, Dickie, died in an automobile accident
in Wyoming. We attended the funeral in Casper, where I met my brother
Michael for the first time and wished that he could live with us, too. But the
fact is, my parents' lives were probably too chaotic to take on another child.
We moved often, sometimes living in motels and run-down rooming houses,
other times living with relatives. By the time I was in third grade, I had
changed schools six times across two states. Thankfully, I knew how to read
before I entered first grade, or I might never have learned at all. Most of the
turmoil in our lives was brought on by my father's alcoholism and the devas-
tation left in its wake. Although he was an incredibly bright and charming
man—and a totally loving father to me and my sister Wendy—the legacy of his
own troubled childhood consumed our lives. I would sometimes awaken in
the middle of the night to find both of my parents gone, my mother either at
work on the night shift at some cocktail lounge or restaurant or looking for my
father who simply disappeared to return days later, hung over and chastened.
During one such episode in 1953, he wrecked his car driving back from Santa
Fe alone late one night and was hospitalized for weeks. Wendy and I went to
live briefly with my mother's sister Mary and her husband John Delaney in El
Paso, Texas. Soon after we returned to Albuquerque, we lost our house and
went to live in an apartment at the rear of my grandmother Petra's house on
12th Street NW, not far from the Old Town plaza.

But that arrangement, too, lasted for just a short time. One night when I was
seven years old, my mother packed all our clothes in some boxes and loaded
Wendy and me in our car, a 1954 red and white Ford convertible, and headed for Denver, leaving my father behind. Though I don't remember them
fighting, I suspect she had finally become fed up with the chaos his drinking
injected into our lives. We got as far as Santa Fe, where she stopped at the La
Fonda Hotel, telling me to wait in the car while she went in to get something
to eat. I fell asleep in the backseat, with Wendy sleeping soundly on a pillow
in the front. When my mother returned, I asked her if we could stop for the
night, but she was anxious to get back on the road. A couple of hours later, I
awakened to the sound of a horn blasting from a semi tractor trailer, its head-
lights headed straight toward us on the narrow mountain pass. I screamed and
lost consciousness. When I came to, I was barefoot, walking along a dirt road.
Our overturned car was behind me, and I was heading toward the sound of my
baby sister, wailing loudly further up the road. When I reached her, she was
scared but didn't have a scratch on her body. Apparently, the car door had

flown open when my mother, who had fallen asleep, jerked the steering wheel to avoid a head-on collision as she awakened to my scream. Wendy sailed out on the pillow, unhurt, but my mother was not so lucky.

I tried to stop cars on the highway, waving wildly while holding my baby sister. Two cars slowed long enough to see me and the upturned wreck behind me, but sped off rather than stopped. Finally, an old jalopy pulled up. The family inside were like something out of the *Grapes of Wrath*, their belongings tied to the roof of the car, kids of all ages climbing all over each other in the backseat, their parents in front, looking poor and disheveled. The woman took Wendy from me, and the man went down the road to examine the wreckage. "Did you find my mother?" I asked when he returned. "We gotta get an ambulance here quick," was all he said.

My mother's injuries included broken vertebrae, a broken shoulder, an ankle so badly mangled it had to be put back together with metal screws, and a one-inch hole in her skull. When the ambulance arrived, they found my mother lying on the ground outside the car, my white, First Communion dress stuffed into the gash in her head. Though I have no memory of it, I must have discovered her body and tried to stop the bleeding with the dress pulled from one of the boxes in the car. I had relatively minor injuries, some cracked ribs and facial cuts and bruises from being thrown through the roof of the convertible or the front windshield. I stayed in the hospital in Springer, New Mexico, about a week and then went to Delta, Colorado, to stay with my great aunt and uncle, Velma and Glenn Speed, the couple who had raised my mother. My mother stayed in the hospital, encased in a body cast for weeks, and when she finally came home, she was unable to walk for months.

Whatever it was that drove my mother to want to leave Albuquerque, the sentiment only intensified after her accident. Although we stayed another year, living again in the small adobe house behind my grandmother's, the summer following her accident, we left Albuquerque for good. This time, my father was with us, driving the 439 miles to Denver in an old, gray Hudson, which had replaced our wrecked Ford convertible, boxes squeezed tightly into every available inch of the car. My grandmother had packed bag lunches for us to eat along the way, hard-boiled eggs, fried chicken, seedless grapes. My father taught me to look for out-of-state license plates, and I spent much of the ride reading and watching the scenery gradually change. From the high desert terrain of Albuquerque, with its pink and brown earth interspersed with low-growing sage brush, the land turned to the piñon-scattered Sangre de Cristo panorama north and east of Sante Fe, making the mountains appear blue rather than the blood red of their name. Finally, as we came over Raton Pass and into southern Colorado, the temperature dropped, and the Rockies loomed large in the west. My father entertained us with stories of Francisco Vasquez de Coronado and Juan de Oñate, who had originally explored this region—reminding us that we were descended from Pedro Gomez Duran y Chaves—born in 1550 in a village near Llerena, Spain—who had accompanied Oñate's first expedition to New Mexico in 1600.

But I was growing more homesick by the mile. When we finally arrived in Denver, driving up to our apartment on Clarkson Street, not far from Denver's gold-domed capitol, I was tired and cranky. The apartment, a third-floor attic, smelled of boiled cabbage, and the linoleum floors in the small kitchen slanted at a perilous angle. A dumbwaiter in a cabinet in the kitchen suggested that our apartment had housed the domestic staff for the original inhabitants of this large, single-family dwelling from the turn of the century. Now the building was occupied mostly by working-class families crowded into little apartments, including Charlotte Baker, a girl about my age who lived with her parents in the basement. Charlotte's dad was a construction worker, even taller than my six-foot-two father, with a southern drawl and quick smile. At a time when Mexican Americans weren't always welcome in the homes of Anglos, the Bakers befriended us and made us feel at ease.[1] Not all of our neighbors were as friendly. A younger boy who lived across the alley in a huge house surrounded by a tall brick wall used to play with me almost every day, tagging along outside wherever I went. But one day when I asked if I could come and see his house, which seemed to me a grand mansion, he told me he'd have to ask his mother first. He came back quickly, stopping short of the backyard to our apartment house. "She says I'm not supposed to play with Mes'cans," he yelled from the alley and quickly disappeared back behind his brick wall.

I was as confused as I was hurt by this explanation. I had never thought of myself as Mexican, a term my family reserved for those who came from "Old Mexico," like my cousin Jennie Guzman's husband, a very successful and well-respected man in our family. But it soon became clear to me that Mexicans were looked down on in Colorado—and that included me. It took me until I was nine years old to bump into such prejudice for the first time, thankfully too late to internalize it or to let it wear me down. Years later, I read a quote from the African American novelist Zora Neale Hurston that summed up my own attitude: "Sometimes I feel discriminated against," she wrote in the 1920s, "but it does not make me angry. It merely astonishes me. How can any deny themselves the pleasure of my company?"[2] After my neighbor was forbidden to play in my backyard, I took to playing in the alley alone or with Charlotte, bouncing a rubber ball against the brick wall that surrounded his property.

Sometimes he'd open the gate and stare wistfully; other times he'd call me names and run inside. He seemed to have no other friends, and I soon tired of taunting him.

Before I came to Colorado, my ethnicity had never affected my life. Most everyone I knew, certainly most of my family members, were "Spanish"—the term we most often used to describe ourselves and our co-ethnics, when we used any at all. But the term didn't have much to do with color or surname or even what language we spoke. I knew my mother looked different from my father, with her fair skin, hair, and eyes. I knew she was an "Anglo," but then so was the Negro girl in my first grade class, as were the Ilfelds, Domenicis, and Khourys—prominent Jewish, Italian, and Arab families in town. Several of my grandmother Petra's brothers and sisters had blue or green eyes and milky white skin. I had cousins named Booth and Wagner, and almost no one in my generation spoke Spanish well, if at all. Being Spanish meant that your family had come to New Mexico more than 250 years ago. They hadn't been there as long as the Indians certainly, but they weren't newcomers like the Anglos, most of whose families arrived after 1848. When I came to Denver, however, I was constantly being asked, "What nationality are you?" Even my fourth grade teacher in my new school, Cathedral Elementary, asked me the question in front of the whole class on the first day of school. "I hope you said 'American,'" my mother replied when I told her about it that evening. I had, but it didn't seem to satisfy the teacher, who insisted, "Are you Mexican or Spanish?"

For months after we arrived in Denver, I despised the city. I refused to drink the water, unless it was boiled and made into tea. I hated the cold and the snow in the winter, and I missed my aunts, uncles, and cousins, and most of all, my grandmother Petra. My mother's mother Eva—whom we all called Susie— lived in Denver, which is why we came there in the first place. But Eva was unlike anyone in my father's family. Her manner was formal, almost elegant. She wore a hat and gloves to work everyday as a bookkeeper at St. Luke's Hospital and spoke with a trace of an English accent, the source of which remains a mystery to me, since her family were pioneers in Wyoming. Her grandmother, Laura, and mother, Lucy Etta, arrived in Wyoming in a covered wagon from Kahoka, Missouri, in the 1880s. Eva's father, George Clements, was a stock drover, born in 1861 in Illinois, who came west to Wyoming as a young man. He worked on the big cattle ranches along the border of Wyoming and Montana, and for a time on the Crow Reservation. "There's not much work about it," he wrote his wife in a letter dated July 6, 1899, "but a good deal of sneaking around trying to catch the Indians killing beef." Eva was only eight years old when she saw her father dragged home by his horse, which had thrown him, impaling him on the horn of his saddle. He died, several days later, and was buried outside Parkman, Wyoming.

Before the end of fourth grade, we moved again, this time to a basement apartment only a few blocks away on Sherman Street, just down the street from the Capitol. Like the Clarkson Street apartment, this one, too, was in a grand old brick mansion built after Denver's gold rush era, when the city was flush with new wealth. The entryway to the apartment building had a large foyer, with dark oak paneling and a big, pillared fireplace mantle, where I would stack the mail for the building's residents. There was also a window seat beneath the large stained glass windows on the staircase. I loved to sit on the cushions beneath the giant purple iris and long green spiked leaves, which stretched almost to the second floor ceiling. I read *Jane Eyre, Wuthering Heights,* and other nineteenth-century romances, all the while imagining that the apartment house we lived in was still a mansion, with its parlors and French doors and grand staircase. Instead, we lived in two rooms in the basement with a cramped kitchen, though we, too, had a lovely wood mantle in the small living room, though the fireplace itself had been tiled over so that no fires could be lit.

My father became the apartment house manager shortly after we moved in, taking over the duties from the absentee owner, an old man named Tex who stayed in a tiny room no bigger than a large closet on the second floor when he came to visit. There were only two bathrooms shared by the five apartments in the building, and it became my duty to allot times for bathing on a sign-up sheet posted on the bathroom doors. Each family could reserve hours on alternating days. I'm not sure the system worked all that well, because each family had multiple children. Our family was luckier than the others since we, at least, had a toilet in the furnace room next to the bedroom, though I was terrified of walking past the huge boiler when it was blasting through the cold, Colorado winters. I could see the flames leap up in the furnace through cracks around the boiler door and hear it belch to life in the middle of the night through the thin wall between it and my bed.

The other families in the building were much like my own, working-class men and women with young children. The men worked at manual jobs—like my father, who painted houses. Most of the women stayed home with their youngsters. One couple were recent immigrants from Germany. Wolfgang, the husband, was a dark and vulgar young man who often bragged about his father, who had been a Nazi soldier, to everyone's disgust. His wife, Helga, wore her hair in long blond braids and could be seen early every morning, exercising in the backyard with her two tow-headed children, wearing only their underwear no matter how frigid the temperature. Once when the little boy was playing with me, I noticed deep, purple bruises across his back. I told my father, who confronted Wolfgang. "If you ever lay a hand on that boy again, I'll take that belt and use it on you," he yelled at the terrified German. My father, who never walked away from a fight and loved to boast about his physical prowess, abhorred men who hit women or beat children. In all my childhood, I never received so much as a spanking from either of my parents.

Despite the occasional spat between families living under, essentially, the same roof—sharing common bathrooms, and for two apartments, a common kitchen—life on Sherman Street was supportive and enriching. I was ten years old when we moved in, already older than the other children in the building, so I often found myself making friends with the parents, most of whom were in their early twenties. By the time I was twelve, I was joining the adults at card games, usually poker or blackjack, in one of the upstairs apartments, occasionally beating them at penny-ante games, to the delight of all. As an adult, I never buy so much as a lottery ticket. But as a child, I loved to gamble, though it may have been the company more than the game that intrigued me. I enjoyed the conversation of adults and liked to talk politics even then, though I would often just parrot my father's opinions. "Ike was a great general, but he hasn't done much as president," I'd pronounce, with great conviction. "All he does is play golf." During the hot summer months with no air conditioning, several families would sit out on the large front porch swing, talking into the late evening.

On one such sweltering night, July 22, 1959, my father and I were on the porch with our neighbors when the phone rang. I ran to answer it, bolting down the stairs to our apartment. My mother was at work at the restaurant where she was night cashier, and my sister Wendy, then six, was in the hospital. Five weeks earlier, on my twelfth birthday, Wendy had become ill. We had come back from my birthday party when Wendy called me to come look in the toilet off the boiler room. The bowl was filled with blood. My parents rushed her to the hospital, where she was diagnosed with Bright's disease, then an incurable kidney disorder. She had been in the hospital ever since, except for a few days over the 4th of July holiday.

"Hello, this is Dr. Rice, who's this?" the voice on the other end of the line asked. When I answered, he replied brusquely, "Tell your parents Wendy has gone into heart failure. They've got to get here as quickly as possible."

I hung up the phone, shaking, and ran upstairs. I felt numb. My sister was dying, and I was the one who had to deliver the message to my father. I still cannot fathom what possessed the doctor to give a twelve-year-old such information to pass on. For the first time in my life, I saw utter terror in my father's eyes as I repeated the doctor's words. He grabbed me and rushed to our car, shouting to one of the stunned neighbors, still sitting on the swing, to call my mother at work and ask her to meet him at the hospital. We drove frantically the few miles to my grandmother Susie's apartment en route to the hospital, where he dropped me off, explaining hurriedly to her what had happened.

For the next hour or so, I waited with Susie. She made tea for us both and suggested we say the rosary together. "Hail Mary, full of grace, the Lord is with thee," we intoned out loud, our fingers kneading the beads as we knelt by her bed. There was nothing more we could do. Then the phone rang. Before she had put the receiver back down, I knew it was over.

"She's gone, dear," Susie said, wrapping her arms around me. I felt utterly alone and abandoned, having lost yet another sibling.

It was after midnight when my parents finally arrived to pick me up. My father's face was ashen. My mother seemed in a stupor. She clutched a hospital bag with Wendy's things in it: a doll, some books, the blue cotton pajamas she'd been wearing, still damp with the fluid from her lungs.

"Rudy went out in the hall to talk to the doctor and I was holding her in my arms," she told my grandmother. "She said 'I'm so tired, Mommy,' and just closed her eyes. And then there was this terrible noise in the back of her throat—I guess what they call the death rattle—and all this fluid started coming out of her nose. And that was it." Her words were slow and thick. My father just sat there, shattered.

Officially, Wendy's death was attributed to congestive heart failure. But by the time she died in my mother's arms, she had developed pneumonia, and her kidneys had shut down completely. In a matter of a few weeks, she went from a seemingly healthy, playful six-year-old to one whose entire system failed, all at once. The effect on my parents was devastating. I was sure they would never be able to smile or laugh again. Remarkably, my father didn't drink anything for weeks, perhaps months. They went about their routines as before, going to work, coming home, watching television, but the joy just went out of their lives—and mine.

I withdrew inward to protect myself from the pain of losing those close to me. In the process of inuring myself to loss, however, I made it difficult for anyone to get very close to me either, developing an emotional reserve that has remained with me all my life. Years later, when I became a public figure, my critics often commented on my "cool, composed" demeanor, with "an image as ice queen always in control."[3] I believe that the grief I experienced throughout my childhood gave me a kind of steely resolve, which helped me through the difficult days I would later face in my career. With increasing stoicism over the years, I simply would not allow myself to feel hurt. I became almost impervious to the insults and attacks my controversial stands on issues would provoke, infuriating those who disagreed with me all the more.

When I started school again in the fall, my classmates treated me like a curiosity. Most of them had never known anyone who had died and had no idea what to say to me. School had always been a kind of refuge. I was popular with other kids and generally well liked by teachers. In the strict environment of a 1950s Catholic school, I excelled at following the rules and pleasing the adults while managing not to alienate my classmates. After Wendy's death, I became more withdrawn and intensely religious, attending daily mass in the school chapel, praying at recess instead of playing. I wore my hair pulled back in a bun and looked every bit the gawky adolescent. The following summer, I went to Delta to stay with Auntie Velma and Uncle Glenn, this time traveling alone by bus across the Continental Divide to Colorado's western slope.

Visits to my great aunt and uncle were an oasis in my childhood. Their lives were as steady as mine was tumultuous. Glenn was a foreman at the Holly Sugar plant in Delta. Auntie was a homemaker. She drove Glenn to work every morning in their shiny 1956 green Oldsmobile and picked him up at the plant gate when the whistle blew at four o'clock. We ate meals at the dinner table in their large kitchen, with vegetables picked out of Auntie's backyard garden: sweet corn, green beans, lettuce, and tomatoes. On Friday nights, we went to the Elks Club, where Auntie ordered a "stinger," a green concoction that smelled sticky sweet, and Glenn drank a few beers. Their lives revolved around Glenn's work and social fraternities and Auntie's church activities and garden. In the evenings they watched Lawrence Welk on television, while I read from the collection of Reader's Digest condensed books on their shelves. Their home life was the picture of middle-American normalcy, which I longed to emulate.

But those reprieves, too, came to an end when Auntie died from cancer when I was in high school. By this time, however, my parents' own lives had become more stable, at least financially. My mother began working at Neusteter's, at the time the finest department store in Denver, which meant that she worked days rather than nights, and my father's painting business picked up so that he occasionally had to hire other workers to meet the demand. We moved three more times while I was in high school, first to a three-story brick house on Logan Street, across from the governor's mansion, where I became friends with Governor Steve McNichols's son, Bob. Like the

Sherman Street building, this house had been built around the turn of the century and featured beautiful fireplaces in every room, dark oak paneling, stained glass windows, and even a maid's back staircase leading to the second floor from the butler's pantry in the kitchen. We sublet rooms to afford the rent, but the house offered the illusion of not merely middle-class status but wealth, so that most of my friends had no idea how tenuous my family's hold on middle-class life actually was. When the owner sold the property, we moved to a duplex in east Denver, and the following year, to a larger duplex a few blocks away.

I continued to attend Cathedral, which had not only an elementary but a high school, taught mainly by Sisters of Charity and diocesan priests. In eighth grade, the nuns moved me into math and English classes with the high school students, and throughout high school they insisted that I take accelerated academic classes. I wanted nothing more than to be in classes with my friends, learning how to type and take shorthand, how to sew and cook, but the nuns gave me no choice. At the end of every semester when I filled out my requests to take bookkeeping or stenography or home economics, the three-by-five-inch index card came back with those classes marked through in red and Latin, trigonometry, or chemistry in their place. The tracking system then popular in American education (and still popular in Catholic schools) divided students into two groups, depending on their standardized test scores. Those who scored well on tests were tracked into academic courses, and those who didn't went into a vocational track. Liberals have always opposed such practices, on the theory that they discriminate against minorities. In my case, academic tracking, based on my test scores, pushed me to achieve beyond my own limited expectations, without which I doubt I would be where I am today. Years later, the economist Thomas Sowell, who is black, told me of his similar experience attending schools in New York City.

Despite my lofty test scores, however, I was far from a model student. By ninth grade, I had begun to miss school frequently, often days at a time. But instead of roaming the stores or movie theaters or getting into trouble, I spent my time at home, holed up in my bedroom with books. In retrospect, I was probably both bored with school and clinically depressed. But I managed to read a great deal, systematically working through authors I liked. My father introduced me to books early on. I remember going to the Albuquerque library on Edith Street with my father when I was only four or five; its lovely Spanish architecture and tiled floors were a cool refuge from the summer heat. And one of my first memories of Denver was of my father taking me to the modern glass building across from the state capitol that housed the Denver Public

Library. Every week or two, we went there together, each of us checking out a large stack of books, which he would devour as eagerly as I.

In high school, I was enamored with W. Somerset Maugham, John Steinbeck, Tennessee Williams, Eugene O'Neill, and Federico García Lorca, authors and playwrights my father introduced me to. I was drawn to somber tales of human misery, which made my own life seem idyllic by comparison. I was especially fond of Maugham's *Of Human Bondage.* The novel begins with Philip Carey, a club-footed child, being handed into his dying mother's arms and follows his torments as he faces rejection throughout his life, eventually triumphing. I read the novel two or three times in high school. My father also encouraged me to read Dostoyevski, Tolstoy, and Gogol—his own favorites—but I found the Russian names confusing and the historical background too challenging and did not take them up again until I became an adult. By the time I finished high school, I had managed a decent survey of nineteenth- and twentieth-century literature, but my grades in school were mediocre to terrible.

Although I was a constant source of frustration to my best teachers, I was nonetheless well liked among the students, winning some elective office each year I was in school. I had two groups of friends. The St. Philomena crowd, named after the parish in East Denver where they lived, was made up of the serious students and athletes from middle-class, mostly Irish, families. But I was also friends with the school's small group of black students, many of whom lived in Denver's Five Points area, named after a nearby intersection just north of the school. Because it was run by the city's Catholic archdiocese, Cathedral High School drew its students from all over Denver: the Italian Northside, the Mexican American Westside, the more affluent South Denver, and the middle-class East Denver. The wealthiest Catholics sent their children to one of the city's private Catholic schools, Regis High for boys or Loretto Heights for girls, instead of the parish-run institutions like Cathedral. Although most Cathedral students came from large families—typically five children or more—there were a handful of kids, like me, who came from smaller ones. And there were even one or two among my classmates who came from what we none-too-kindly called "broken homes."

My parents were strict, even by the standards of the time, which were much more rigid than today's. I was allowed to attend school social events, but I had to be home immediately afterward. My father was always waiting at the door when I arrived—never a minute late—though his rules didn't stop me from saying I was going one place and ending up somewhere else. I had only one serious boyfriend in high school, Bill Weber. He was a nephew of my aunt and uncle, Mary and John Delaney, with whom I had lived in El Paso, though not a blood relative of mine. Bill's mother, Jean, didn't approve of our relationship. Some of my friends thought she objected because I was Mexican American, but I believe she simply thought we were too young to be so seriously involved. There were only a few incidents in high school in which my ethnicity was ever an issue. When I was invited to a party at the Cherry Creek Country Club by a boy whose parents were members, several of the girls at the party made snide remarks in the ladies' room. "I didn't know they let Mexicans in here," one snotty girl announced in a voice meant for me to hear. And in my senior year, a boy whom I expected to ask me to the prom invited someone else, because—as his best friend explained—the boy's father didn't let him date Mexicans. I thought it was an odd prejudice for an Italian, especially one whose skin was much darker than mine. However, my own parents had their prejudices as well.

For much of high school, one of my best friends was a black student named Monica Scott. Monica and I were in French class together, and we used to love to hang out in the bathroom at lunchtime with the handful of other black girls in our class, practicing the Watusi, the Twist, and the Mashed Potato to imaginary James Brown music. On weekends, Monica would sometimes sleep over at my house, and my father would drive us to basketball or football games. But my parents would never let me sleep at Monica's house, worrying that her neighborhood wasn't safe enough. Then, in my junior year when one of Monica's friends got her driver's license, Monica suggested they pick me up to drive me to the football game. My parents balked. "It's not a good idea," my mother explained, sheepishly. "I know Monica is a nice girl, but people will get the wrong idea if you hang out with colored girls all the time." I was humiliated by my parents' prejudice, but I couldn't stand up to them. I told Monica I was sick and stayed home from the game altogether. Still, my parents didn't object when I joined Student C.O.R.E. (Congress on Racial Equality) and marched in a large demonstration in front of the downtown Woolworth's, protesting the chain's refusal to allow blacks to sit at lunch counters in stores in the South. My father voiced horror and disgust over the treatment of blacks, which was becoming an almost nightly item on the television news during the mid-sixties, with its pictures of Bull Connor and other lawmen setting police dogs and fire hoses on peaceful demonstrators, Southern governors blocking schoolhouse doors, and angry mobs of whites shaking their fists at frightened black children.

The civil rights movement seemed a distant, almost exotic struggle. The brutal murders of civil rights workers Michael Schwerner, Andrew Goodman, and James Chaney in Mississippi in the summer of 1964 horrified the nation but seemed far removed from the Colorado of my youth. Nothing remotely like it ever occurred in the relevantly tolerant Denver community. Denver's small black population in the mid-1960s was typical of most western cities, having developed largely after World War II when returning Negro soldiers and their families went to places like Los Angeles and Denver in search of greater economic opportunities. Like many northern cities at the time, Denver had no formal segregation in housing, education, or employment, but both blacks and Hispanics were still relegated mostly to low-paying jobs and lived in poor neighborhoods with inferior public schools.[4]

My black classmates, however, came from an elite group: black Catholics. Conversion to Catholicism was frequently a sign of upward mobility for blacks, just as conversion to Protestantism has often been for Hispanics. But in the case of black Catholics, conversion brought an immediate benefit. The parochial school system—then, unlike now, attended exclusively by Catholic children—offered the best hope of an affordable, high-quality education for youngsters who might otherwise be consigned to poor-quality and unsafe public schools.

My Hispanic classmates were a more mixed lot. Most came from working-class families, though one boy who took me to school dances once or twice, was from a wealthy family. His father drove a Mercedes-Benz, the first Mercedes I had ever seen in an era in which hardly anyone drove imported cars.

My first identification with the civil rights movement came from my sympathy with the struggles of black Americans for equality, not with my fellow Mexican Americans. I was too young to join the Freedom Rides, made up of idealistic white college students who gave up their summers to help blacks register to vote in the Deep South. But I followed the efforts of Roy Wilkins Jr., then president of the NAACP, Martin Luther King Jr. and Ralph Abernathy of the Southern Christian Leadership Conference, and A. Phillip Randolph, president of the Brotherhood of Sleeping Car Porters and organizer of the 1963 March on Washington. No comparable civil rights leaders emerged from the Hispanic community, except perhaps Cesar Chavez, whose efforts to win bargaining rights for farmworkers during the 1960s were more a labor issue than a civil rights cause. The plight of urban Mexican Americans and Puerto Ricans never rose to the same level of awareness in the national consciousness at the time—nor in my own—as that of blacks, perhaps because their situation was similar to that of previous immigrant groups, who ultimately succeeded despite widespread, if temporary, discrimination. Yet a growing Chicano movement was coalescing in Denver by the late 1960s,[5] led not by a religious or union leader but by a local bail bondsman, Rodolfo "Corky" Gonzales.

Gonzales, a former professional boxer, was a charismatic and controversial figure who had made a good living out of getting people out of jail when they were arrested for anything from public drunkenness to major felonies. My father didn't think much of Corky, who was, in his opinion, a rabble-rouser more intent on getting attention for himself than doing much for "his people." Gonzales developed his reputation as a civic leader in large part because of his involvement in two high-profile cases of alleged police brutality by the Denver police department. Off-duty police officers often acted as bouncers in bars in Denver's toughest neighborhoods, wearing their uniforms and badges and carrying service revolvers to keep rowdy patrons in line. On July 7, 1962, Edward Larry Romero, a nineteen-year-old Mexican American man, was shot in the back outside a bar in a Mexican American neighborhood by an off-duty policeman after he ran away while being evicted from the bar. According to Ernesto Vigil, who wrote about the incident in his book *The Crusade for Justice*, the cop who shot Romero reported he heard someone shout, "Look out, he's got a gun," but no gun was ever found. Two young Mexican Americans watching from a nearby house later claimed that Romero, while he lay dying, asked the off-duty policeman why he had been shot since he had done nothing. "If you didn't do nothing, what did you run for?" the witnesses reported the cop answered.[6]

The police officer was cleared of any wrongdoing and returned to work less than one week after the incident. Gonzales led community protests that called for an independent police review board to be set up, an idea the leading mayoral candidate in the 1963 election, Thomas Currigan, championed but failed to deliver when elected. A year later, another Mexican American died after an altercation with off-duty cops at a local bar. This time, the young man, nineteen-year-old Alfred Salazar, died after being hit in the head with a police baton and put in a jail cell without medical attention. Corky went to the jail with Salazar's mother to secure his release from jail and found him incoherent. Gonzales had him transported to Denver General Hospital, where he died from a skull fracture. The death was ultimately ruled an accident when an autopsy revealed that Salazar had an exceptionally thin skull, half the normal thickness. Nonetheless, Gonzales managed to mount an impressive protest, a march by several hundred activists on City Hall, thus sealing his reputation as an effective community organizer.

Gonzales and his followers at the Crusade for Justice came to represent the face of radical Chicano politics in Denver. They favored street demonstrations, bombastic rhetoric, and peasant garb, sporting Mexican serapes and, occasionally, bandoliers across their chests. Within a few years, these activists would join the ranks of the Black Panthers, the Brown Berets, the Weather Underground, and other violent left-wing groups. I sympathized with the Crusade's criticism of brutality by the Denver cops, which I had witnessed in my own family. My father's cousin Arthur, who sometimes lived with us, was an alcoholic whose only crime was occasionally falling asleep outside a bar. Once, while he slept on the sidewalk, the Denver cops beat him so badly his lungs collapsed and he nearly died. But despite their focus on a real problem in the community, I didn't believe in the Crusade's tactics or their hostility to America. Even the term they adopted to identify themselves—Chicano— seemed foreign and ugly to my ears. The word Chicano was popularized by Pachucos, Mexican American gang members in the 1930s who spoke their own semiliterate Spanish dialect.

There was another, more fundamental reason why I did not identify as strongly with the struggles of the nascent Mexican American civil rights movement. My own experiences of prejudice and discrimination were relatively minor—petty slights and name-calling that never interfered in any major way with my life's ambitions or aspirations. Had I grown up in South Texas, or had I been darker-skinned or less articulate, perhaps my experiences would have been different. But as it was, being a Mexican American did not seem an absolute barrier to opportunities in the community in which I grew up. Although many of my Mexican American classmates did not go on to college, a great many of my Anglo peers didn't either. And it is difficult to know what role, if any, discrimination played in those decisions. My own sense is that fewer Mexican American parents encouraged their children to attend college, a problem that persists to this day. My parents were typical in this regard.

Despite taking calculus and chemistry in high school, I had no plans to attend college after I graduated. My parents never urged me to go to college, and in any case, they didn't have the money to pay the tuition, much less room and board. Although my high school counselor recommended me for a scholarship at a local Catholic women's college, nothing came of it, which was not surprising given my mediocre high school grades. By the time I was ready to graduate, I had done nothing to apply for college. Sister Jean Patrice, the school principal, summed up the prevailing sentiment of my frustrated teachers when she handed me my final report card in the school gym: "I hope you're not planning on wasting your parents' hard-earned money on college with grades like these, young lady." Still, she felt some responsibility to help me on my way in life, and she recommended me to a local department store looking for teen models. I won a competition for the slot, which secured me an astronomical salary of fifteen dollars per hour for modeling sportswear for Joslin's, a store just down the street from Neusteter's where my mother worked.

At five feet four and a half inches, I was not destined to make it in the world of high fashion, but during that summer after high school, my picture adorned newspaper ads and a local teen magazine. I modeled the first bikini featured in a Denver fashion show, a very modest affair that barely exposed my navel but sent my father into a fit. Modeling seemed far more glamorous from afar than it did up close, especially in Denver, where I nearly froze during the shooting of outdoor swimsuit ads when the spring snows had barely melted and roasted while modeling ski outfits when the temperature climbed into the nineties. Nonetheless, my short stint as a model landed me a permanent job at Joslin's, first selling ladies clothing and then as the receptionist in the store beauty salon. And it was this job that ultimately led me to college.

The University of Colorado Denver Center was located in an old run-down office building barely one block from Joslin's in downtown Denver, miles away from the beautiful sandstone and red-tiled roofs of the Boulder campus. In August, Frances Lee, an old grade school friend, came by to have lunch with me on her way to enroll for classes at CU. On a lark, I not only accompanied her to the registrar's office but filled out an application myself. I had not taken the required entrance exams, so I signed up to take them the following week. I took a copy of the class schedule home to peruse and found several courses I thought I might enjoy, including one that would change my life. In addition to a college math course, taught by a professor who lived across the street from my home, I enrolled in two English courses and Introduction to Modern Dance for one credit. My dance teacher was a woman named Rhoda Gersten, a middle-aged bohemian with a wild mane of hair who had once danced in the Martha Graham company in New York City. Her class met in a storefront dance studio in East Denver during the evening. I rode the bus there after work, one of some two dozen students fulfilling a physical education requirement. But Rhoda was unlike anyone I had ever met. Graceful, despite a matronly figure, she fairly burst with energy and creativity.

One day after class, Rhoda announced that she was looking for volunteers to assist in an arts enrichment program for underprivileged kids in Park Hill, a mostly black neighborhood in East Denver. The program, run by one of Denver's new anti-poverty agencies, operated out of a Catholic school, Curé d'Ars, on Saturday mornings. I offered to help teach drama to the elementary school children enrolled in the program. A few days later, Rhoda called me at home. "I'd like to discuss the Curé d'Ars program," she said. "Can you come to my house some afternoon this week?" I was flattered by the invitation and promptly accepted, but when I arrived for the appointment, something seemed amiss. Rhoda's house, not far from her dance studio, was a short bus ride away from my own but different from any house I'd ever been in. The walls were covered by African masks and Matisse cutouts, every inch of surface space was occupied by books and magazines in disarray, and stereo components lined one wall but no television was in sight. It was a far cry from my own neat, conventional home, with crocheted doilies on the arms of the couch and chairs, a framed print of George Romney's "Miss Juliana Willoughby" on the wall, books on their proper shelves, and the furniture arranged around a large console television at the center of the living room. Like her house, Rhoda's conversation was eclectic and disorganized. She jumped from one topic to another, barely touching on the tutoring project that was the ostensible reason for our visit. Then, she shifted gears abruptly.

"Linda, I'd like you to meet my son, Chris," she announced with no one yet in sight. As if by prearrangement, Chris emerged from the hallway, tall, handsome, but bashful. "He'll drive you home," she said. And with that our meeting was over, the real reason for the invitation now apparent. But Chris didn't drive me home. Instead he drove me to the White Spot restaurant on East Colfax.

"I'll have to call home," I explained.

"Tell them you'll be late, real late," he said, handing me a dime. When I returned, we sat in a booth sipping coffee for hours.

After dozens of attempts at matchmaking for friends and family, including a previous effort to interest Chris in another student in her class, Rhoda had finally succeeded. And my life took a dramatic turn.

2

From Teenage Bride to Campus Activist

*Few are they who are so happy as to have passed their youth
without committing any damnable sins, either by dissolute or
violent conduct, or by following some godless and unlawful
opinions.*

—Augustine, *City of God*

FROM THE MOMENT WE MET, Chris took over my life. It would be years before I
would assert my own opinions, make my own decisions, or dissent from him in
any important way. In our early, heady days together, he was the driving force
in our relationship.

Born the middle child of five, Chris was, from his earliest years, the one who
organized everyone in his amazingly disorganized family. Rhoda had little
patience for the mundane tasks of running a household. Dirty dishes overflowed
the sink, and the leftovers in the family refrigerator displayed more colorful varieties
of mold and fungus than I had ever imagined existed. "Exposure to germs
improves the immune system," Rhoda would say, explaining away the mess.
Chris's father, Jerry, was as fastidious as Rhoda was disorderly. Though every
other surface in the house was cluttered with two decades of newspapers and
magazines, photographs and books, Jerry's desk was tidy, every piece of paper
and implement in its proper place. Unlike Chris, Jerry was a small man, barely
five feet, six inches tall. With a gray goatee and kind blue eyes, he looked every
bit the rabbi he had almost become. The only son of Polish immigrant parents,
Jerry had a prodigious intellect. At the age of three, he was already reading
Hebrew, and by eighteen he had graduated from City College, a feat made even
more impressive by the fact that he simultaneously attended the Jewish
Theological Seminary. Instead of pursuing the rabbinate, however, he decided
to study medicine at New York University Medical School. By the time I met
Chris, Jerry was already at the top of his field, the chairman of the department
of rehabilitation medicine at the University of Colorado Medical Center in

Denver and the incoming president of the American Congress of Physical Medicine and Rehabilitation.

Though Jerry made a good living, he insisted on saving enough money from his physician's salary to ensure that he would be able to pay tuition for five children through graduate school. His frugality meant that the family lacked the usual amenities. They drove old cars and wore secondhand clothes, and their furniture looked as if came from the local Goodwill. Chris's wardrobe came mostly from thrift shops—a fact that deeply embarrassed me when we first dated. He would show up for our dates in some ancient, ratty sports jacket with too-short sleeves and mismatched slacks, making me feel ridiculous in my stylish outfits. Worse, he drove a gray 1950 Chevy, with the upholstery in such tatters that little bits of foam rubber worked their way through the fabric and stuck to my clothes. I emerged from each ride speckled with tiny yellow particles, as if I'd been through an artificial snowstorm.

But Chris's clothes and car were more than a reflection of his family's thrift. They made a political statement as well, a rejection of the bourgeois values that I aspired to. He was, he informed me on our first date, "an atheist and a socialist." I'm not sure which identification shocked me more. I not only attended mass every Sunday but had toyed with becoming a nun. I applied and was accepted by the Sisters of Charity of Cincinnati during my senior year in high school but decided against joining when the nun sent to interview me warned that I would never get over being attracted to men. Twelve years of Catholic school had also imbued me with a hatred of communism and everything associated with it, including Karl Marx. From grade school on, I learned of the evils of the communist system, in often horrific detail. Stories of missionaries tortured by the Red Chinese were the fare of classroom discussion: tales of priests and nuns with their fingernails extracted, slowly impaled by bamboo shoots, subjected to every manner of degradation and deprivation. And like many Americans of that era, I was a faithful viewer of Bishop Fulton Sheen's weekly television program, where he regularly inveighed against atheist communism. But Chris's brand of socialism was entirely new to me.

"I'm a Yipsel," I heard him say.

"A what?" I asked.

"A member of the Young People's Socialist League.[1] It's the youth arm of the Socialist Party, founded by Eugene Victor Debs and headed by Norman Thomas." I had never heard of either man. "We're anti-communist socialists. Democratic socialists hate the communists," he told me, "and they hate us." This was news to me, but I decided to put aside any skepticism. Despite having written an essay titled "The Red Crusade" when I was thirteen, in which I warned of "the disease of Red infiltration, a disease which un-arrested could mean total abolition of democracy as we know it today, and the introduction of a socialistic, communistic government," under Chris's tutelage I came to believe that socialism wasn't such a bad thing after all. Economics was not a subject I'd ever given any serious thought to. The idea that there should be more equal distribution of wealth in society sounded benign from my vantage point at the bottom of the economic ladder, though I never stopped to consider what it might mean to my incentive to climb higher.

Chris's influence over me extended far beyond politics. I met him at the end of my first semester in college. Having started college at sixteen, he was already in his third year at CU in Boulder when we met, though he had dropped out for a semester and was living at home temporarily. I had no clear idea of what I wanted to do with my life, no plan even to enroll as a full-time student. Within weeks of our first date, Chris had convinced me that I not only had to finish college but go on to graduate school as well. Until I met Chris, I don't think I even knew what a Ph.D. was, much less how to go about earning one. Suddenly, I needed to worry about grades, something I had not done since elementary school. My first semester college grades were inauspicious, two A's, including one from Rhoda, a B, and a D in math. I would have to do better. For the first time in my life, I became a serious student.

With Chris's prodding and help, I applied to transfer to Boulder in the fall of 1966. Lyndon Johnson's new anti-poverty programs paid my way. I was able to obtain Work-Study grants, as well as federal loans and a small scholarship from the university, without which it would have been difficult, if not impossible, for me to attend school full-time—for which I still harbor fond regard for President Johnson. The Work-Study programs in which I participated once again put me into Denver's black community.

In the summer of 1966, America's cities were poised for civil disturbance. A riot in Watts, a black neighborhood in Los Angeles, the previous summer had left 34 dead, more than 1,000 injured, 4,000 arrested, and more than 1,000 businesses looted or destroyed.[2] Between 1964 and 1968, more than 250 Northern cities experienced riots in black neighborhoods. Denver authorities were taking no chances and enlisted the local War on Poverty program to try to keep the lid on the black and Mexican American neighborhoods. Corky Gonzales had been appointed head of the Denver War on Poverty by Mayor Currigan in 1965 but was fired less than one year later for leading a noisy protest against the Rocky Mountain News, which accused him of showing favoritism in hiring Mexican American youth for the Neighborhood Youth Corps. But despite some concern among Mexican American civic leaders that their community might soon experience the civil unrest afflicting black neighborhoods across the country, North Denver and the Westside, where much of the Mexican American community lived, remained calm. My new Work-Study assignment took me instead to Five Points and Park Hill, black neighborhoods that city officials feared might erupt.

Denver's Operation Cool It was meant to keep young blacks off the street and out of trouble over the long hot summers by sponsoring community dances on the weekend where teenagers and young adults could gather with supervision. Chris and I were hired as chaperones for a series of such dances in the tough Five Points area. I'm not sure what anyone thought two white teenagers could do to prevent trouble, but the pay was good and the assignment promised to be fun as well. What better job than being paid to rock 'n' roll on a warm summer evening? We lasted one week. My parents were terrified about letting me go into Denver's most notoriously troubled neighborhood, but at over six feet, Chris promised at least some protection for me. When we arrived, the community center was brightly lit and festive; money from the War on Poverty paid not only our salaries but provided for decorations, music, and refreshments. Slowly, kids began to arrive, but far more young men than women. For the most part, they seemed little different than the black kids who attended my high school: polite, well-dressed, hardly the types who were throwing Molotov cocktails and looting shops in places like Detroit, Cincinnati, and Newark. Although several of the young men asked me to dance, Chris got the message from the hostile looks and snide remarks that there would be trouble if he, in turn, danced with the few young black women present. At one point, Chris went outside for a cigarette and I joined him. First, one of the locals approached, asking Chris for a match. Then a couple of other young men approached.

"Hey, man got a dollar you can lend me?" the tall, smiling, but somewhat menacing fellow in his early twenties asked.

"No, can't say as I do," Chris answered, with me hanging tightly onto his arm.

"How 'bout a quarter then? You got a quarter, don't you?"

"Nope." Chris sounded relaxed, friendly, but I was scared. It was dark, we didn't know any of these guys or anyone else for that matter, and we were greatly outnumbered. Chris threw his cigarette butt on the ground, crushing it with his foot, and casually walked with me past the three men back into the dance hall. I was impressed.

"You handled that well," I said.

"Yeah, well I don't think we want to stick around too much longer," he warned.

Soon the guys who had hassled him outside were back in the hall. As Chris and I danced, they made wisecracks about the "po' white boy" from the sidelines, nothing particularly threatening, but unsettling nonetheless. By 1966, the civil rights struggle had become more complicated. Images of Southern policemen unleashing dogs on peaceful black demonstrators had been replaced on the evening news with pictures of rock-wielding blacks breaking store windows and setting fire to buildings in the North. Alongside the voices of the Reverend Martin Luther King Jr., the NAACP's Roy Wilkins, and the Urban League's Whitney Young, Americans were hearing the angry rants of Malcolm X, the newly formed Black Panthers' Huey Newton and Bobby Seale, and the Student Nonviolent Coordinating Committee's (SNCC) Stokely Carmichael. Black radicals cast all whites as the enemy, with liberals who had demonstrated on behalf of equal rights held in the same contempt as the likes of Governor George Wallace or Bull Connor. Though we were in no real danger, I decided maybe it was best not to tempt fate, and the Operation Cool It dance was my last venture into Five Points for awhile, to the great relief of my parents. I spent the rest of the summer and the next working at the Southwest Denver Community Center, where again I taught drama and art to poor black kids in a program Rhoda set up.

In the fall, Chris and I both headed for Boulder. His parents bought Chris a tiny trailer to live in, twenty-eight feet long and eight feet wide. I moved into a boardinghouse a few blocks from campus. Like most universities of that era, the University of Colorado exercised a strict policy of *in loco parentis*. CU's rules determined where unmarried students could live, what hours they were required to be in their rooms at night, and strictly forbade co-ed visits in dormitory rooms at any time. Although I lived off-campus, my boardinghouse had identical rules. As a second-year student, I was allowed to stay out until 10 P.M. on weeknights and midnight on weekends; when my grades put me on the honor roll my second semester, my curfew increased by an hour. A resident assistant conducted bed checks nightly, although it was still possible to "sign out" for overnights so long as they were to the homes of responsible married couples—and there were always obliging older friends if the need arose.

The decrepit state of Chris's trailer, which shook ferociously in Boulder's frequent chinook winds, kept me at the boardinghouse most nights. But by the end of the year, the rules themselves had begun to break down so widely everywhere on campus and off that our R.A. didn't even bother to keep up pretenses. Her own boyfriend spent most nights in her room on the first floor, and it was so easy to sneak out of the walk-out basement where my room and three others were located that our floor was virtually empty much of the time. Fear that my parents might call unexpectedly did more to keep me at the boardinghouse than the university's increasingly ignored rules. My father was quite capable of driving the forty-five minutes it took to get from Denver to Boulder in the middle of the night to check on me, so I was more cautious than the other girls, but by no means perfect.

The mid- to late sixties were a time of great upheaval on American campuses across the country, with often violent protests wracking many universities from coast to coast. What began with Mario Savio and the Free Speech Movement at Berkeley in 1964 had spread rapidly to other campuses, spurred on by a growing antiwar movement as the United States' role in Vietnam escalated. By the end of 1965, there were nearly 200,000 U.S. troops fighting in Indochina, and in 1966, the United States began bombing Hanoi and firing into Cambodia. As the war expanded, the protests against it proliferated. Yet it was still possible to attend college during this period—even on a campus known for its political activism, like Boulder—and remain almost oblivious to the goings-on. The university regularly held "teach-ins" on the Vietnam War, and the campus quadrangle was often filled with students haranguing each other on the political issue du jour. One group of students regularly snaked through the halls of the University Memorial Center with their Viet Cong flags, chanting "Ho, Ho, Ho Chi Minh, the Viet Cong are going to win." I had grown up with tremendous respect for the military. My father had talked of his time in the Air Force as the most rewarding period of his life, and many of the kids I went to school with were from military families stationed at Denver's three military bases. I believed that our soldiers fighting in Vietnam were heroes. The protesters, on the other hand, seemed dirty, disrespectful, and unpatriotic. I had no desire to join in their antics and developed an intense dislike for the entire antiwar movement and its followers. But, for the most part, I could ignore them; I was preoccupied with schoolwork and my new relationship with Chris. The closest I came that year to experiencing the radical politics then bursting out on universities across America was in the lunchroom of the University Memorial Center.

Chris introduced me to "Red Square," a motley corner of the school cafeteria, on my first day on campus. Though students could sit anywhere they chose in the large room that took up nearly the entire basement of the UMC, by tradition, CU's fractious left-wing students gravitated toward three large round tables in the darkest corner of the room to eat meals, drink coffee, smoke, or just hang out. The Yipsels dominated the tables, though they were by no means the largest left-wing group on campus. The Trotskyist Young Socialist Alliance (YSA), the Students for a Democratic Society (SDS), and even the

Communist Party were well represented in Red Square, provoking noisy arguments among the diners, especially on the subject of Vietnam. The Yipsels
largely supported U.S. involvement in the war—though all the males were
happy to take student deferments so as not to have to fight in Vietnam. The
Yipsels viewed the war as a struggle against Soviet-inspired and supported total-
itarianism, not some indigenous peasant revolt against imperialism, then the
romanticized leftist version of what was going on in Southeast Asia. I mostly
listened to the debates in Red Square, being too ignorant to engage in the
often fierce polemics. Most of the participants were sociology or political science majors. As an English literature major, I often found the arcane discussions of socialist economic and political theory impossible to follow.
Nonetheless, most afternoons after class I would head for Red Square to meet
Chris. Shy and unsure of myself, I rarely spoke to anyone, preferring instead
to sit, sipping endless cups of coffee, reading literature.

By Christmas break, my relationship with Chris was coming to a head. I
wanted to get married as soon as school let out for the summer. Chris wasn't
so sure he was ready for marriage—an entirely sensible position for someone
who had just turned nineteen. But it was clear that if I moved home again for
the summer, our relationship would suffer. I would be back to midnight cur-
fews, my father waiting up for me at the door when I returned home from our
dates. Neither of us relished the impending loss of my newfound independence. On Christmas eve, Chris asked me to marry him. I accepted immediately and was anxious to tell the world, but we waited to announce our engage-
ment for several weeks. We chose to make the announcement at the wedding
of Chris's older brother, Steve, who was just completing medical school at the
University of Colorado Medical Center, where their father taught. I stood in
the reception line next to Chris at Temple Emmanuel synagogue as he introduced me to the wedding guests as his fiancée, Linda Chavez.

"Linda Javitz? Nice Jewish name," one family friend announced loudly, in
an obvious dig. Steve, too, married a Gentile—though one who converted just
prior to the wedding. Intermarriage, even among Reform Jews like the
Gerstens, was still the exception in the 1960s, not the commonplace phenomenon it has become in the decades since. Chris and I had barely discussed
where we would get married, knowing the options were limited. Since moving
to Boulder, I had stopped going to mass except on weekends I spent at home,
but my Catholicism was still deeply ingrained in the way I thought about the
world. I hadn't stopped believing; I had just learned to live with a certain
amount of guilt for those conflicts I couldn't rationalize away. Chris's parents
offered to have our wedding in their home in a civil service, but I was intent

on a religious ceremony. The Catholic Church allowed Catholics to marry non-Catholics, so long as the couple agreed to raise their children in the Church. I knew Chris would never agree to that, nor to the Pre-Cana sessions, the religion-based premarital counseling that was required of all couples. Instead, we decided to explore getting married at Temple Emmanuel, where Chris's parents were members. I agreed to meet with a new young rabbi, whom we hoped would be sympathetic to our plight. But he dashed our hopes in the first meeting.

"You'll have to convert. The process will take about six months if you're willing to drive in twice a week to meet with me for private lessons. Since you are under twenty-one, you'll have to get signed permission from your parents," he said.

There was no way that I was going to broach this subject with my parents. Even though neither of them were practicing Catholics, having been previously divorced, they would have been deeply chagrined at the thought of my converting. Besides, as a full-time student in Boulder, I couldn't possibly come into Denver twice a week during the school year—and Chris would have to drive me, since I had not yet learned to drive. When Chris told his mother what the rabbi had said, she called the head of the congregation, Rabbi Earl Stone, who was far more accommodating when we met a week later.

"I don't see it as my job to throw up roadblocks," he explained to Chris and me in obvious reference to his younger, more traditional colleague's stipulations. "I'll give you a few books to read. You'll come see me once a month. We'll talk for an hour or so. I'll ask you a few questions. That's it." I was greatly relieved. My conversion would be a mere formality, and in the process I would study Judaism, which had always interested me anyway—or at least that is how I rationalized my decision at the time.

In fact, the process was every bit as simple as Rabbi Stone described. I went in to meet with him in his study at Temple Emmanuel a half dozen times over the next several months. Although he gave me a few books to read, which described holidays and rituals, there was little in them about religious doctrine. And our private tutoring lessons weren't much more elucidating. Rabbi Stone spent much of the time telling me funny stories—and took special delight if some of them made me blush. Meanwhile, the preparations for our wedding proceeded. With the exception of picking out my wedding dress, Rhoda and Chris made most of the major decisions, even picking out our flatware and dish patterns together. The reception following the wedding was to be a simple affair, a light buffet of cold cuts and fruit to be held in the basement of the synagogue.

Chris and I were married at Temple Emmanuel on June 15, 1967. Just before the wedding, I went to the synagogue, along with Chris and his seventeen-year-old brother Dennis, to meet with Rabbi Stone. In a brief ceremony in the empty sanctuary, Rabbi Stone admitted me into the Jewish faith, with Dennis as the witness. Afterward the rabbi presented me with a copy of the prayers to be said when lighting the candles before the Sabbath meal. In all, the whole process took less than five minutes, but it was to cause me great anguish over time. My expedient conversion brought me no closer to Judaism, which I never practiced beyond cooking a Passover meal occasionally, and simply alienated me from my Catholic faith. Though I continued to attend mass sporadically at Christmas and Easter, it would be years marked by much inner conflict before I would formally return to the Catholic Church.

Like any father giving away his daughter in marriage, my father looked more sad than happy as he walked me down the aisle, but, on the whole, my parents were pleased with my marriage. I kept my conversion secret from them, but they had no objections to my marrying a Jew. They liked Chris and his parents. My father especially enjoyed having around a young man with whom he could watch football and talk sports, and both my parents seem pleased that I was marrying the son of a prominent Denver physician.

After a three-week honeymoon of camping at national parks across the Southwest, Chris and I moved in with his parents, where we slept on a fold-out sofa in his mother's basement dance studio. I was anxious to set up housekeeping on my own and longed for privacy away from Chris's large family. Although I got along well enough with both Rhoda and Jerry, living with the Gerstens was trying. Meals were noisy affairs, with Rhoda rambling on about some harebrained scheme guaranteed to earn fame and fortune for Chris and me. "You should go into news broadcasting together. Someday they'll need someone to replace Huntley and Brinkley, and you two would be perfect," she suggested. Or, "Maybe the two of you could become forest rangers and then try to get *Life* magazine out to do a story on your adventures in the wild." Rhoda's flights of fancy could send Jerry into fits of laughter or provoke a mercurial rage, where he'd pound the table with his fist to end the discussion. I had never experienced anything like these dinner-time dramas. In my parents' house we generally ate our meals on TV tables while we watched the news. Conversation consisted of requests to turn the volume up or down.

In the fall, we moved back to Boulder, this time to a small garden-style apartment about a mile from the north end of campus. Living under the same roof with Chris for the first time, my study habits increased dramatically. Most evenings we spent at our apartment, reading, writing, or quizzing each other in preparation for exams. Although most of my classes consisted of English literature, I took two classes with Chris, psychology and sociology. We were competitive with each other and ended up earning identical grades in both. Though schoolwork left us little time for much of a social life on weekdays, we spent weekends with our friends, most of whom were married and already in graduate school. Two couples had recently had babies, and Chris especially liked to spend time playing with the infants. Chris loved babies. He couldn't get enough of them and told me when we got married that he wanted nine children. Although I had envisioned waiting until I was in my mid-twenties to have my first child, Chris was anxious to get started on our family immediately. The fact that we were penniless—living off student loans, my Work-Study jobs, and a small stipend from Chris's father—was no deterrent. By the time the spring 1968 semester started, I was pregnant. If all went as planned, I would have the baby between summer session and the start of the fall semester, and I wouldn't miss any school. We would take turns caring for the infant, alternating our classes so that one of us would be home while the other was on campus. But, of course, nature had its own timetable.

I began to feel ill almost immediately, and not with the kind of mild nausea the pregnancy books I was reading described. My "morning sickness" lasted twenty-four hours a day for nine months and consisted of gut-wrenching vomiting that would leave me faint and drenched in sweat. Even after my doctor prescribed Bendectin to control the worst vomiting, I could sometimes barely drag myself out of bed. I was hospitalized twice during my pregnancy for complications. I managed to finish the semester anyway, but then had to fight the university financial aid office, which insisted that I would have to work full-time in the fall after the baby was born or lose my aid. I complained that my grades were higher than some of the students I knew who were receiving full scholarships.

"We give scholarships to the students we anticipate will finish college. As a married—and pregnant—woman, your prospects of doing so aren't good," the officious young financial aid officer explained. "But I suppose we can increase your loan to make up the difference if you can't work. Of course, you'll have to start paying the loan back immediately if you drop out," he said.

Today, such comments would invite a fat law suit for sex discrimination, but the attitudes toward female students were often condescending at the time. And the financial aid officer wasn't the only one on campus convinced that the university was wasting a perfectly good education on a pregnant woman who would never complete her degree. When I had not yet delivered my baby by the time the fall semester began, I signed up for a light load of classes, including an honors seminar in astronomy for non-science majors, which met only once a week in the evenings. On the first night of class, barely able to squeeze my enormous belly into the desk, I told the professor that I might miss a couple of weeks of class when my baby was born. And he informed me that if I missed more than one class all semester, I would flunk the course. It was almost impossible to fail honors courses. Once you got in, you were virtually guaranteed to receive an H, equivalent to an A or B, or at worst, a P, for passing. I had never heard of anyone actually flunking an honors seminar, which were restricted to students who were already on the dean's list. The class met on Wednesdays. I delivered my son David on October 1, a Tuesday, and I was back in classes again the following Monday. When I showed up for my astronomy seminar on Wednesday, eight days after the birth and suddenly slim again, the professor said not a word—though he could not have failed to notice the change in my appearance in a class of a dozen students.

Despite my valiant efforts to continue my education without missing a beat, I was feeling overwhelmed by the end of the semester. I had obtained my driver's license a week before David was born—from a clearly anxious examiner who was happy to ignore my shaky driving skills as long as he could get out of the vehicle before I went into labor. I began shuttling to and from campus each day, sometimes with the baby in an infant seat ready to be handed off to Chris, who would meet me right after his classes let out. I was trying to nurse the baby, study, attend classes, cook, and clean—all on about three hours of sleep a night. David developed colic and would fall asleep only if taken for long rides in our 1960 Buick Invicta. Once we turned off the engine, his wailing would begin anew. What's more, we had moved from our small but nice apartment near campus to an old, dingy converted storefront miles away so that the baby would not have to sleep in our bedroom. Rhoda had convinced Chris that an infant would suffer irreparable psychological damage if he slept in the same bedroom as his parents—a notion I found preposterous. But with Sigmund Freud and Rhoda allied against me, I lost the argument, and we moved to the drab three-room apartment when David was born. Even after my father painted the rooms in bright shades of melon, avocado, and lilac, the place was depressingly gloomy and I found myself sinking deeper and deeper into depression. The final blow came when both Chris and I fell victim to the Hong Kong flu epidemic, which claimed 34,000 American lives that year, making it one of the deadliest in U.S. history. The two of us lay in bed for days, unable to keep any solid food down and wracked with 102-degree fevers that alternated with body-shaking chills. My mother took the Greyhound bus up from Denver on her day off to help clean the apartment and care for David, who, mercifully, remained healthy. By the time I was able to get out of bed, I was so far behind in my class work and so thoroughly exhausted that I withdrew for the semester. Having been only a part-time student my first year in Denver, I was already a full semester behind schedule for graduation. Now I would fall even farther behind.

A few weeks of rest revived me, however. By the beginning of spring semester, I was ready to get back to classes full-time. Though still not sleeping through the night, David had nonetheless become a delightful infant, easily adapting to our crazy schedules. Chris and I would often study late into the night, taking a break at 1 A.M. to head to the Doozy Duds, an all-night laundromat near campus, baby in tow, the backseat of our Invicta piled high with dirty laundry. When the spring snows finally melted, Chris took David to campus with him to let him crawl on the lush grass outside the Hellems Building, where most of my lit classes met. I could sit against the windows and stare down at the two of them frolicking on the quadrangle that stretched from Norlin Library to the edge of campus while I tried to listen to a boring lecture on Samuel Pepys's *Diary*. David, with his huge brown eyes and golden curls, was a co-ed magnet, and I would often find Chris and David waiting for me surrounded by a group of adoring female students.

The CU campus was teeming with political activity during the spring of 1969. U.S. involvement in the Vietnam War peaked in April at 543,000 troops, spawning campus and city demonstrations across the country. The Tet Offensive—the surprise communist attack on South Vietnamese towns during the Vietnamese New Year's celebrations a year earlier—marked a turning point in American public opinion about the war. When North Vietnamese and Viet Cong troops captured cities throughout the South—including parts of Saigon and Hué, South Vietnam's second-largest city—it was clear that the United States was not winning the war, despite LBJ's claims. Even though U.S. troops were able to recapture the cities, it had become obvious that Vietnam was a quagmire and we had to get out. Even Yipsel hardliners were forced to become critics of the conduct of the war, made easier by Richard Nixon's assumption of the presidency in January. We all had a visceral hatred of Nixon. Anything he did or said was automatically suspect, including his assertion during the campaign that he had a "secret plan" to end the war. _____

The antiwar movement itself was also becoming less monolithic. The Mobilization to End the War, a national umbrella group active on campuses and in cities across the nation, the SDS, and other leftist groups favored unilateral U.S. withdrawal. Indeed, most of the New Left favored a Viet Cong victory that would crush and humiliate the U.S. military and South Vietnam, which they regarded as a puppet regime. But there were growing numbers of Vietnam critics who were not merely anti-American. With no clear end to the fighting in sight and victory over the communists a chimera, even some hawks were beginning to think the best the United States could hope for was a dignified withdrawal. The Yipsels around the country became active in a group called "Negotiations Now," a coalition of social democrats, liberals, and some civil rights leaders, who urged a negotiated settlement with the North Vietnamese, as opposed to the unilateral U.S. withdrawal favored by the hardcore Left. When the Boulder Yipsel chapter set up a table in the University Memorial Center to gather signatures on a Negotiations Now petition, I agreed to man it for a couple of hours between classes. But the Negotiations Now position pleased neither the Left nor the Right. SDSers and Young Americans for Freedom alike heaped abuse on me as they walked by the table. My volunteering was short-lived. After David's birth I rarely did anything on campus unrelated to my classes, but that was about to change.

Campus life was now dominated by the left-wing groups on the CU campus, and it was impossible to avoid running into the radical politics they espoused. In addition to the ubiquitous antiwar groups, the Black Student Alliance had become increasingly visible and militant. BSA members reveled in intimidating white students on campus, adopting the slogans and symbols of the growing Black Power movement. Dressed in black T-shirts, muscles bulging, their huge Afros making the tallest men appear near-giants, a small group would march into the UMC cafeteria in military-style formation, cutting through groups of unnerved "honkies" like Moses parting the Red Sea.

But blacks were still a small minority on the CU campus. The student population in the late 1960s was overwhelmingly white and affluent. In all my years as an undergraduate on the CU campus of some 16,000 students, I encountered only one other Mexican American in any of my classes, and not many more blacks. In 1969, the racial makeup began to change when the university, at the prodding of the BSA and the fledgling United Mexican American Students (UMAS), decided to expand an affirmative action program, which had begun the previous summer with fewer than seventy black and Mexican American students. The Summer Tutorial Program (STP) was scheduled to grow to three hundred blacks and Mexican Americans for the summer 1969 session.

I saw the notice for a UMAS meeting to discuss the impending program posted outside the cafeteria one day. Curious and feeling a bit left out of the political maelstrom swirling about me on campus, I decided to attend the meeting that evening. The group, gathered in a small room in the UMC, was almost entirely male, made up of upperclassmen and a couple of graduate students. The president of the group, Phil Hernandez, wore glasses and a white dress shirt, unbuttoned at the collar. He was warm and engaging. Few of the students present looked the part of campus radicals. They were, for the most part, far more clean-cut looking than the average Boulder politicos. I felt at home immediately. Despite Chris's increasingly Bohemian look—with his long scraggly hair, mustache, leather pants, and Indian moccasins—I continued to wear matching skirts and sweaters, courtesy of my mother's discount at Neusteter's, my hair coiffed, lipstick on my lips, and mascara on my lashes— making me fit in more with the sorority crowd than my fellow Yipsels in Red Square. But the UMAS members looked similarly straight-laced and middle-class. Whereas the BSA members seemed eager to emulate the likes of Huey Newton and Bobby Seale, the UMAS leaders had not yet discovered Ché Guevara. The stated political agenda of UMAS was "to further education on Mexican-American cultural and historical contributions to the U.S. among the Spanish-surnamed and the Anglo population," hardly the stuff of revolution.[3] Not even my father, who bristled at the mere mention of the word Chicano, could object to my promoting these aims.

Although the university had agreed to admit one hundred and fifty new Mexican American applicants, it was not altogether clear where they would find them. It was not as if the university were turning away hundreds of Mexican American applicants each year. Few Mexican Americans bothered to apply to the school in the first place. Next to the Colorado School of Mines, an engineering school in Golden, Colorado, CU is the most academically rigorous public college in the state. The high school dropout rate for Mexican Americans in Colorado was extraordinarily high in the 1960s. Well over half of Mexican American students never made it to high school graduation. And even the most ambitious students usually ended up enrolling in night school if they wanted to continue their education, as I had initially, or attended one of Colorado's less competitive colleges. Out of my own high school graduation class, only four of the twenty or so Mexican Americans who graduated went on to four-year institutions. The CU administration had its work cut out for itself to fill the allotted slots, despite generous financial aid packages being offered to successful applicants, so UMAS stepped in to help recruit young Mexican American high school seniors, especially in southern Colorado, which was home to one of the largest Mexican American populations in the state. And I went along for the ride, literally.

Setting out in groups of two or three, UMAS members traveled the state in search of promising recruits. We visited high schools, met with school counselors, interviewed potential applicants, and even hit the local hangouts. In Pueblo, Colorado, a mill town one hundred miles south of Denver, I went into pool halls and drive-in restaurants, trying to spot potential recruits. Everywhere our message was the same. "I did it. You can, too. It's not as tough as you think." The girls were especially difficult to reach. If they had any ambition, their parents were likely to discourage it, especially if it meant moving away from home.

Boulder's reputation didn't help. Many Mexican American families had boys in Vietnam, and they had little use for the flag-burning campus radicals they saw on television. But they feared the drug scene and sexually permissive culture even more. By the mid-sixties, the campus had a thriving countercul-ture. Marijuana, LSD, mescaline, psilocybin, amphetamines, and even hero-in were widely available among the hippies on campus, many of whom were mere hangers-on, having taken to heart LSD guru Timothy Leary's advice to "tune in, turn on, drop out." It took all our powers of persuasion to convince protective Mexican American parents to allow their daughters to come to CU. I could certainly empathize with what these girls were going through. My par-ents weren't thrilled to see me move away from home either, especially not to Boulder, and were much relieved when Chris and I married, so that he could presumably protect me.

In the end, UMAS met its recruiting goals, but I had the impression that it was because the university accepted virtually every Mexican American who applied, no matter how ill-prepared. Meanwhile, I was getting ever more involved in UMAS, eventually becoming a member of the executive commit-tee. With a baby at home and a full load of classes, I was stretched thin, but I believed that what UMAS was doing was important. I wanted to encourage others who'd come from working-class backgrounds like mine to aspire to more than a steady paycheck. The work ethic in the Mexican American com-munity was high, but education was valued too little. Few Mexican American families encouraged their kids to go to college, even after financial aid became more widely available. I hoped I could make a difference in the Mexican American community through my UMAS involvement, so I put in the extra hours, often taking David with me to meetings on campus. But as I became more active, I noticed that UMAS had begun to change, too. Many of the orig-inal leaders, like Phil Hernandez, were becoming less influential, and others who had a more confrontational approach were taking over. In order to accommodate the burgeoning affirmative action program, the university recruited a new director, a sociology professor from South Texas, Salvador Ramirez, who brought with him a different, more radical style of leadership.

The rotund Ramirez earned the nickname *"el huevo"* not only because of his egg-shaped build but because he had the *huevos*—or balls, in the Spanish vernacular—to take on the CU administrators. Sal's methods were antagonistic. His classes, which were required for every Mexican American student enrolled in the summer program, became propaganda seminars where students learned to distrust the *gabachos*—the popular slang term for whites—and to wallow in the history of their own oppression.

As the only English major in UMAS—probably the only Mexican American majoring in English literature on campus at the time—I took on the responsibility of putting together the English tutoring sessions for the summer students. It was clear from the beginning that many of the students would flunk out once they enrolled in regular classes on campus. Few of the kids were Spanish-speaking. Like most third-generation Mexican Americans, most spoke only English, but they spoke—and wrote—it badly. One student routinely wrote "jallo" for yellow, much as he pronounced it. Others had never learned how to write complete sentences, had no idea what nouns or verbs were, and had never read anything but comic books. I'm not sure their math skills were much better, but at least they could avoid classes requiring math. Writing was a different matter. There was no way they would make it through CU unless their writing skills improved.

At a UMAS executive board meeting, I offered to go to the chairman of the English Department and plead for a special remedial freshman English course to be taught by UMAS-approved instructors, a plan that won quick endorsement. By the time I made my presentation to the English Department, I had devised lesson plans and selected a text to use with the incoming freshmen, a "programmed learning" approach to English as a second language (ESL), which allowed students to progress through a series of simple lessons at their own speed. I chose an ESL text, even though English was not a second language for the great majority of students, because it taught simple grammar and syntax rules to adults. Many of the students I encountered seemed to have had no basic training in either, certainly none that left any lasting impression.

I was surprised at how quickly the department chairman approved my plan, but I shouldn't have been. No one in the university knew what to do with these new students. The majority of them were admitted despite high school grades and test scores substantially below par. The whole design of the program ensured that students would attend special classes for at least their first year on campus—and as it turned out, many continued to take ethnic studies courses that kept them isolated throughout their years on campus. Mexican American students in the Equal Opportunity Program (EOP) lived together in the dorms, took at least nine of their twelve scheduled hours of classes together, attended UMAS meetings, rallies, and tutoring sessions as a group, and became a cohesive faction on campus. The BSU operated a similar program for black EOP students, which was no less isolated, and if anything, more militant than the UMAS program. The only time the two groups got together was for the regular protest marches to Regents Hall, where the university's administrative and financial aid offices were located. The BSU and UMAS were united in their animosity toward the CU administration, which was ironic in that it was the largesse of those same administrators that paid for the EOP's staff salaries, not to mention the scholarships for EOP students.

The English Department allowed me to teach the UMAS classes even though I had not yet completed my undergraduate degree and had no teaching experience, aside from my volunteer efforts for Rhoda a few years earlier. In a special arrangement, the department accepted me into the Ph.D. program while I was still working toward my B.A., so that my last semester in college I earned credits toward both my undergraduate and graduate degrees simultaneously. The arrangement—not so unusual since I was one of the top students in the department—allowed me to teach the freshman English course. Still, the university was doing no one a favor by putting such an inexperienced teacher in charge of some of the most challenging students on campus. It was all that I could do to keep my head above water, trying to help students make up in a few weeks what they had missed through twelve years of miserable public education.

For the most part, my students were sweet kids, and I found myself acting more like a big sister and counselor than a college instructor. When students stayed after class to talk, they were more likely to discuss problems with boyfriends or girlfriends than grammar or syntax. Many of the students were far away from home for the first time in their lives, with exciting, new opportunities available—and even more temptations. Several of the girls became pregnant their first semester on campus, sparking heated discussions on the UMAS executive board over whether the EOP freshmen should be encouraged during orientation to take advantage of birth control services available at the University Health Center. Sal Ramirez, a liberal on all other subjects, was a conservative on this one. He opposed any UMAS effort to get the girls information on birth control, insisting that it would alienate their parents. In the end, UMAS intervention may not have made much difference. Most of the girls believed that it was doubly sinful to plan ahead to engage in sex, which taking the pill implied. They would rather take their chances getting pregnant than admit they intended to have sex. I fully understood their moral dilemma, but I was impatient that they were throwing away an opportunity to improve their lives that might never come again.

Pregnancy wasn't the only danger students faced in their new environment. Drugs had become so commonplace on campus that it was impossible to cross the quadrangle on a warm spring day without inhaling the pungent aroma of marijuana from groups of students sitting on the steps of Norlin Library or lounging on the grass. And some of the students in the UMAS program had gone way beyond marijuana. I had students come to class tripping on LSD or high on amphetamines. One day, one of my most engaging students showed up in the middle of my lecture and motioned me out into the hall. His eyes were dilated and his speech thick, but it was his arm that caught my attention. A baseball-sized, festering ulcer had formed on the inside of his elbow where he had clearly been shooting up heroin or speed.

"Roberto, you've got to get to the health center. You could lose that arm," I said.

"I can't, man. They'll kick me out of school. They'll throw me in the can. Can't you do something?" he begged.

I dismissed class early and called the health center on the boy's behalf. They assured me his treatment would remain confidential, and I persuaded him to get to the clinic. He was back in class after a few days, his arm bandaged, but with the same stoned, glazed look to his eyes. I was beginning to feel that we had done a disservice to many of the kids in the UMAS program—and their parents, whom we had promised that the university would watch over their kids. College was supposed to change the students' lives, open up new opportunities to them, allow them to leave behind the gangs, drugs, and teenage pregnancies endemic in their communities. Instead, CU had simply exposed them to new temptations. I'd seen professors pass around joints in class and casually light up in front of students outside the classroom. At least at home, their parents would have tried to discourage their behavior, whereas many of the adults in the permissive Boulder environment condoned or even encouraged it.

I was also becoming increasingly frustrated with the new leadership in the UMAS program. What started out as a modest program to help marginal students acclimate to the rigorous demands of a college education was turning into an indoctrination camp. Chicano Power was the slogan of the day, and Ramirez and his Texas cronies seemed more interested in turning the students into Brown Berets than helping them learn the skills to make it in the university. The whole philosophy of the program was changing. Ramirez seemed to believe the university should accommodate to the students, not the other way around. Despite year-round tutoring and special remedial classes, many of the students were flunking out. The response of UMAS was to demand that students be allowed to remain in the program despite failing grades. Failure to maintain a 2.0 grade point average normally put a student on academic probation. If a student's grades dropped below 1.8 for two semesters, he was out, barring special appeals. UMAS initially fought for a 1.6 cutoff and then argued that a 1.0 should be sufficient. Furthermore, UMAS was pushing for an entirely separate Chicano studies curriculum for the students. The BSU was demanding the same for black students, in essence calling for segregated environments for black and brown students within the university. And of course, UMAS and the BSA wanted some say in who would teach the courses. In UMAS that meant limited involvement of the *gabachos*. I soon found myself on the losing side of arguments on these issues.

"What is the point of bringing these kids to a college campus and then isolating them from the rest of the students? They could have stayed behind in their old neighborhoods if they were just going to hang around with the same crowd they've known all their lives," I argued. "It's like we're creating our own ghettos here. And all this emphasis on Chicano studies isn't going to help them get good jobs when they graduate either. Then we make matters worse by letting them get away with murder when it comes to grades. A lot of these kids are basically flunking out, and we're protecting them from the consequences of their actions," I fumed. I was speaking from experience. I had become a good student when I realized I had something to gain from studying hard and doing well, but that hadn't happened until college. But these kids would never learn that lesson. I feared that, in trying to protect its students, UMAS was actually ensuring that they never succeed.

At first, Ramirez and his "Texas mafia" tolerated my views. I was one of the few women in any leadership role, and the guys—who relished their super-macho image—seemed almost amused at my outspokenness. They had the votes, after all, so my impassioned pleas to uphold standards and integrate students weren't any real threat. But I was becoming suspect. I already had two strikes against me: I was married to a white man—a Jew, no less—and I espoused "white" values. Worse, I had helped several whites get jobs in the tutoring program I managed, and I fought to keep them from being replaced with less-qualified Chicanos.

The issue came to a head in the summer of 1970. The UMAS honchos called me to a meeting one evening to inform me that there would be changes in the tutoring program and that Earl Schwartz, my good friend and a graduate student who had worked in the program from the beginning, was on his way out. Sal Peralta, then president of UMAS, had already threatened Schwartz. Peralta, a tall and imposing character, pulled Schwartz out of an STP staff meeting we were all attending in the basement of Temporary Building 1 to warn him to get out of the program or "face the consequences." To make sure Schwartz understood what those consequences might be, Peralta had brought along a group of ex-convicts from Canyon City prison, now part of the UMAS program, who stood ominously nearby.

The message to me was no less graphic. Richard Falcon, one of the UMAS leaders, sat across from me during the meeting playing with a switchblade the whole time. Falcon—gaunt, with a cruel, pock-marked face and a thick black mustache—had always seemed to me more like a street thug than a college student, but he was well regarded by others in UMAS, especially for his fiery rhetoric. He sat staring at me, his lips curled menacingly, holding the pearl-handled knife in front of his face as he released and retracted the long silver blade. Falcon scared me—unlike a lot of the new UMAS crowd, I hadn't grown up in the barrio. The Catholic schools I had attended expelled anyone who got into trouble, so I had no experience with hoodlums like Falcon. But I held my ground and argued on Schwartz's behalf, refusing to bow to the obvious attempt to intimidate me. Frustrated, Falcon repeatedly stuck the knife-point into the table. I left the meeting angry but unable to do anything. The next morning when I opened my front door to get the newspaper, I found a dead cat, its limp body laid out across my front stoop.

Years later I would remember this little drama when Falcon was killed in a confrontation with a filling station owner in Orogrande, New Mexico, near the Texas border. On August 30, 1972, Falcon was on his way to the national convention of La Raza Unida Party, a Texas-based, separatist political party, when he stopped his overheating car at a filling station owned by a white member of George Wallace's American Independent Party, Perry Brunson. The two got into a fight and Brunson shot Falcon, he claimed in self-defense. The case instantly became a cause célèbre for the militant Chicano movement. Falcon became a martyr, and the failure to convict Brunson (who was charged with involuntary manslaughter and acquitted) was touted as proof of a rigged justice system. I doubted it. My own experience with Falcon suggested that he was a man who courted trouble, and I could easily see him provoking a fight.

Falcon was not the only former UMAS member to meet a violent death. In 1974, four years after I left CU, six UMAS activists blew themselves up while trying to place bombs on campus in two separate incidents within a 48-hour period. In each case, the bombs exploded in the cars the UMAS kids and their companions were driving, completely destroying the vehicles and killing all but one of the occupants, who suffered severe burns and had to have his leg amputated. Four of the six who died were from Texas, part of the militant group that took control of the UMAS program.

By the time I left Boulder in August 1970, I had become deeply alienated from the program I had helped to create. I still believed that disadvantaged students deserved a chance at a college education, even if their grades and test scores didn't measure up to the usual admissions standards. But I also knew that if these kids had any hope of succeeding, it would take hard work to make up for years of educational neglect. Ranting against the "racist" system that had produced their failure in the first place would not get them anywhere. Nor would indoctrinating them with the notion that they were society's victims. Worst of all, teaching them to mistrust and hate whites for their role in "keeping Chicanos down," as the mantra of the day went, would make it difficult for these students to succeed in the larger world once they left the insular life of a college campus.

I was beginning to see the dark side of affirmative action—a term that was just beginning to be used. Initially I believed affirmative action programs would extend a helping hand to those who might not otherwise learn about available opportunities and might lack the skills to be able to compete for them. But the more I witnessed what went on in the programs, the more I questioned whether they sometimes did more harm than good. Still, I had no firsthand experience of what it was like to be a beneficiary of affirmative action—but that was soon to change. When I entered college in 1965, there were no affirmative action programs to assist me or others like me, although financial aid for economically disadvantaged students of all races was becoming much more widely available. But by 1970, affirmative action programs based on race and ethnicity had proliferated broadly, with new programs being offered everyday. I would soon learn that affirmative action could be a double-edged sword, even for its intended beneficiaries.

Although I had been accepted as a graduate student in English literature at CU, I knew that I would not be able to complete my degree in Boulder. After graduating with a B.A. in political science in 1968, Chris had decided that he wanted to pursue a graduate degree in clinical psychology, which necessitated his earning a second undergraduate major in psychology over the next two years. Graduate programs in clinical psych were highly competitive, and CU's was ranked among the best in the country, so Chris held out little hope that he would be accepted there.

In January 1970, we began applying to schools around the country with two criteria: Chris had to be accepted in the psych program, and I not only had to be accepted in a Ph.D. program in English but had to earn a full fellowship or teaching assistantship. Chris's father would pay for his graduate school tuition and half of our living expenses, but I would have to pay my own way and our son's. One of my professors had nominated me for a prestigious Woodrow Wilson Fellowship, but even if I won, no money came with the honor, although graduate schools usually gave money to Wilson fellows whom they accepted. As it happened, I won only an honorable mention in the Woodrow Wilson competition and was very worried about paying for graduate school when I came across an advertisement for a new Ford Foundation graduate fellowship for blacks, Mexican Americans, Puerto Ricans, and American Indians. The notice, pinned to the bulletin board outside the English Department office, announced a generous fellowship program: full tuition and fees at any institution of the winner's choosing, plus a $3,500-a-year stipend, which was about a thousand dollars higher than most other fellowships offered.

I applied and was ecstatic when I received a telegram in early spring notifying me that I had been selected as a finalist. The letter, which followed a few days later, informed me that the foundation would fly me to New York for a personal interview, covering all my expenses. I had never flown in an airplane and was nervous about leaving my eighteen-month-old son behind. But my parents offered to take David, while Chris's parents agreed to pay for him to accompany me, turning the trip into a short second honeymoon. The foundation paid for me to stay in a midtown New York City hotel for one night. I was put in a room with another female finalist, a first-generation Mexican American from California whose father was a physician, while Chris stayed with our friends Ray and Joy Willis who had recently moved to Long Island. I barely slept that night, my first ever in a big hotel. In the morning, I awakened early and walked the few short blocks to the tall, glass skyscraper that housed the Ford Foundation, arriving so early for my interview that the guard had me wait in the giant atrium for nearly an hour. I sat nervously, thumbing through the first copy of the *New York Times* I had ever seen. When the guard finally sent me up in the elevator I had already gone over in my mind a hundred times all the possible questions the panel might ask me. A few months earlier, I had sat for a similar interview for the Woodrow Wilson Fellowship, and I was convinced that I had blown it on a question about the fourteenth-century Italian poet Francesco Petrarch. I spent time cramming for the Ford Foundation interview by going over all my literary anthologies, memorizing facts and rereading passages. From the moment I entered the room, it was apparent that my studying was wasted.

Immediately I sensed an uneasiness from the three interviewers—two Anglo men and a Puerto Rican woman, as if I were not quite what they expected. The lead figure, a balding, middle-aged man in a tweed sports jacket, invited me to sit in an empty chair in a small semicircle in the large, ornate room, with an imposing conference table and desk at one end. He started off by asking me to tell them about my background and why I deserved the fellowship. I described growing up in a working-class family in New Mexico and Colorado, how I'd worked my way through college, managed to stay in school even after I married and gave birth to a son. Then I described my involvement in the UMAS program. I explained how I persuaded the English Department to set up a special section of freshman English for the incoming Mexican American students and described the difficult balancing act I'd undertaken to teach, take care of my son, and finish my own degree simultaneously. "It will make a huge difference in my academic life if I don't have to work while I pursue a Ph.D.," I explained.

When I finished, the bald man smiled solicitously. "You speak English so well," he said. "No accent at all," he added, addressing his colleagues almost as if I weren't in the room. "But why did you decide to study English literature instead of Spanish literature?"

I could barely believe my ears. I started to answer, mumbling something about Lope de Vega and a course I'd taken in seventeenth-century Spanish drama.

"You do speak Spanish, don't you?" the other man, a bespectacled fellow with a mustache, interrupted.

"I didn't grow up speaking it. My grandparents sometimes spoke Spanish, and I understand it a little. But most young Mexican Americans in Colorado speak English as their first language," I added, defensively. The Puerto Rican woman, a small, auburn-haired matron, leaned toward me and proceeded to say something in Spanish. I froze. Despite having taken Spanish in college and having grown up hearing it, I could barely make out the words. They sounded like gibberish. It didn't help that the woman's accent was distinctly Caribbean, the endings of words were lopped off, and the cadence was less rhythmical than the standard Mexican inflection.

"I'm sorry, could you repeat your question?" I asked.

Instead, the woman said to her colleagues, shaking her head, "She doesn't speak Spanish."

The bald man smiled, unctuously. "I was curious about your GRE scores," he said, changing the subject abruptly to my performance on the graduate record exams required by most graduate schools.

I had done miserably on the math section of the GREs, scoring below the 40th percentile, which had little effect on my chances of getting into an English lit program, since my verbal and English literature scores were respectable, in about the top 10 percent of students taking the exams. Still, I thought I could have done better.

"I probably should have retaken the GREs," I said. "The night before the exam, I was up all night with my baby. He had colic for his first several months," I offered, apologizing for not doing better on the tests.

He seemed confused. "The problem isn't that your scores are too low," he said.

Now it was my turn to be puzzled.

"The purpose of this fellowship program is to help educationally disadvantaged students. Judging from your GREs and everything I've heard today, I'm not sure you need our help."

I was utterly dismayed. Of course I needed their help. Without financial assistance there was no way I could attend graduate school. And most schools offered teaching assistantships instead of straight fellowships, which would mean that I would have to continue to work and attend school while struggling to raise my son. Didn't my work with UMAS count for anything? Wasn't I exactly what the Ford Foundation should have been looking for: an economically disadvantaged student who earned good grades, performed well on achievement tests, and had a history of trying to help others?

Apparently not.

"Anyone have any additional questions?" he asked the others. Then, turning back to me, he said, "You're going to do just fine. You'll make it on your own no matter what happens." All three interviewers stood up, signaling that my ordeal was over. I thanked them and left the room, fighting back tears. The interview had lasted no more than fifteen minutes. I knew there was no chance I'd be given the fellowship. I hadn't lived up to their image of what a disadvantaged Mexican American looked, sounded, or behaved like. My skin wasn't dark enough. I lacked a tell-tale accent. I'd chosen to study Samuel Beckett instead of Octavio Paz. And worst of all, my test scores were too high. These three knew perfectly well that Mexican Americans don't do well on standardized tests; therefore I must not be an authentic Mexican American. I was furious. My roommate from the night before brushed by me as I stepped out of the elevator.

"Good luck," she said cheerfully.

"Yeah, you too," I muttered, wondering whether she would fit their ethnic stereotypes better with her darker skin and slight accent, even if her father was a physician and mine a house painter.

Predictably, I didn't get the Ford Foundation fellowship. I received the usual form letter complimenting me on the tremendous achievement I'd earned just by becoming a finalist in the competition. I crumpled it up and threw it in the trash. Meanwhile, my acceptance letters to graduate programs were coming in. Unfortunately, my first choice, the University of Chicago, accepted me, but without financial aid—which made me even more bitter about the Ford Fellowship fiasco. And Chris was having less luck getting into a graduate program in psychology. Finally, we both had what we needed: Chris was accepted into a master's program in clinical psych at Pepperdine University in Los Angeles, and I received an offer of a fellowship from the University of California at Los Angeles for a Ph.D. in English lit. The award letter informed me that I had been chosen for an "Academic Advancement Program" fellowship offered by the university, which would cover most of my expenses. The name sounded suspiciously like an affirmative action program. It was one thing to teach in such programs, as I had. But I'd never been a beneficiary of affirmative action. Now this letter made it appear that I had been accepted into a graduate program at UCLA similar to the undergraduate program I had been teaching in at CU—one meant for students who couldn't make it into the university on their own. With my grades and test scores, I didn't need an affirmative action boost. I could compete fine on my own—just as the Ford Foundation representative had suggested. Any implication to the contrary was downright insulting. I decided to call the UCLA English Department to discuss my status. The chairman of the department sounded friendly and eager to have me in his department. But when I asked whether I had been considered for a regular department fellowship or even a teaching assistantship, his response was blunt.

"I have only a handful of T.A.'s and fellowships to give out. Why should I waste one on you when you are automatically eligible for the AAP?" he asked.

"I understand," I said, "but the fact is that a fellowship awarded on merit means something very different than one awarded as part of an affirmative action program."

"From the department's vantage point, everyone wins by your accepting the AAP award," he argued. "Besides, we've already notified our department fellowship recipients and they've accepted. I suppose we could look into a T.A. position if you're interested."

"I had hoped not to have to work and go to school," I said, deciding not to mention my son David, which experience had taught me usually made matters worse. I thanked him and said that I was looking forward to joining the graduate program and hoped we would meet soon. But I felt cheated.

It is possible, of course, that had I been considered for an academic fellowship I might well have lost out anyway. As it was, I resented not being given the chance to find out if I measured up or not. I needed the money nonetheless, so I accepted the AAP grant, ignoring the sting of stigma I felt accepting it. My experiences in Colorado had made me very wary of affirmative action, and I was about to discover exactly how corrosive the policy could be for everyone involved: students, teachers, and the institutions themselves. My experiences at UCLA in the coming year would profoundly influence not just my personal life but the role I would play in public policy in years to come.

3

Affirmative Action Nightmare

The mafia calls its code of silence omerta, *because the penalty for speaking against the mob is death. The left's penalty for defection (in those countries where it does not exercise state power) is excommunication from the community of saints. This is a kind of death, too.*

—David Horowitz,
Hating Whitey and
Other Progressive Causes

THE PEPPERDINE CAMPUS IN 1970 stood like a fortress in the heart of South Central Los Angeles. Surrounded by six-foot-high walls, the university was a tiny white enclave in the middle of a deteriorating black neighborhood, bordered by South Normandie Avenue on the west and Vermont on the east. A conservative Christian school, Pepperdine required all students to attend chapel one evening a week. At the west edge of campus, married student housing consisted of several wooden, two-story, World War I–era "temporary" barracks, which had been converted into small apartments. Since Chris and I had a child, we were entitled to a two-bedroom unit, which was really two one-bedroom apartments with a connecting door. Consequently, we had two small kitchens, two bathrooms, two living rooms, and two exterior doors, giving us ample, if dilapidated, space. The yard in front of our apartment was barren, the grass long ago trampled to dust, a few rusty playground fixtures the only adornment. David, now two years old, spent his days riding his tricycle along the crumbling cement walkway outside our front door or climbing the old jungle gym in the courtyard.

Chris and I still managed to take turns caring for our son, alternating our class schedules so that one of us was home with him at all times, but it was getting more difficult to do so since both of us now had jobs in addition to our course work. Chris worked the graveyard shift at a nearby halfway house for mental patients, dispensing medicine and ensuring that the residents remained on the premises overnight. On the nights that Chris was at work, I lay sleepless in bed, listening to the sound of sirens and occasional gunshots from the surrounding neighborhood. Crime was rampant in the area of run-down bungalows and strip malls, which looked deceptively calm in the daylight but was transformed by gangs and drug addicts when the sun went down. When I did manage to fall asleep, I was sometimes awakened by the bright glare of police helicopter searchlights shining through my window as they pursued fleeing criminals through the alleys and streets near the school. Even though Pepperdine maintained its own security guards, I never felt entirely safe behind its walls.

My days, on the other hand, were spent far away from the South Central L.A. ghetto, with its liquor stores, barred windows, and boarded-up houses. Three days a week, I awoke at 6:00 A.M. to make my way in my old Buick Invicta up the "405" freeway to UCLA. I got off at the Sunset Boulevard exit, where I drove east for two miles past the multimillion-dollar homes of Brentwood and Westwood to the north gate of the campus. Spread out across four hundred acres of rolling hills and palm trees, the red-tiled roofs of the buildings gave the campus the look of a Mediterranean village. But despite its bucolic vistas, UCLA was not exempt from the violence that wracked American campuses in that era—some of which flowed directly from the streets of South Central L.A., Compton, Watts, East L.A., and other ghettos and barrios of greater Los Angeles, thanks to well-meaning but hopelessly naive college administrators. In addition to the regular affirmative action program on campus, UCLA had set up a special program for young black and brown men coming out of prison, admitting dozens of felons as college students. But earning a GED behind bars hadn't necessarily turned some of these ex-cons into model citizens, and the mix of criminal element and radical politics on campus predictably turned bloody.

A little more than a year before I arrived on campus, on January 17, 1969, gunfire erupted in Campbell Hall, which housed the administrative offices and classrooms of UCLA's "High Potential Program." Two brothers, G. P. and L. J. Stiner, both ex-cons and members of a black nationalist group on campus known as the United Slaves, or simply US, shot and killed John Huggins and Alprentice "Bunchy" Carter, UCLA students and local Black Panther leaders. The fight broke out after a meeting of the Black Student Union to discuss the selection of a director for the newly established Black Studies Department. Elaine Brown, one-time head of the Black Panther Party and a UCLA undergraduate in 1969, recalled the incident in her memoir A *Taste of Power: A Black Woman's Story:*

I climbed the stairs and never heard the first shot that ripped into John's back—only ten feet away from the assassin. I climbed the stairs and never heard the second shot that blasted into Bunchy's powerful chest. . . . I heard the sound of feet moving fast down the marble corridor. Fearful whisperings rose above the sound of running feet. Then gunfire again and more gunfire. One, two shots at a time. Short bursts of fire, very loud, horrible echoes. . . . More shots rang out. I heard glass break, then the crash of more breakage. Students were leaping through the huge windows to escape.[1]

In Brown's telling, guns were almost as ubiquitous among the radical black students on UCLA campus as they were in South Central L.A. Indeed, the rivalries resembled traditional gang conflicts, with each group sporting its own "colors" and vying for turf. The black nationalist US members dressed in dashikis and shaved their heads in imitation of their leader Ron Karenga—a college professor best known for having invented the pseudo-African holiday Kwanzaa, celebrated today by many blacks in December. The Panthers wore paramilitary uniforms, black leather jackets, and berets and had close ties to predominantly white radical groups, which was anathema to the ultra-nationalist US members. The Panthers were largely a Northern California phenomenon, and Karenga's local US thugs didn't want these interlopers invading their territory—especially when the Panthers tried to hone in on the protection racket US had going with the university.

In order to stave off unrest on the UCLA campus, the university administration had decided to establish a multi-hundred-thousand-dollar Black Studies program, which US and Karenga controlled. But the Panthers were fomenting dissent among the BSU members to pick their own leaders. In the meeting that sparked the bloodbath in Campbell Hall, the BSU voted to establish a committee to negotiate with the university over who would direct the program, rather than giving the job to Karenga's hand-picked candidate. The United Slaves and the Black Panthers settled the matter as gangs usually do: through the barrel of a gun, and in this case several guns, including a sawed-off shotgun, a 9 mm Browning, and a .44 magnum, all of which Elaine Brown described as being present in Campbell Hall on January 17, 1969.

When I arrived on campus in the summer of 1970, the memory of the incident had already faded. The only visible evidence of the gun battle was an ugly brown smear on a stairwell wall in Campbell Hall. Though barely recognizable as blood, the stain was preserved as a monument to the fallen students—or so I was told by Winston Doby, the director of the High Potential Program, who led me on a tour of the building as he was recruiting me to teach in the HPP. Earlier—about a week before my classes at UCLA were to begin—I had received a telegram from the university asking me to contact the HPP immediately. Although my fellowship had made it theoretically possible for me not to work while I attended graduate school, the HPP salary would make our lives much easier. It meant that I would have to teach two classes a week, but I had been carrying a full load and teaching for the previous year at CU for far less money. It would make my schedule more complicated and leave little time for studying at the research library on campus, but I decided to accept the offer anyway.

Many of the students in the High Potential Program were older than the kids I had taught in Boulder, and HPP mixed students of all ethnic groups together in certain classes rather than segregating them as UMAS had. I taught a composition class made up of Chicano men in the ex-offender program and another class that was essentially a reading discussion group made up of regular HPP students. Both classes were more challenging than any I had taught at CU. There were eight young men in the composition class, most of whom were a good deal older than I. Their spelling and grammar were atrocious, and they had great fun at my expense. They took every chance to embarrass me. Dangling modifiers became "dangling motherfuckers" in their jargon, and I soon found out that open-ended writing assignments usually turned into fantasies of what they would like to do to me if they could get me alone sometime. Not quite knowing how to handle the situation, I decided to correct the spelling and syntax and return the papers with a note suggesting the writers ought to learn how to spell the sex acts they described. I also decided to forego the short skirts and hip-hugger slacks then in fashion in favor of more conservative dress, at least on the days I taught class, but I often felt vulnerable when the classroom door closed and I faced the group of sometimes leering young men.

The students in my reading class were less provocative but no less challenging to teach. I had students of all races in the class, including one or two Anglo kids from poor, rural backgrounds, a middle-aged American Indian couple, and several blacks and Mexican Americans. The Indian couple were heartbreaking. They were the most serious and devoted of any of the students, but they read at a grade school level. I have often wondered what happened to them, if they made it through four years at one of the best colleges in the country, and if so, whether that said more about the university's indifference to standards than it did about their own power to overcome their disadvantages.

The text we used in the class, *Mixed Bag: Artifacts from the Contemporary Culture*,[2] was typical of the era: hip, multicultural, and interdisciplinary. But I soon found that not only were the selections in the text—everything from Sophocles to Lenny Bruce—way over the heads of most of the kids but the topics themselves—race, violence, religion, family, and death—provoked anger and hostility among the students. Classroom discussions quickly degenerated into name-calling between groups of students. With no sense of irony and lots of racial grievances, real and perceived, most of the students found it impossible to empathize with characters and situations beyond their own racial experience. But that didn't stop me from trying. In a discussion of one of the readings—comedian Lenny Bruce's routine "Just How Do You Relax Colored People at Parties?"—I asked students to consider whether Bruce wasn't guilty of the racial stereotyping he was poking fun at.

"When Bruce sets up these characters, he makes the white guy an idiot and a bigot—and a blue-collar worker to boot. But the Negro—as Bruce identifies him—is well educated, sophisticated, and infinitely tolerant," I said. "The white asks questions like 'I guess you know a lot of people in show business, huh. . . . You know Aunt Jemimah? . . . ' Or: 'I haven't got any fried chicken or watermelon, ahhh, raisins, or rice, whatever you people eat.' Do you think maybe Bruce himself is engaging in a little racial or, perhaps, class prejudice?"[3]

"Hell no," Robert, one of my black students yelled out. "Honkies think all the brothers eat watermelon and fried chicken all the time."

"Yeah, look at that fat honky Archie Bunker," Sandra piped in, referring to the character in Norman Lear's hit show *All In the Family*. "He's always talking about 'colored people this and colored people that.' I don't know why they put that shit on TV in the first place."

"I noticed both of you used the term 'honky,'" I replied. "Maybe some people find that term offensive, just like the derogatory words that are used to describe blacks or Chicanos or Indians. Aren't you showing your prejudice?" I asked, hoping to make students see that bigotry wasn't the preserve of any particular race or ethnic group.

"You a honky, too," a female voice from the back of the room called out, which set the students to laughing hysterically. The Chicano kids in the class seemed to think the remark was particularly funny. The UCLA Chicano students were both tougher and more militant than their counterparts at CU. Many of them came from the barrios of East L.A. and viewed me as an outsider. I talked funny—"like a *gabacho*," as one student pointed out in class, which meant I spoke standard English without an accent. I also used my married name, Gersten, which didn't help. And I didn't speak Spanish, unlike many of my students who were first- and second-generation Americans. But perhaps their reaction had less to do with me personally than it did with the shift taking place in the organized Chicano movement, especially in California, which had become increasingly radicalized as Mexican American groups joined the antiwar movement and vied with violent black groups like the Black Panthers for national attention.

On August 29, 1970, just about the time I arrived in Los Angeles, Mexican Americans rioted in East Los Angeles. The riot erupted during a march of more than twenty thousand through the streets of East L.A. to protest U.S. involvement in Vietnam. The so-called Chicano Moratorium was the largest minority demonstration against the war of the entire era. Groundwork for the march had begun nearly a year earlier when Rosalio Muñoz, former UCLA student body president, refused to be inducted. Calling on Chicanos every-where to launch a "moratorium" to oppose the war, he issued the following statement, an odd combination of pride in the valor of Mexican American sol-diers and hatred for the system for which they fought:

> I accuse the government of the United States of America of genocide
> against the Mexican people. Specifically I accuse the draft, the entire
> social, political, and economic system of creating the funnel which
> shoots Mexican youth into Vietnam to be killed and kill innocent men,
> women, and children. . . . I accuse the entire American social and eco-
> nomic system of taking advantage of the machismo of the Chicano
> male, widowing and orphaning the mothers, wives, and children of the
> Chicano community, by sending their men into the front lines where
> our machismo has given us more Congressional Medals [of Honor],
> Purple Hearts, and deaths in proportion to the population than any
> other race or ethnic group in the nation. This is genocide.[4]

The Chicano Moratorium drew participants from all over the Southwest, including a large contingent from Colorado's Crusade for Justice, with Corky Gonzales at the helm. According to Ernesto Vigil, who chronicled the protest march in his book *The Crusade for Justice*, the riot began when police respond-ed to complaints from neighborhood merchants that protestors were stealing from them. Chasing suspects into Laguna Park on Whittier Boulevard, the police wielded clubs and set off tear gas into the crowds gathered to hear Moratorium speakers, according to witnesses. The melee soon spread beyond Laguna Park to Wilmington on the west and Riverside on the east, an area of about ten miles. Gonzales and one of his companions were arrested on weapons charges as they fled the scene on a flatbed truck, two among more than four hundred arrests made that day. Although Corky would later be convicted and serve time in the L.A. county jail, his involvement in the Chicano Moratorium became a mere footnote. It was the death of a local TV reporter, Ruben Salazar, that stunned the Mexican American community in Los Angeles that day.

Salazar was a popular journalist, a reporter for the *Los Angeles Times* and news director of a local Spanish-language television station, KMEX. Salazar was covering the protest and resulting riot when he apparently ducked inside a bar, the Silver Dollar Café on Whittier Boulevard. Police, responding to reports of an armed suspect holed up in the bar, shot tear gas into the building. The ten-inch tear gas projectile hit Salazar in the head, killing him instantly. Although there was never any evidence to suggest Salazar's death was anything but a tragic accident, conspiracy theories abounded afterward. As one of only a handful of Mexican American journalists at the time, and one who often wrote pieces critical of the Los Angeles Police Department's treatment of Mexican Americans, Salazar soon became a martyr to many in the Chicano movement who believed he'd been murdered by the L.A.P.D.

UCLA administrators, worried by the unrest in the Mexican American community, were anxious to demonstrate their sensitivity and goodwill. In response to student demands, the university created courses in Chicano Studies in the political science, history, and sociology departments. They also established a Chicano library, run by a graduate student from Chile. Finally, the English Department decided it would offer a sophomore-level "Chicano Literature" course—but had little idea about what would be taught or who would teach it. In 1970 there weren't enough novels, short stories, poems, or essays published by Mexican American authors to fill a syllabus for a twelve-week course. Nor was there anyone on the faculty to teach the course—especially since MEChA,[5] the Chicano student association, insisted that all of the new Chicano Studies courses had to be taught by Mexican Americans. The English Department approached me, since I was the only Mexican American in their Ph.D. program. Despite my total unfamiliarity with the field, the department made me a handsome offer. I would be paid as a regular faculty member at the lecturer level— nearly twice as much as I earned in the High Potential Program for teaching just half as many hours; plus it would give me another teaching credential, which would make it easier for me to secure a faculty position once I completed my doctorate. I accepted the offer but soon discovered that I had struck no bargain. Nothing I had encountered in my teaching assignments to that point had prepared me for the problems I would face in the classroom in the spring of 1971.

By the time I began teaching Chicano Literature 200, Chris had dropped out of graduate school, disillusioned with the clinical psychology field, and returned to his primary interest in politics. Chris began working full-time registering voters for a new AFL-CIO-funded grouped called Frontlash. The AFL-CIO was heavily involved in a special election for the state legislature that would determine control of the California House and was pouring money into voter registration efforts to try to affect the outcome of the race. Chris spent most of his days at shopping centers in largely Democratic neighborhoods, signing up new voters on the spot, for which he was paid twenty-five cents per signature by the county voter registrar's office—and an additional fifty cents by Frontlash if the new voters lived in the district where the special election was being held. This money, coupled with my income from teaching, made us suddenly flush, and we could afford to move from our slum duplex on the Pepperdine campus. We found a ground-floor, two-bedroom apartment on South Barrington Avenue, just a few miles from the UCLA campus. The building, occupied for the most part by young singles, was only a block away from a lovely park, where I could take David to play in the afternoons. There were restaurants nearby and a small shopping center with a supermarket stocked with wonderful fresh produce and expensive cuts of meat, unlike the stores in South Central that sold fatty hamburger brown with age, bruised apples and bananas, and wilted lettuce, all at premium prices. Life was unfair, especially for the poor, but I hated my brief interlude in South Central L.A. and complained often to Chris that I felt like I had been thrown back in time to the worst of my childhood venues—except that not even then had I ever experienced the level of fear and crime rampant in South Central L.A. Now that we had escaped the dreary poverty- and crime-ridden neighborhood, I vowed never to allow myself to end up in a place like that again.

Being closer to campus made it easier to get to the library to prepare for the Chicano lit course I was about to teach, which I did over the winter break. However, there were few sources to draw on, and I had no real idea what I was doing. The English Department made it clear that I was on my own and seemed not to care that the syllabus was so thin. Although a huge body of excellent Latin American literature existed in English translation, the Chicano students wanted a course devoted exclusively to works written by Mexican American authors. I chose two contemporary novels, *City of Night*, by John Rechy, and *Chicano*, by Richard F. Vasquez. Rechy, whose mother was Mexican, was a talented writer, but only the first chapter of his memoir touched on his ethnic background. Rechy described the poverty of his El Paso childhood, living with a mother whose love couldn't protect him from a violent, sexually abusive father who gave the boy a nickel each time he fondled the eight-year-old. Most of the book dealt with Rechy's life as a promiscuous homosexual who earned his living as a male prostitute.

The other book I chose for the course—*Chicano*—though more traditional in its subject matter, was a second-rate novel in which the heroes were hard-working Mexicans and the villains, hard-hearted Anglos. The beautiful Mexican American heroine of the novel falls in love with a rich Anglo college student who seduces her and then forces her to have an abortion, which was still illegal in 1970. Predictably, the abortion causes the heroine's death, but only after she spends her last hours trying to protect her selfish Anglo lover from being implicated in the criminal investigation into the abortion. The plot and characters were better suited to an afternoon soap opera than a college literature class, but it was one of the few novels published by a Mexican American author at the time. I also assigned Corky Gonzales's poem "I Am Joaquin," an epic about a Mexican "Everyman": "I am Joaquin / lost in a world of confusion, / . . . My culture has been raped / I lengthen the line at the welfare door / and fill the jails with crime," Gonzales wrote, blaming all Chicanos' woes on "Strangers / Who changed our language / and plagiarized our deeds / As feats of valor/of their own."[6] In addition, I chose several short stories from a new publication called *El Grito*, more radical screed than literary magazine. I considered most of the materials racist pap and intended to use the discussions to challenge the worst ideas. To that end, I supplemented the readings with analysis—such as there was—of Chicano culture, including several books written by non–Mexican American authors.

Despite my efforts to give students an authentic "Chicano" literary experience, the class got off to a bad start and quickly went downhill. Of the thirty or so students enrolled, only about a half-dozen appeared to have any interest in reading of any kind. When I tried to organize classroom discussions of the assignments, it quickly became clear that most of the students hadn't bothered to look at the books at all. One group of students sat sullenly as I lectured or audibly talked to each other as if I wasn't there. Finally, the ringleader of the dissident group, Richard, spoke up.

"This is bullshit. I don't need to read Chicano literature. I *live* Chicano literature," he said. "And you—you don't even know how to say 'Chicano,' Mrs. Gersteeeen," he said, drawing out the last syllable in case anyone in the class had failed to notice it was a Jewish name.

With that the class erupted in hoots and hollers, slapping their desks and stomping their feet.

I could feel my face turn crimson. "You may not like the way I pronounce 'Chicano,'" I said, in the nasal tones that characterized my students' barrio pronunciation, "but at least I know something about Chicano literature because I've actually read it."

"She got you, man," another of the boys chimed in, drawing appreciative assents from the others.

For the moment, I'd taken back control of the classroom. But not for long. The students sensed they could intimidate me, and I felt shaky and frightened, despite my bravado. A week later, I encountered more trouble when I wrote a list of reference books on the chalkboard. Among the books was a short work on the Pachuco dialect, a hybrid Spanish and English slang spoken originally by "zoot-suiters" in the 1930s, which had become very popular once again among young Chicanos throughout the Southwest. The book, published in the 1950s as a master's thesis by a University of Arizona graduate student named Baker, traced the origin of the dialect to first-generation Mexican immigrants of the Depression era. Naively, I thought students might actually enjoy learning the etymology of words like *cholo, pocho, ese,* even *Chicano,* which they regularly sprinkled through their conversation. I was wrong.

The dust from the chalk had barely settled on the board when Richard jumped to his feet.

"I ain't reading no *gabacho* books. They got nothin' to teach me." And with that he turned his back to me, still standing. One by one, other students stood up, and in almost drill-like precision, turned on their heels to present a phalanx of backs to me. Only a half-dozen students remained in their seats, but I decided to try to teach the class anyway.

"The point of a college education," I lectured, "is to acquaint yourselves with ideas and people unfamiliar to you. Just because someone has a different background from you doesn't mean he doesn't have something important to teach you." I kept my voice low and steady. "The Baker book is the only thing written on the Pachuco dialect. Maybe someday one of you will write a better book, but not by refusing to read everything that has already been written on the subject, no matter who wrote it."

Any hopes I had of using reason to deflect the students' anger vanished as the standing students began stamping their feet in unison, creating a clamor that resounded throughout the building. Within minutes, puzzled professors were peering through the small window of my classroom door.

"What are you teaching in here, a flamenco class?" one befuddled man asked me when I went out to tell them what was going on. As I was explaining that I had a class protest on my hands, the stomping students began marching out in military formation, leaving all of us standing in the hall shaking our heads.

I reported the incident to the English Department but got no sympathy or help there. The message came down loud and clear: "You're on your own. Handle it." At twenty-three years of age, younger than many of my students and clearly less wise in the ways of protest politics or the streets, I was ill prepared to manage the situation. A few of the protestors trickled back into class over the next few weeks, but most never returned. I began to dread teaching the class, whose subject matter held no particular interest for me in the first place. The books, stories, and poems I was using were clearly inferior to anything I had ever studied in a college classroom, and I thought it was a waste of everyone's time to create a Chicano literature course when the literary output didn't even exist. Once again, it seemed college administrators were caving in to unreasonable demands. And by my going along with it and agreeing to teach the course, I was contributing to the problem.

I managed to finish the class, but with no enthusiasm. Only one student in the class made any real effort to do the assigned work. And by the last week of class, barely a half-dozen kids bothered to show up at all. I knew that I was going to have to flunk about half the class, especially since most of the protestors hadn't bothered to formally drop the course. I posted notices in Campbell Hall offering students the opportunity to drop the class, even though the usual period to do so had elapsed. I gave the High Potential Program office a list of students who had never shown up for a test or handed in any papers, warning them that unless the students dropped the course, they would receive F's, but only a few students took me up on the offer. I ended up flunking a dozen students. I was surprised that I received no complaints when grades were posted, but I surmised that many of the students may have dropped out altogether or had gone home for the summer without knowing their grades.

Meanwhile, the summer had some surprises in store for Chris and me. Since moving to the apartment on Barrington Avenue, Chris and I had become good friends with several people who worked in the labor movement, including Jim Wood, the local Frontlash director. Impressed with Chris's Frontlash work, Jim suggested that Chris apply for a one-year, paid internship at the AFL-CIO in Washington. The AFL-CIO offered internships in each of its departments, and Chris decided to apply for an internship in the AFL's Committee on Political Education—COPE—which coordinated the labor federation's involvement in political campaigns and fund-raising. Chris made it onto the list of finalists, and Mary Zahn, COPE's longtime assistant director—a gravelly voiced, chain-smoking woman who reveled in her status as one of the few "broads" in a top position at the AFL-CIO's headquarters in Washington—flew out to L.A. to interview him. A few weeks later, the phone in the kitchen rang at 6:00 A.M. It was Mary Zahn calling to offer Chris the position.

"Well, what did you say?" I asked when he crawled back into bed.

"I turned it down."

"You did *what?*" I nearly shouted in disbelief. Since he had dropped out of graduate school, Chris had been at loose ends. Although he worked part-time, his life lacked the structure that school had always provided, and I was becoming impatient with his lack of focus, especially since I continued to carry a full academic load and also work. He seemed not to know what he wanted to do with his life, in sharp contrast to our early days together when he was the ambitious one. After all, he was the one who insisted that I become a serious student and that I go on to graduate school. If it had not been for Chris, I might well have been content to stay at Joslin's, working in the beauty salon and taking a CU extension course now and then. Now it was my turn to provide him with the motivation he needed.

"I want you to call her back and accept the job. Right now," I said.

"O.K.," he replied, looking a little surprised by the uncharacteristic tone of my voice.

When he returned to the bedroom, he told me that he would have to leave for Washington in less than two weeks.

"I'm not going with you—at least not until I complete the first half of my course work," I said. In the few minutes Chris was on the phone, I had decided that I wasn't willing to pick up and move again, with no clear plan in sight for my own future. I could barely believe my own assertiveness. But I was a little resentful of having moved to Los Angeles primarily to suit Chris's academic plans, especially after he had abandoned them so quickly once we got there. Now I wasn't so sure that the same thing might not happen again, and I didn't want to be uprooted once more after a lifetime of moving from place to place. If I stayed at UCLA through two more quarters, I might be able to complete an M.A., whereas if I tried to transfer into another Ph.D. program, most of my credits would be lost.

With Chris moving to Washington, I was going to have to find someone to care for David, a responsibility Chris and I had always shared. UCLA had a model day care center run by the school's early childhood development program, to which I applied immediately. Summer slots were more readily available, so I had no difficulty securing a place for David, but I was anxious about leaving him there. At two and a half, David was a bright and engaging child who instantly won friends among adults as well as children his own age. But many of the children at the center were mere infants, left to sleep most of the day in little plastic cribs like the ones hospital nurseries place babies in right after birth. Even though UCLA had an exceptionally low ratio of staff to children, I worried that David wouldn't get the attention and love he needed. I had never felt guilty going off to school for my own classes or to teach when David was a baby because Chris was there to take care of him, and he was a wonderful father. This was altogether different; I was turning my son over to strangers, and I wasn't sure that it was the right thing to do.

However, my worries were allayed when I watched him happily playing with the other children and being showered with attention by the teachers. Once a week, I volunteered at the center, which required parents to spend a few hours each week helping out, easing the burden on staff and providing opportunities for parents to interact with their children while they were in day care. The center was located on the west edge of campus, so it was convenient to drop him off on the short commute between our apartment and my classes, and if I had time during the day, I could visit at lunchtime as well.

Chris left on July 1, and for the first time in my life, I was living on my own—albeit with a two-year-old. Life was incredibly more complicated with no one to help out around the house, share chores, or keep me company. I found myself having to do things I'd always relied on Chris to do—like taking care of our old, increasingly unreliable Buick. Before Chris left, the alternator on the car had gone out unexpectedly, but instead of replacing it, Chris had decided to buy a portable battery charger, which we could attach to the battery and recharge it overnight, for about a third the cost of a new alternator. It was a real hassle running a heavy-duty extension cord out the bedroom window to the car parked beneath and attaching the charger to the battery cables. As long as I remembered to plug the contraption in after every short trip I made in the car, it worked almost as well as a new alternator. The problem was that I sometimes had to make longer trips, and I occasionally forgot to fully recharge the battery, so I was never sure I'd make it home. Finally, after weeks of this routine, the battery just wouldn't hold a charge, and the car stopped dead in its tracks on a dangerous curve on Sunset Boulevard as I was driving David home from the day care center. With cars whizzing by at what seemed like sixty miles per hour, I pulled David out of the car, still strapped into his little car seat, and sat him on the grass in front of one of the million-dollar homes I passed every day, while I stood helplessly by the car peering under the hood. Thankfully, one of the other teachers from the High Potential Program saw me as he drove by on his way to the freeway and rescued us. He drove me to a filling station a few blocks from my apartment, where I promptly ordered the car towed—and a new alternator.

With the end of the summer session, the regular HPP students began drifting back to campus, and with them came more trouble for me. The English Department had hired a talented young professor from Texas, Ray Paredes, to teach Chicano literature, so I was back to teaching composition, a subject I was far more comfortable with. I had settled into my new life, juggling all the responsibilities of caring for my son, attending my own classes, and teaching others, and was looking forward to a visit from Chris in September, when we had planned to take a long weekend drive up the coast to Yosemite National Park. Then, one crisp fall morning, I went out to my car with David in tow. As we approached the vehicle, I noticed a swarm of flies hovering around the open window on the driver's side. Picking David up in my arms to put him in his car seat, I opened the car door.

"Mommy, somebody pooped in our car," he yelled out in excitement. I pulled back in horror. Indeed, someone had ripped open the seat on the driver's side and dumped a hideous liquid mixture of excrement and water in the gash in the upholstery. The smell gagged me, and I quickly covered David's face with my hands. I went back inside the apartment and called the HPP offices to notify them of what had happened and that I would not be in to teach that day. I sat David in front of the television to watch *Sesame Street* and went into the kitchen to find rubber gloves and disinfectant. I spent the next two hours attempting to clean the car, intermittently choking on the stench as I hosed down the seat, cutting away at the foam rubber inside the upholstery to create a small crater. I didn't know how I would ever be able to drive the car again without replacing the entire seat, which I couldn't afford. I poured Lysol into the upholstery, hoping the smell of disinfectant would at least cover the reeking mess. I soon discovered that the two malodorous substances simply coexisted, with the fecal matter still detectable under the harsh chemical smell of the Lysol. The Buick had become a big white albatross, which I desperately wanted to dump but still needed to get around sprawling L.A. As if the stink from the car were not reminder enough of the hostility I engendered from some quarter, I was soon subjected to even more torment.

Within days of the attack on my car, I started getting threatening phone calls warning me that if I didn't watch out, I'd find a bomb in my car. Even though keeping the car windows rolled up overnight made the smell so strong that it was almost impossible to drive the car in the morning, I had to start doing so. I also placed tiny pebbles on the hood of the car so that I could be sure no one had tampered with it. Every morning, I came out to the car, alone, and checked to make sure the pebbles were still in place. Then I looked under and around the car to see if any explosive devices had been placed there. Finally,

I gingerly opened the door, rolled down the windows, and started the engine, holding my breath not just from the foul smell but from fear. Only then did I go back into my apartment to get David so that we could head for campus.

But the harassment didn't stop with my car. I came home one evening to find that my electricity had been shut off. When I called to find out what the problem was, the utility company told me that service had been terminated at "my" request. Apparently, someone posing as me had informed the electric company that I was moving and requested that service be stopped. David and I waited in the dark for repairmen to come and turn the lights back on. Then pizzas started coming—by the dozens, one company after another showing up at my door day after day until the delivery boys finally wised up to the pranks. And when I went to sleep at night, I was often awakened by the sound of sticks being dragged across my apartment windows. The police were little help. They offered to teach me how to use a gun if I bought one, but I decided that it was too dangerous to keep a loaded gun around a two-year-old. Instead I borrowed a six-foot-long African spear from a Yipsel who had served in the Peace Corps. At the first sound of sticks against glass, I raced out of the apartment in my nightgown, spear in hand, screaming every foul epithet I could think of as the car sped down the alley. It's a wonder my neighbors didn't have me arrested or sent off to a mental institution.

I had no idea who was harassing me. It was hard to imagine what I could have done to engender such hatred, but I was fairly certain it was one of the students I had flunked the previous spring. I couldn't imagine that any of them would have reacted the same way toward an Anglo teacher. Their anger toward me was more visceral. I suppose, in their eyes I was a traitor. I had married an Anglo, adopted Anglo values, and was accepted in the Anglo world—which they claimed to reject, but which many of them, no doubt, feared would never accept them. I remembered the rage of the students who had stood in my class that spring, stomping their feet before they'd marched out en masse. They seemed infuriated that they weren't able to drive me from the room, crying. I worried that maybe one or more of them were now responsible for these latest attacks and would feel driven to up the ante further until I was physically hurt—or worse, David was. Alone—with my husband thousands of miles away and no one to protect me—I felt incredibly vulnerable and afraid.

No one in the English Department or the High Potential Program was interested in helping track down the perpetrators, so I turned to MEChA, the Chicano student group on campus. Luis Ortiz, a fellow HPP instructor who taught math, suggested that I approach the MEChA leadership and ask for their help. Luis, a native of Jalisco, Mexico, was one of my few friends in the

HPP program. He was one of a handful of immigrants affiliated with the program. Unlike the American-born Chicanos in the HPP, the Mexican students and teachers harbored fewer racial grievances. They were, on average, better prepared academically than their American-born counterparts and less self-conscious about their ethnicity. Luis got an agreement from the head of MEChA to address the issue at the next meeting. I later learned that the message was delivered unambiguously: "If we find out who's doing this, we're going to beat the crap out of them." The incidents stopped immediately. For all my misgivings about MEChA, I was deeply grateful for their intervention.

As the end of the quarter approached, I decided that I did not want to stay in L.A. any longer. I was still frightened, even after the attacks stopped, and I was lonely. I missed Chris terribly, and the phone bills between Washington and L.A. were bankrupting us since we talked nearly every night. I was also disillusioned with school. I had set out to study early-twentieth-century English and Irish literature at UCLA, but my academic advisor persuaded me to shift my focus to contemporary American literature, arguing that as a Mexican American, my job prospects as a specialist in American literature would be better. But it wasn't just the change in focus that disheartened me. I was surprised to find that graduate school consisted almost entirely of reading literary criticism — much of it pedantic — rather than literature itself. The reason that I had decided to pursue a Ph.D. in English was because I loved reading literature. Now, instead of reading Joyce or T. S. Eliot or Thomas Hardy, I was reading a bunch of academics I had never heard of and whose opinions didn't interest me. I found myself bored and discontent with graduate school — and totally disgusted with teaching. So I made plans to join Chris in Washington, abandoning, at least temporarily, any hope for a Ph.D.

Having worked in affirmative action programs for two and a half years, I knew that I could not continue teaching in an environment that rewarded ignorance, made students the arbiters of what would be taught and who would teach it, and was better suited to political indoctrination than genuine learning. More and more, I felt alienated from my students, my fellow teachers in the affirmative action programs — the university itself. I had started out hoping to inspire underachievers like myself to reach beyond the world they grew up in. I had been content merely to get by in high school. I had hoped for nothing better than a nine-to-five job that paid well enough to live decently, and I assumed that I would follow in my mother's footsteps, moving up in the world of retail sales. Maybe one day I would become a department manager in a clothing store, but that was as high as I had aspired. College changed everything. It opened up new vistas for me. For the first time, I realized that I could control my own destiny. I didn't have to settle for what opportunities came my way. I could go out and create them for myself. I also discovered that the harder I worked, the more I could achieve. I wanted my students to see those same possibilities. Instead I found myself confronted with kids who sincerely believed that the world was out to defeat them. They blamed racism for all their problems and would never consider that their own behavior might be partly to blame for their failures.

Affirmative action began with the premise that blacks and, later, Mexican Americans, Puerto Ricans, and other disadvantaged minorities deserved a helping hand. Years of officially sanctioned discrimination had created an uneven playing field in which not everyone had the same opportunity to succeed. But most affirmative action programs, like those in place in major colleges and universities by the early 1970s, tried to level that playing field by ignoring the huge skills gap that existed between disadvantaged blacks and Hispanics, on the one hand, and middle-class whites, on the other. These programs were doomed from the start. If anything, they enhanced racial and ethnic tensions and animosity and reinforced stereotypes. At both the University of Colorado and at UCLA, I witnessed firsthand the devastating impact these programs had on academic standards, on race relations, and on the intended beneficiaries as well. These kids came into school with huge handicaps, but instead of recognizing their academic deficiencies and trying to do whatever it took to improve them, many of the affirmative action students I taught preferred to wallow in self-pity. Their attitude—as much as their social, economic, and educational disadvantages—would make life difficult and success elusive.

I left Los Angeles for Washington having little idea of what I would do with my life. I knew that I would never teach again, so long as colleges remained in the grip of affirmative action policies I'd come to disagree with so fundamentally. I had no plans to complete my Ph.D. and little interest in politics, but I assumed I would find a way to make a living. Until then, Chris's income would support us. At least we would all be together again. With David now a rambunctious three-year-old, I was anxious that he have his father and that we be a family once more. For the moment, that was more important than what would happen to my career.

Luis Ortiz drove David and me to the airport in my beat-up Buick. I had promised to give the car to the United Farmworkers Union, and Luis was to deliver it for me. Cesar Chavez's oldest son, whom we all called "Polly," had been in one of my classes, and I had traveled to Chavez's home in Delano with a group of students and HPP teachers one weekend. But my Buick Invicta, which had been the source of so much vexation, let me down once again. The car died after Luis dropped us off at the Los Angeles Airport terminal, and he abandoned it on the L.A. freeway. I imagine it on the side of the road, stripped of its wheels and chrome—just waiting to be transformed into a "low-rider" by one of the *vatos locos* from East L.A.—a fitting end to what had become the symbol of my sojourn in the Chicano world.

4

Watergate, Nixon, and Me

*If a man will begin with certainties, he shall end in doubts;
but if he will be content to begin with doubts, he shall end in
certainties.*

—Francis Bacon, *Advancement of Learning*

CHRIS WAS WAITING FOR DAVID AND ME at Dulles Airport when we arrived in
Washington just days before Christmas 1971. He had already rented a small
house on Fern Street in upper-northwest Washington, in one of the city's only
truly integrated neighborhoods. Our house stood on the east side of Georgia
Avenue, the dividing line between a largely working-class neighborhood and
Washington's Gold Coast, named for the large mansions that lined 16th Street,
a mere four blocks to the west. The larger neighborhood, known as Shepherd
Park, had changed populations over the years. Once, mostly Jewish families had
lived in the big brick and stone houses on the west side of Georgia, which
accounted for the presence of several synagogues along 16th Street. Then, over
time, members of Washington's large and growing black middle class gradually
moved into the area, and many whites began moving out to the suburbs—a
process that accelerated after the 1968 riots that tore the city apart following
Reverend Martin Luther King Jr.'s assassination.

Chris learned about Shepherd Park from his coworkers at the AFL-CIO and
decided to search there for a place to rent. I was pleased with the neighborhood
but unhappy with the house he'd found. It was run-down, with peeling paint
and stained carpeting, and a family of squirrels had made a home on the back
porch. I felt like we had moved back to South Central L.A. after our brief interlude "uptown" in our spanking new apartment in Brentwood. But Chris was so
pleased with his choice—a bargain at $245 a month—that I kept my disap-
pointment to myself. At least we now had a decent car, a used, but still elegant,
white 1964 Mercedes with blue leather seats, which Chris had purchased for
$750 through the AFL-CIO credit union. He had practically worn it out before

I even arrived in Washington, however, driving almost every weekend to Connecticut, where his brother Steve lived and practiced psychiatry.

It should have been a happy time for me, finally reunited with my husband and with free time on my hands for the first time since I had graduated from high school. I could read novels or take David to museums or Candy Cane City, a large playground in nearby Rock Creek Park. But I was miserable. Less than a week after I arrived, my grandmother Petra died from cancer in Albuquerque. I decided not to go to her funeral, which would mean leaving Chris again when we had been back together for so short a time. But the decision left me feeling guilty and homesick, torn between my old family and my new one. Petra had been a constant source of love and laughter throughout my childhood. I enjoyed playing practical jokes on her, especially when she fell asleep on the living room couch as we watched television together. One time I buried her in leaves and tried to convince her that she was in heaven when she awoke. She played along, flailing her arms about, muttering in Spanish, "*Madre de Dios,* I see an angel." When we had no place to live, her house was my refuge. I remembered the smell of pinto beans simmering on the stove and her sitting at the kitchen table kneading red chile peppers in a bowl of water until her hands turned raw. Now she was gone. I felt a sense of disloyalty, both to her and my father, for not paying my final respects in person. And I worried that my father would see my absence as one more sign, like going to college and moving away, that I had left my family's circle.

I was also gripped by a growing anxiety about the future. I had no idea of what I was going to do with my life. I wanted to work, but hadn't a clue about what I could do in Washington, where everything seemed tied in one way or another to politics. Ever since I had met Chris, he had pretty much decided what path my life would take. Now he had moved us to Washington, where I was even farther away from family and friends than I'd been in Los Angeles. Never mind that I was the one who pushed him to take the AFL-CIO job in the first place; I still felt that I'd been dragged from city to city, just as I'd been moved from place to place as a child. I also felt dependent on him in a way that made me feel strangely insecure. For the first time in our marriage, he was the sole breadwinner—and I wasn't sure I liked it. I never felt entirely secure having someone else take care of me. I decided that I must get a job quickly. I searched the classified ads and sent my resumé out to dozens of firms, with little luck. Finally, Chris arranged for me to meet with Don Slaiman, the assistant director of the AFL-CIO civil rights department.

One of a generation of young, well-educated, idealistic, often socialist Jews who joined the labor movement in the 1930s and 1940s, Slaiman rose through the ranks to become an official in the AFL-CIO in 1959. He was famous for getting jobs in the labor movement for the many young Yipsels who sought out his counsel. Several of the AFL-CIO interns, in addition to Chris, were Yipsels, as was AFL-CIO president George Meany's assistant, Tom Kahn. Slaiman was their official guru and loved to hold forth from his office down the hall from Meany's. Slaiman—who loved fine food and fast horses—took me to lunch at Chez François, a French restaurant near the AFL-CIO's Lafayette Square headquarters, to discuss my future. He ordered coquilles St. Jacques for me and then proceeded to help himself to what was on my plate, all the while lecturing me about ambition.

"Go slow. Find a job that will get your foot in the door, and then work your way up the ranks," he said, soaking up my sauce with his baguette. "And be careful you don't get in over your head because someone needs to hire a Mexican American to fill a quota," he warned. I suppose it was good advice, but it irked me. I would take the best job I could find, and I wasn't going to worry about a prospective employer's motives.

Slaiman's antagonism toward affirmative action shouldn't have surprised me, however. The labor movement, which had been crucial to the passage of the 1964 Civil Rights Act, now found itself at odds with many in the civil rights movement over the issue of affirmative action. In 1969, the Nixon administration had used affirmative action to try to break the control of some of the building trades unions involved in government construction by implementing the Philadelphia Plan—which set quotas for bringing blacks into the traditionally all-white construction unions. In its aftermath, the AFL-CIO and its member unions often found themselves fighting some of their former allies over the true meaning of the 1964 Civil Rights Act's guarantee of equal opportunity and nondiscrimination. Slaiman assumed, wrongly, that I was sympathetic to quotas, no doubt because I was Mexican American. But I told him I had seen enough of the problems with affirmative action programs at CU and UCLA to make me skeptical of their benefits, even for those they were intended to help. I was offended by his patronizing tone, though I later learned that he talked the same way to all the eager young socialists who sought his help. However bruised my feelings, I was grateful that Slaiman set up interviews that led to my first job in Washington.

Interstate Research Associates (IRA) was one of a burgeoning number of minority-owned firms doing business with the federal government. The founder, Raul Yzaguirre, was a Mexican American from the Rio Grande Valley of Texas who had worked in the Washington bureaucracy for a decade, mostly in the migrant education field. He would later become one of the most powerful Latino leaders in the country when he became president of the National Council of La Raza in 1973. A smart, burly fellow, Raul offered me a job right off the bat—but at a discount. He couldn't afford to pay me as much as I had been making at UCLA, he said. I accepted the position writing government proposals anyway, thankful for a paycheck and to be out of the house after six weeks of looking for a job without much success. My gratitude soon turned sour when I discovered that although I was the highest paid woman on the small staff, I earned far less than any of the men in the firm. I was furious and marched, unannounced, into Raul's office on the second floor of the old Georgetown warehouse building on Grace Street.

"You pleaded poverty when you hired me," I said pulling up a chair. "Now I find out that every guy in the place makes more than I do—by thousands of dollars."

Raul looked uncharacteristically sheepish. "How did I know you'd even work out," he said.

"Yeah, well I've worked out just fine. I've already written one grant proposal that's been funded, and I've only been here a couple of months," I said, not backing down.

He smiled. "You're really angry."

I prided myself in never losing my temper, but I wasn't going to let him get away with paying me less than I deserved.

He offered me an immediate raise and more down the road.

"I'll think about it," I said, to his surprise, and walked out the door.

In fact, I had already set my sights on a new position—or more accurately, Chris had done so on my behalf.

Although I had little interest in politics before coming to Washington, I knew I had better get interested if I was to succeed here. And Chris was there to prod me along. In early spring 1972, we attended a party thrown by one of Chris's coworkers for Dolores Huerta, the secretary-treasurer of the United Farm Workers Union, and her husband, Richard Chavez, Cesar Chavez's brother. Huerta and Chavez had come to Washington to gin up support for the union's national lettuce boycott. With the help of the Kennedy family and several Hollywood stars, the union had been moderately successful in using a consumer boycott of table grapes to force California growers to recognize the union as the bargaining agent for the mostly Mexican migrant workers who picked grapes in the state. The boycott had become a cause célèbre in left-wing circles, and no self-respecting liberal would dare serve California grapes at his table. The Farm Workers were now trying to do the same thing with lettuce as they tried to organize workers in the lettuce fields. But average

Americans were reluctant to give up their iceberg lettuce, and the boycott wasn't going well. Chris spent the evening convincing Huerta that what the union needed was someone loyal to them working at the Democratic National Committee's newly established Office of the Spanish-Speaking. It seemed like a hard sell to me, but Huerta sounded interested.

At Chris's prodding, Huerta called DNC chairman Larry O'Brien and urged him to hire me as Polly Baca Barragan's assistant director. Married to a former Catholic priest, Polly grew up in a middle-class family in Greeley, Colorado, where—like me—she never learned to speak Spanish, making her post as director of the Office of the Spanish-Speaking a bit awkward. Understandably, Polly was cool to the idea of hiring me. She had no previous relationship with me and viewed me as a competitor rather than an ally. She told me that she would be leaving the job after the Democratic convention in July, but warned me that I could not, under any circumstances, seek to replace her.

"The office needs somebody who speaks Spanish and knows the community," she said. I couldn't argue with her. In fact, the idea of becoming a professional ethnic had little appeal to me. I had no pretense of becoming a Chicano leader and saw the job at the DNC as a stepping-stone into mainstream politics. Despite Polly's reservations, Larry O'Brien didn't want to offend Huerta, and I got the job.

The tension with Polly did not diminish through the weeks, though we managed not to be together in the office all that often. She spent most of her time traveling around the country to meet with Mexican American activists. Occasionally, I traveled in her place, to Arizona and California where I met with local leaders. They were a varied lot: small businessmen, lawyers for Chicano advocacy groups, labor leaders from the United Auto Workers and the Steelworkers, an occasional Chicano radical. Some were ethnic hustlers only interested in persuading the DNC to throw money their way; others seemed genuinely committed to helping their communities have a voice in American politics. But the job was turning into a bad fit for me. I was neither an adept political organizer nor a particularly good listener, so I often found the meetings a waste of time, both for me and those who hoped to gain a measure of political influence by meeting with me. And I wasn't turning out to be of much value to Dolores Huerta—or the labor movement—either. I felt like I was watching the really important political fights from the sidelines, despite being a supposed insider. It was an important lesson: Power wasn't always where you expected to find it in Washington. Although I was working for what seemed to be the center of the Democratic Party universe—the Democratic National Committee—the fight for the soul of the party was being waged elsewhere, in the party caucuses and committee meetings far from the DNC's Watergate offices.

The Democratic Party had been badly split by the Vietnam War. Older, New Deal Democrat politicians—like Hubert Humphrey and Henry "Scoop" Jackson—and much of the labor movement backed U.S. involvement, whereas antiwar politicians—like Eugene McCarthy, Robert F. Kennedy, and George McGovern—and the entire New Left argued for an immediate U.S. withdrawal. The cleavage went beyond disagreements about the war, however. The New Left was seeking a realignment in American politics. They wanted to forge a new alliance to replace the broad New Deal coalition, which had included labor, blacks, farmers, and Jews. The "New Politics" coalition would be made up of university students, many of them pro-communist radicals from the Students for a Democratic Society and other far-left groups; the growing feminist movement; and the "disenfranchised"—blacks, welfare recipients, and homosexuals. The New Politics activists regarded not only Republican businessmen and Southern segregationists as the enemy but the labor movement itself. The New Politics faction argued that labor unions now represented workers who had become well-paid reactionaries, resenting higher taxes to pay for more welfare and resisting affirmative action programs that threatened their jobs. The answer, according to historian Ronald Radosh was "'to weld the McCarthy, Kennedy, and McGovern Democrats' into a force that could overcome labor to reform the party from within."[1] The way to do that was by rewriting the rules for selecting delegates to the party convention, thereby controlling who would become the party's presidential nominee.

The new rules for delegate selection set up by the McGovern Commission— named for the commission's chairman and soon-to-be presidential nominee, Senator George McGovern—would determine the selection of the 1972 presidential nominee. The rules called for proportional representation for both minorities and women, although—in what would come to be characteristic double-talk on the issue—they included a footnote that rejected "mandatory imposition of quotas." As Ronald Radosh pointed out, "McGovern himself boasted, in an interview with the *National Journal*, that 'the way we got the quota thing through was by not using the word quotas.'"[2] Labor unions, which had historically played a powerful role in picking delegates, now stood to have their power seriously diminished, as feminists and minorities filled the slots that in the past would have gone to union representatives. But the labor movement had no intention of going quietly into the night. The AFL-CIO led the fight against the McGovern reforms in party caucuses and rules committee hearings across the country. In a booming baritone voice, Al Barkan, the legendary director of

COPE, inveighed against his new rivals in the Democratic Party: "The blacks. The women-libbers. The hippies. The homo—" pausing, taking a deep breath, and dragging out the syllables, "—sexuals." The New Politics coalition represented everything that Barkan and the middle-aged, blue-collar, mostly male, mostly white workers in the AFL-CIO feared.

Many of my friends in the Young People's Socialist League had also joined the fight against the takeover of the Democratic Party. Many of the Washington Yipsels worked for unions, the largest contingent at the American Federation of Teachers, or in AFL-CIO front groups, such as Frontlash. Most of the Yipsels were supporting the candidacy of "Scoop" Jackson, a pro-defense, socially conservative Democratic senator from the state of Washington. But the Yipsels' unquestioning support of Jackson irritated me. Even though I agreed with Jackson's position on defense issues and quotas, I didn't like his stand against mandatory school busing. I knew that being opposed to racial quotas didn't mean that you were anti-civil rights, but I was highly skeptical of those who were opposed to busing. I just couldn't understand why busing provoked such strong resistance. What was wrong with transporting kids across town if necessary so that they could attend integrated schools?

My views were strongly rooted in my own experience. I believed fervently in integration. In my view, the only way that America could ever overcome its history of racial discrimination and suspicion was by blacks and whites living, working, and going to school together. Attending school with blacks from first grade on had inoculated me against the racial prejudices and stereotypes common at the time. So long as blacks and whites continued to live in separate communities, busing for the purpose of racial integration seemed to me the only alternative to insure that children got to know each other across racial lines at an early age. The Supreme Court had recently upheld a controversial busing plan in Charlotte, North Carolina, in which black students from the largely black inner city were bused to outlying Mecklenburg County, and white suburban students were bused into the city. Soon busing would become a fact of life in many cities in the North—including my hometown, Denver—and would provoke a tremendous backlash among whites, and eventually blacks as well.

In 1972, only 13 percent of whites and a bare majority of blacks—56 percent—supported mandatory busing, which ultimately doomed the policy as whites fled the cities in droves, leaving the schools even more racially isolated.[3] I knew the statistics, but it would be years before I would come—reluctantly—to change my position on busing. I realize now that Jackson was prescient in his understanding that forced busing would lead to even greater racial animosity and more racial isolation. But at the time, I found Jackson's position on busing off-putting and decided to throw my support to Hubert Humphrey, the 1968 Democratic presidential nominee and former vice president under Lyndon Johnson. Humphrey was an old-fashioned liberal who—like Scoop Jackson—represented a strong anti-communist and pro-defense position, but whose credentials on civil rights were impeccable.

As the convention approached, it became clear that neither Humphrey nor Jackson had much chance under the new McGovern rules. It was looking inevitable that the New Politics movement was about to score a big victory: the nomination of George McGovern to be the Democratic presidential candidate in 1972. But it would be a pyrrhic victory, one that most astute political observers believed would insure the re-election of Richard Nixon. I left for Miami and the convention knowing that my remaining time at the DNC was short. There was no way that I would work for George McGovern—I wasn't even sure I could vote for him in good conscience. I considered McGovern a dangerous man who was, at best, naive about the threat of communism, or worse, a fellow traveler. I still considered myself a liberal Democrat, but the party itself was changing in ways that was making it increasingly difficult to maintain my loyalty, much less enthusiasm. I was still anti-communist to the core and believed that the spread of communism in Asia, Africa, and Latin America was a serious threat to world freedom. I couldn't reconcile my own views with the Democrats' increasingly soft stance on the communist menace. And I wasn't happy with the party's embrace of racial quotas, either, which I found demeaning as well as unfair.

I arrived in Miami a week before the convention began. The DNC head-quarters were housed in the Fontainebleau Hotel, a grotesque monument to bad taste on Collier Boulevard, but my hotel, the Flamingo, was two blocks away, a seedy fleabag frequented by the many prostitutes who had flocked to Miami to ply their trade to convention delegates. The Miami heat in July was oppressive, unlike anything I had ever experienced, with temperatures soaring into the upper nineties and humidity almost as high. Worst of all, the air con-ditioner in my hotel room, a rattling window unit that kept me awake at night, froze up after an hour or two, making it not only noisy but totally ineffective at lowering the temperature. But as convention activities got under way, I spent little time in my room anyway. On several nights, I worked nearly round the clock—producing campaign material for the Latino delegates whom I hoped would take the material back to their communities to use against the Republicans. Polly, glad that I was not out lobbying for her job, gave me few assignments and left me alone to do what I wanted.

I enlisted the help of two politicos, a young attorney with the Farm Workers, Art Torres, and a legislative aide to Senator Ted Kennedy, Mark Schneider, who helped me type and xerox hundreds of copies of a pamphlet I had written: "Promises, Promises: A Nixon Fact Sheet." "Nixon was full of campaign promises to the Spanish-speaking community in 1968," I wrote. "Today, after four years in office, he is still making those same promises," outlining the administration's shortcomings on creating jobs, lowering unemployment, improving education, and reducing poverty—the standard liberal litany. While most of the DNC staff were out partying to the early morning hours, we labored away in the deserted, but delightfully air-conditioned, offices at the Fontainebleau past 1:00 A.M. When we finished, I walked, exhausted, the short distance to the Flamingo, hoping not to be mistaken in my leotard and blue jeans for one of the "ladies of the evening" who were drumming up business along Collier Boulevard.

The Nixon administration's outreach to Mexican American voters had become an obsession with me, even before the convention. It was clear that Richard Nixon understood the Mexican American community better than any Republican before or—until George W. Bush—since. Having grown up in a middle-class home in Whittier, California, a small town near Los Angeles, Nixon was familiar with Mexican Americans in a way most politicians at the time were not, Republicans or Democrats. Even Robert Kennedy—whose photo hung, along with that of his slain brother President John F. Kennedy, in many Mexican American homes—had treated Mexican Americans as downtrodden migrant workers and Cesar Chavez as their spokesman. Nixon recognized early on that a growing number of Mexican Americans were entering the middle class and that the Republican Party had some appeal, especially among the growing ranks of Mexican American men and women involved in small business. He also understood that Mexican Americans—though only about 4 percent of the population in the early 1970s and an even smaller percentage of voters—could tip the election in some important states like California and Texas, where they were heavily concentrated. In 1968, Nixon won only 6 percent of Mexican American votes, 11 percent fewer than he had won against John F. Kennedy in 1960.[4] He did not want a repeat of that poor performance, which some analysts believed cost him Texas in '68, and set out to ensure that he would do better.

In 1971, Nixon appointed an educator from his hometown of Whittier, Henry M. Ramirez, to head up a newly invigorated Cabinet Committee on Opportunities for Spanish-Speaking People.[5] The committee's purpose was to oversee programs to benefit Mexican Americans, Puerto Ricans, and Cubans, including hiring more Latinos in government jobs through a plan dubbed the "Sixteen Point Program." Nixon shrewdly realized that his best hope in wooing Latino voters was to appoint Mexican Americans and other Latinos to high-ranking administration jobs, where they could be empowered to act as the president's, and the party's, ambassadors in the Mexican American community.

By the beginning of 1972, Nixon had appointed more than fifty Mexican Americans to top posts in his administration, including Phillip V. Sanchez as head of the Office of Economic Opportunity and California businesswoman Ramona Banuelos as U.S. Treasurer. Democrats, who had been taking Mexican American votes for granted for years, never came close to matching Nixon's record. The "appointments do little but window dress an otherwise indifferent administration," I wrote in my Democratic convention critique of Nixon's record, but, in fact, they proved a useful tool in mobilizing Latino votes in the 1972 election. And though I didn't recognize it at the time, I had more in common with the Mexican American businesspeople who supported Nixon than I did with most of the Latinos I was working with in the Democratic Party. But a few more years would pass before I would be able to admit this, even to myself. In the meantime, I had a job to do—fighting Nixon's inroads into the Latino vote.

A few weeks before the Democratic convention, I had noticed a small news item in the *Washington Post* about congressional hearings on the federal government's record of hiring of Latinos. The chairman of the subcommittee that held the hearings, Representative Don Edwards, was a Democrat from San Jose, California, and a well-known liberal. I called his office to see if I could get some information for the anti-Nixon pamphlet I was preparing for convention delegates and was surprised to be invited to meet with the congressman's top legislative assistant, Alan Parker. When I arrived in Edwards's office on the second floor of the new Rayburn House Office Building, Parker was joined by the chief counsel of Edwards's subcommittee, Jerome Zeifman. Both men were eager to help, promising to open their files to me, letting me look at unpublished subcommittee transcripts and other material that would help me build a case against the Nixon administration, which I was able to use in the pamphlet I was preparing. I couldn't believe my good fortune, but I was also puzzled. Both men were treating me as if I were the answer to their prayers.

"How would you like a job?" Jerry Zeifman asked after I'd been with them about fifteen minutes. Zeifman was an odd fellow. He looked like a somewhat disheveled W. C. Fields and talked in hushed, almost conspiratorial tones.

Parker jumped in to explain that Mr. Edwards, as both men referred to the congressman, had recently been redistricted. He now represented a sizable Mexican American population and was desperate to hire "someone who understands the Chicano community," as Parker euphemistically put it. I knew of course what they meant was that they needed someone with a Spanish surname.

"We had a young woman in here yesterday who we were interviewing for the job, but every other word out of her mouth was a curse word," Zeifman said, leaning over as if he had just imparted state secrets.

I wondered if the woman hadn't been trying to appear more authentic by adopting street vocabulary to please these two, especially if they'd made it clear that ethnicity was the job's chief qualification.

"Well, what do you think?" Zeifman prodded.

"I'm not really looking for a job," I answered. The whole thing seemed so ironic. A few months earlier I was desperately looking for work and nothing was coming my way, and now people were offering me jobs I hadn't even applied for.

"Would you at least think it over?" Parker said. I told them I would get back to them after the Democratic convention. They took me in to meet Mr. Edwards, a distinguished, tanned politician who looked as if he had stepped straight out of central casting. We exchanged a few pleasantries, and I agreed that I would call Jerry Zeifman when I returned to Washington from Miami. In the meantime, they would hold open the job.

On the night George McGovern won the Democratic presidential nomination—after midnight, long after most Americans had gone to sleep—I sat on the convention floor thinking about my conversation with Edwards's staff. I had known from the outset that the DNC job would be temporary, and here was a real opportunity to get my foot in the door on Capitol Hill, just as Don Slaiman had suggested. But would I be just a token Mexican American on the subcommittee staff? That might be the way they thought of me now, I decided, but I would prove my worth. As "Happy Days Are Here Again" played and balloons and confetti dropped in the convention hall, I was already making plans to accept Zeifman's offer. In a little more than six months, I'd gone from a political neophyte in a new city to a prized job on Capitol Hill. Whatever doubts I had about the move to Washington had disappeared, and I felt incredibly fortunate.

With the exception of the staff director, Bess Dick, there were no women on the professional staff of the House Judiciary Committee in July 1972 when I came aboard, even though the Judiciary Committee had been the congressional birthplace of the Equal Rights Amendment. I was also the first non-lawyer hired on the professional staff, which by tradition had always consisted entirely of attorneys, as did membership on the committee itself. Although I would work on the subcommittee staff for Congressman Don Edwards, salary decisions were made by the full committee staff director. Mrs. Dick had begun working for Judiciary Committee Chairman Emanuel Celler years earlier, starting off as his personal secretary and, after finishing law school at night, eventually becoming staff director, the most powerful job on one of the most powerful committees in Congress.

Jerry Zeifman took me in to Mrs. Dick's office to introduce me. She was a tiny attractive woman, then in her sixties, sitting behind a huge oak desk. Jerry had made the case that the committee needed someone who could write up committee reports—the formal documents issued at the conclusion of both legislative and oversight hearings. He didn't mention a word about Edwards needing a Latino on his staff, I was relieved to hear. Instead he argued that the lawyers on the staff produced reports that were unreadable. Congressman Edwards's subcommittee dealt largely with oversight of certain government agencies and, most important, with federal civil rights enforcement, and Jerry especially wanted subcommittee reports that could attract press attention to Edwards's work. Since the subcommittee didn't hold the purse strings—as, for example, an appropriations subcommittee would—its only real power was to draw attention to abuses within federal agencies and bring public pressure to bear. It would be my job to make the subcommittee reports lively and interesting so that they would generate more attention and, therefore, make the subcommittee more effective. Mrs. Dick seemed to like the idea.

"What are we talking about as a starting salary?" she asked.

"I've been making $14,000 a year in my current job, but that is less than I was paid when I was teaching at UCLA." I said. "I made about $18,000 on a full-time basis there," I added, though, of course, I had only worked half-time.

She reached into her desk and pulled out a copy of the *Congressional Record* and began thumbing through it.

"I think $16,000 looks about right. That's what we seem to be paying our starting lawyers. I thinks it's best if you make as much they do if we want to give this new job the proper level of status and respect," she said.

In fact, everyone who worked on the Hill eagerly pored over the listing of staff salaries printed in the report of the Clerk of the House, which appeared in the *Congressional Record* twice each year, allowing each employee to figure out where he or she ranked in the pecking order. I was relieved that I would not encounter the same situation I had at Yzaguirre's shop, where I was the highest paid woman but still earned less than any of the men on staff.

When I looked up the list of fifty or so Judiciary Committee employees, I was surprised to learn that several women were among the highest-paid employees on the committee, even though they were clerical staff. On Capitol Hill, a good secretary was as important to a politician's success as any member of his staff—perhaps more so. At least on the Judiciary Committee they were rewarded accordingly. Salaries varied widely among the personal staffs of individual members of Congress (who had cleverly written themselves out of every law they passed to govern the practices of other employers, including the Equal Pay Act, which guaranteed that women must be paid the same for doing the identical job). Some members of Congress paid scandalously low salaries to their staffs, men and women, but committees, on the whole, paid better. Still, women were few in number in professional roles, especially on committee staffs—though that, too, would change dramatically during my few short years on the Hill.

I began work in late July 1972, joining the small staff of Subcommittee No. 4, as it was then known, later to become the Subcommittee on Civil and Constitutional Rights. My office was a tiny windowless room in the basement, with three government-issue desks crammed in along with several large filing cabinets and bookcases. I felt claustrophobic, almost buried in the huge mausoleum-like Rayburn Building. My office mates were a young black lawyer, George Dalley, and a secretary, Alice Jackson, a lovely young woman who had been one of the first black students to integrate the nearby Leesburg, Virginia, public schools. Dalley was particularly helpful, assisting me in learning the ropes of civil rights law. Despite Jerry Zeifman's bravado about my talents and my own determination to prove myself, I was spectacularly ill prepared to take on my new tasks. I knew almost nothing about the legislative process, other than what I had learned as an undergraduate in the one introductory American government course I had taken. However, I was a quick study, and I immediately applied myself to learning everything I could.

I began by reading the Judiciary Committee's own publications, including "How a Bill Becomes Law," a short pamphlet given out to tourists and school children, and *Jefferson's Manual and Rules of the House of Representatives,* a book of parliamentary procedures and precedents that governs the work of the House. I researched the various civil rights acts and checked out books from the Library of Congress on the legislative history of the various acts. After the first Monday in October, when the Supreme Court was back in session, I eagerly delved into the "slip opinions," the small pamphlet-size publications containing the Court's individual decisions, which we received by courier as soon as they were issued.

On January 22, 1973, the day that *Roe* v. *Wade* was handed down, I sat in my basement subcommittee office poring over every word of the 7 to 2 opinion, which guaranteed virtually unlimited abortion rights to American women. It was not an issue I'd ever given much thought to, but as I read the decision, I thought it went too far, striking down laws in states like California and Colorado—which had made abortion legal, though restricted—as well as those that banned the procedure altogether. And I was amazed at how much of the decision dealt not with law or the Constitution but with social history and fetal development, which seemed to me beyond the purview of the justices. Like most Americans at the time, though, I had no idea that the words I was reading would launch a huge social revolution and cause a deep rift in American politics, one that continues to this day.

Most of my study, however, was confined to civil rights law. Within a few months, I had taught myself enough civil rights law to hold my own with the lawyers on the committee with whom I had to negotiate over the wording of subcommittee reports. Nevertheless, as a non-lawyer, a woman, and a Mexican American, I was continually having to prove myself. As I knew from personal experience, affirmative action had created a whole new set of stereotypes that automatically cast doubt on the qualifications of anyone who happened to be black, brown, or female *and* successful. I bristled at the suggestion that I wasn't qualified for my job—though, in truth, I clearly was not qualified initially. As it was, I soon proved that I could handle the job. I learned quickly that I had to work harder than my colleagues, to know more, to outperform others if I was ever to prove myself as more than a token affirmative action hire. My strategy worked. I became Jerry's trusted confidant, in part because, as I was surprised to discover, we both shared deep reservations about racial quotas. Like me, Jerry thought of himself as a committed liberal, but he secretly resented the pressure to settle for staff he considered unqualified.

"Imagine what might have happened if you hadn't come into Mr. Edwards's office that day," he said every time the subject of affirmative action came up.

"To tell you the truth, I figured you would have hired any reasonably competent Mexican American who walked in off the street."

"What do you mean 'reasonably competent.' We would have settled for anyone who could walk and talk at the same time," he said, his eyes twinkling.

"Gee thanks, Jerry, you really know how to build up a girl's confidence," I said. But I knew that the very fact that we could joke about the issue meant that he had no reservations about my competence. In fact, I imagined that a lot more liberals harbored such thoughts, despite their outward support of affirmative action.

When Jerry was promoted to general counsel of the full Judiciary Committee, he demonstrated his trust in me by trying to persuade the new chairman of the committee, Peter Rodino, to hire me as his administrative assistant, the top job in the New Jersey Democrat's congressional office. Rodino balked, ironically, because he wasn't sure whether the tough political bosses in his Italian American district would accept a young woman in so powerful a role.

Sex discrimination was, if anything, more open than racial or ethnic discrimination in the early 1970s. Although discrimination on the basis of sex had been outlawed in employment by the 1964 Civil Rights Act, its inclusion in the law came about as much by mischief as anything else. When a Southern opponent of civil rights, Virginia Democrat Howard Smith, offered a "poison pill" amendment in the House bill adding sex to the list of prohibitions against discrimination, the Johnson administration opposed it on the theory that it might indeed doom the legislation—and a woman, Oregon Democrat Edith Green, led the fight to keep the amendment out of the legislation. The amendment won anyway—168 to 133—thanks to the votes of many Southern Democrats who wanted to see the civil rights bill go down.[6] Though women were making great strides in employment and education, official barriers were still in place in some sectors, as I found out when Chris and I went to buy our first house.

With my Judiciary Committee salary and Chris's new job working for a maritime union and industry group, the Transportation Institute, which he had landed after his AFL-CIO internship was over, we were able to afford to buy our own home. We decided to buy in Shepherd Park and found a small Tudor-style brick house on Hemlock Street built in 1928, just a few blocks from our rented house. The original owner, a widow, still lived in the house. But with stairs to climb to the only bathroom on the second floor and more space than one person needed, she had decided to sell the house and move to an apartment closer to her grown children. We made an offer on the house the day we saw it and eagerly set out to secure a mortgage loan. Chris's faithful payments to the AFL-CIO credit union for the old Mercedes had established good credit, and we both had secure and well-paying jobs that should easily have qualified us for the amount we wanted to borrow, so we assumed we'd have no trouble. But the loan officer at our bank saw it differently.

"I'm sorry, we can't count your wife's salary in qualifying for the loan," the bank officer said, addressing only Chris, as he looked up from our application.

"What do you mean you can't count my salary?" I replied, in disbelief.

"We don't know whether you'll get pregnant and quit your job. Or maybe your husband will decide he doesn't want you to work anymore, and then where would we be?" he said, putting me in my place.

Chris looked like he was about to punch the guy.

"But I've already had one child, and I took off a total of five days. If I do decide to have another baby, I intend to keep working," I said calmly.

"It's company policy. We don't make exceptions," he said, handing us back the application.

"If you don't want our business, we'll go elsewhere," Chris said, as we both stood up to leave.

"I doubt that you'll find anyone who'll make a different decision though. It's pretty much the industry standard. But good luck," he said, dripping with insincerity.

Banks considered married women poor credit risks and their salaries unreliable. It was the same argument I'd heard in college—I might get pregnant and quit. But the bank officer's scenario wasn't so far-fetched, since many employers *required* pregnant women to quit working once their pregnancy became obvious, a practice that was perfectly legal at the time. Broken-hearted, we told the owner what had happened, and she decided to lend us the money herself under the same terms and interest rate as the bank. I had the feeling that it was the plucky octogenarian's way of striking a blow for women.

The feminist movement was in full swing by the early 1970s, but despite my anger at the unfair treatment I occasionally encountered as a woman, I didn't identify much with the feminist icons of the day. Betty Friedan seemed to me embittered and shrill, and her book *The Feminine Mystique* a wild exaggeration of the plight of women, especially the affluent women about whom she wrote. I was outraged by her statement that "the women who 'adjust' as housewives, who grow up wanting to be 'just a housewife,' are in as much danger as the millions who walked to their own death in the concentration camps—and the millions more who refused to believe that the concentration camps existed."[7] The statement was obscene. My mother's fondest dream would have been to be a housewife instead of standing on her feet long hours each day in restaurants and department stores to keep a roof over our heads and food on the table. Although I had made the decision to work, even when I didn't have to, it seemed to me that each woman should be able to make that decision for herself and not be dictated to or made to feel less worthy by her peers.

Most of the women I knew who called themselves feminists had grown up in upper-middle-class homes very different from mine, and I considered many of them spoiled and self-centered. Certainly there existed prejudice against women, as I could testify firsthand, but not every obstacle that any woman ran into could be attributed to sex discrimination. Yet many of my feminist friends were quick to blame every personal failure on sex bias. Still, hoping for a less radical brand of feminism with which I could identify, I decided to attend a meeting of the newly formed Women's Political Caucus on the Hill. The room was full of women in their twenties and thirties who worked at various jobs in the House and Senate, plus a few I recognized from the Library of Congress. There were no other brown or black faces in the room, and I sized the group up, perhaps unfairly, as former Vassar and Radcliffe girls. I listened to the litany of complaints—agreeing with some of what I heard about the difficulty of overcoming stereotypes—but then got turned off when one young woman stood up with her solution for women who worked in congressional offices.

"You know those 'robo-type' machines," she said, referring to the Display Writer IBMs, which typed out form letters to constituents. "If someone invented a machine that could automatically type whatever was dictated, we wouldn't need any secretaries, and women would be freed up to do the important work on the Hill," she declared to cheers from the other women.

"No," I said, standing up to leave. "That would just put a lot of women out of work, who, unlike the women in this room, haven't gone to college." The women looked at me as if I'd just landed from Mars.

It wasn't just what I perceived as the elitism of the feminist movement that turned me off; it was the antagonism toward men and the disdain of motherhood. So many feminists seemed to regard men as the enemy: "male chauvinist pigs," in the popular phrase of the day. I liked men. Most of my friends were men; even as a little girl I got along better with boys than girls. I enjoyed their company and liked their attention, which seemed perfectly natural. So many of the feminists who marched in demonstrations looked not only angry but purposefully unattractive—as if their goal was to alienate the opposite sex. Even Gloria Steinem, who was stunning and sexy, made the ridiculous assertion that "a woman needs a man like a fish needs a bicycle" (which didn't explain why she wore mini-skirts and lightened her perfectly coiffed hair). I believed in equal opportunity for women, but if being a feminist meant rejecting men, I wasn't interested.

Nor could I understand how feminists could be so disdainful of motherhood. Simone de Beauvoir's famous rant—"Since the oppression of woman has its cause in the will to perpetuate the family and to keep patrimony intact, woman escapes complete dependency to the degree in which she escapes from the family"[8]—seemed to me not only unnatural but nihilistic. How precisely did these feminists think civilization, much less feminism, would continue if women stopped having babies? Feminism later accommodated itself to motherhood—ushered in by Friedan's 1981 book *The Second Stage*—but only by encouraging a vastly expanded welfare state to provide for the needs of women and their children. I might actually have found this brand of feminism attractive in the early seventies, when I still considered myself a socialist, but by the time Friedan had changed her mind and Sylvia Ann Hewlett and other second-stage feminists came along, I had become too mistrustful of government to look to it as a woman's best friend.

I couldn't imagine a life without children. I was totally in love with my son. There was simply nothing like the comfort of a baby, soft and warm in your arms, so totally dependent on you for all his needs. Sure, being a mother required some sacrifice, but the rewards far outweighed the difficulties. No matter how tired I was or disappointed and frustrated at work, the minute I picked up David at school, his cheerful jabbering on about the adventures of his day lifted my spirits—which is not to say that balancing motherhood and career was easy in Washington's workaholic environment. I often found it a challenge to find good care for my son. About the time I started working for the Judiciary Committee, David, now four, began attending a private school on Harvard Street in the Adams-Morgan area of Washington. I dropped him off on the way to my Capitol Hill office in the morning, and when school let out at two-thirty, one of his former preschool teachers babysat him in her apartment nearby. But the transition was not always smooth, since he needed a ride from another parent to get there. Car pooling arrangements invariably broke down at the most inconvenient time, and either Chris or I would have to leave work and drive across town to drop him off at the sitter's.

Chris was always willing to share parental responsibilities, but his employers were far less accommodating than mine. Childcare was still primarily a mother's responsibility, even if she worked full-time. When Chris did help out by taking David to the doctor, for example, I was always the one who made the appointment. I was often exhausted, running back and forth between my office and David's school, then rushing out to retrieve him by 6:00 P.M., fighting traffic all the way. By the time we got home, a quick trip to the nearby take-out restaurant was all that I could manage. Since it was impossible to get any serious writing done in my cramped, shared office, I often brought work home with me, tackling it only after David was safely in bed. I had little energy for anything but work and family and managed to totally avoid the Washington social scene, with its cocktail parties and receptions and hordes of lobbyists, which suited me fine.

Meanwhile, my work on the Judiciary Committee was expanding beyond merely writing subcommittee reports. I was put in charge of setting up hearings and preparing questions for witnesses as part of the subcommittee's civil rights oversight responsibilities. The Nixon administration was in trouble over the Watergate break-in, money laundering, and other election shenanigans, and I hoped to turn up the heat with some subcommittee hearings of my own. With the Nixon administration already under fire, I decided this was a good time for the subcommittee to subpoena Henry Ramirez, the director of the Cabinet Committee on Opportunities for Spanish-Speaking People, to see whether he had used his office illegally during the election. Federal law then prohibited federal employees, except those appointed by the president and confirmed by the Senate, from engaging in any partisan political activity, such as campaigning for candidates, and they were strictly forbidden to do so in the course of their official duties. I was convinced, however, that Ramirez and several other Mexican American appointees in the Nixon administration not only ignored the prohibition against campaigning but used government funds to promote the president's re-election. I persuaded Congressman Edwards to hold hearings and set about collecting evidence. On the eve of our hearings, Ramirez reimbursed the government for his air fare and accommodations for the Republican convention, so I knew I was on to something.

The Watergate break-in had turned out to be a good deal more than the "third-rate burglary" President Nixon had called it, and by spring 1973, the Senate was holding hearings that imperiled the president himself. The Senate Select Committee, chaired by North Carolina Democrat Sam Ervin, had subpoenaed the entire files of the Nixon campaign's Committee to Re-Elect the President, or "Creep" as Democrats liked to call it. The files were being held at the National Archives, an imposing gray building on Pennsylvania Avenue, which also housed the Declaration of Independence. I asked Congressman Edwards to request permission for me to examine the papers. When I signed the log in a guarded room upstairs in the archives, I realized that I was the first person to delve into the "Creep" files. In a strange coincidence, I had also been one of the first persons to encounter the Watergate burglars, when I was working at the Democratic National Committee. Coming out of the ladies' room on the afternoon of June 16, I nearly ran into a short, dark-haired Latin man, who seemed very unnerved by the incident. The next morning, I discovered, along with the rest of the world, that five Cubans had been arrested in the early morning hours of June 17 trying to break into Larry O'Brien's sixth-floor office. The fellow who had almost knocked me over was one of them. He had apparently been casing the stairwell leading up to O'Brien's office when I interrupted him.

I wasn't sure what I was looking for in the archive documents. It was more a fishing expedition than anything else, but I soon found a trove of partisan treasure. Sitting in a tiny, almost bare room in the archives, furnished only with a metal table and chair, I sifted through boxes of original documents that came from CREP. There were memos with familiar names throughout: H. R. Haldeman, the president's chief of staff; John D. Ehrlichman, assistant to the president for domestic affairs; and Charles W. Colson, counselor to the president, all of whom had become household names as a result of the Watergate investigation and nationally televised hearings. In all, I found some five hundred pages of incriminating documents, which outlined an extensive Nixon Chicano strategy, most of it legal, but some of it highly suspect. The strategy itself was outlined in a memorandum from Alex Armendariz, an Indiana businessman, to Fred Malek, the deputy director of CREP.[9] In the memo, Armendariz urged the Nixon administration to support the fledgling La Raza Unida Party in Texas.[10] As a result, the administration poured more than a million dollars into a health clinic in La Raza Unida's home base of Crystal City, Texas, and secretly funneled other money into La Raza's coffers.

The Republicans' affinity for La Raza seemed odd, given the latter's radical, anti-white rhetoric. La Raza's founder, José Angel Gutierrez, once told reporters that it might be necessary "to kill the gringo," and the party itself called for the creation of a separate Chicano nation—Aztlan, named after the territory ruled by the Aztecs, which, according to myth, extended into what is now the southwestern United States. However, Armendariz rightly surmised that La Raza would siphon off votes from the Democrats, thereby enhancing Republican prospects for winning the state. In the close 1968 election, a mere shift of an additional 5 percent of Mexican American votes would have delivered Texas to Nixon, and the campaign wanted to ensure that they did not lose the state again in 1972.

Of course, as it turned out, the McGovern candidacy was such a disaster for the Democratic Party that Nixon handily won all but two states. But there was no way of knowing early in the campaign that Nixon's victory would be such an easy one, and Nixon himself remained the eternal paranoid pessimist, which is what motivated so much of the mischief that eventually undid his presidency. In the end, La Raza Unida refused to endorse either McGovern or Nixon—which was just what the Republicans had wanted—issuing a statement that maintained "there is no difference between George McGovern and Richard Nixon. It really doesn't make any difference to us who gets elected."[11]

I also found other evidence of quid pro quos between the Nixon campaign and Chicano militants. Perhaps the most damning was a handwritten letter by a jailed radical, Reies Lopez Tijerina, who had led a 1967 raid on the Tierra Amarilla, New Mexico, courthouse in which two people were shot and others were held hostage. Tijerina wrote to Henry Ramirez: "most of the Spanish-speaking people in the United States would feel grateful if an executive pardon would be granted." Ramirez forwarded the letter to Armendariz, with a notation: "Mr. Tijerina indicated that he would work for us in return for due consideration." Armendariz, in turn, forwarded the letter to the White House. I found the letter in the National Archives in a box of materials from Charles Colson's office. Although Tijerina was never granted a pardon, it appeared that it was under active consideration for a time.

I could barely believe my eyes. Nixon had indeed betrayed the Latino population—but not in the ways I expected. His crime was not that he had spent too little on bilingual education or community services, but that his operatives were pandering to the most radical, Anglo-hating elements in the Chicano movement. This was rank political opportunism at its worst. And it confirmed all my worst suspicions about Richard Nixon. He wasn't a principled conservative but a cynical politician. Nixon's dealings with the Mexican American community fit a pattern. This was, after all, the staunch anti-communist who recognized Red China, arguably a more repressive communist regime than the Soviet Union at the time. Here was the politician who developed a Southern strategy to appeal to disaffected Democrats unhappy with desegregation and who then turned around and imposed racial quotas to get even with unions. Although Nixon could have made his pitch for Mexican American votes by appealing to Latinos' inherent conservative social values and strong patriotism, he chose instead to appoint ethnic hustlers, who weren't very different from their Democratic counterparts, and to secretly fund racist Brown Power fanatics.

Despite my urging that we hold full-scale hearings into Nixon's Chicano strategy, Don Edwards decided not to pursue the matter after our initial hearings on Henry Ramirez, so I forwarded copies of the material I'd found to the Ervin Senate Select Committee through New Mexico Senator Joseph Montoya's office, which led to a day of hearings before the Watergate committee. In addition, I leaked copies of everything I'd found to a young reporter with the *Dallas Morning News*, Tony Castro. Tony and I became friends over the telephone, sometimes spending hours a week gossiping about Washington politics. In time-honored Washington fashion, I soon learned to use him as an outlet for information that I wanted to publicize, but which I couldn't convince Congressman Edward to make public. Castro, in turn, used some of the material I provided in a book he published on Mexican American politics, *Chicano Power*, in 1974.

Congressman Edwards often fell short when it came time to pursue an issue aggressively. I would spend hours preparing detailed questions for witnesses at subcommittee hearings only to have Edwards drop the ball after the initial question or two. Sometimes, I'd barely have a chance to brief him before the hearings, just the amount of time it took to walk from his office in the west wing of the second floor of Rayburn to the hearing rooms on the east side of the building one floor below. Edwards represented an overwhelmingly Democratic district, and he was independently wealthy, which meant that he could take things relatively easy, never fearing a serious political challenge as long as he took care of his constituents' needs. Although Edwards was a kind and generous boss, he seemed to spend little time preparing for subcommittee hearings, which made my job incredibly frustrating. Things got worse once the Judiciary Committee opened its impeachment hearings for President Nixon in April 1974.

My work on civil rights oversight ground to a virtual standstill, since the entire Judiciary Committee was totally absorbed with its constitutional duties in the nation's second impeachment of a president. I could take three-hour lunches or read novels during work hours if I chose, with no consequences— but I was bored and felt totally out of the loop on the most important issue of the day, the impeachment of President Nixon. The Judiciary Committee had hired an entirely separate staff to handle the proceedings, including a young lawyer straight out of Yale Law School named Hillary Rodham. As it happened, the impeachment staff were housed in the old Congressional Hotel, which had been converted to office space and where my office had been moved a few months earlier. Armed guards stood watch, and the elevators didn't stop on the floors where the impeachment staff worked late into the night. The media hung around the front doors to the building, lounging on the grass during the beautiful Washington spring, the reporters, including a particularly brash Sam Donaldson, flirting with the women who went in and out of the building. After a few months of mind-numbing inactivity, I decided to look around for another job.

Senator Alan Cranston—like Don Edwards, a liberal California Democrat—was about to lose the only Mexican American on his staff, a young lawyer with whom I was friendly. Outside of the New Mexico delegation, there were probably fewer than a dozen Mexican American professionals employed throughout Congress in 1974, and most of us knew each other, at least casually. I decided to apply for the legislative assistant slot being vacated in Cranston's office, assuming I'd have an excellent shot at it with my two-plus years of experience on the Judiciary Subcommittee. I sent over a copy of my resumé and several samples of my writing and soon received a call from Cranston's administrative assistant, Roy Greeneway. The staff of powerful United States senators are powers themselves, often making the crucial decisions about what goes into legislation and even recommending to senators how to vote on critical bills. Lobbyists and constituents rarely get to spend significant time meeting with members of Congress and must make their case to congressional staff, many of whom develop huge egos as a result. Greeneway struck me as a prime example of this type. Gruff and overweight, he sat behind his desk in Cranston's office like a pasha receiving tribute from his underlings.

I came into the interview confident and prepared. My only drawback was that I was no longer a California resident, though I had maintained my voting residency there through the 1972 elections, voting absentee. Members of Congress usually preferred to hire staff from their home states, in part because they were more likely to understand local issues but also as a form of patronage. Having lived in California for a while and having worked for a California congressman, I wasn't too worried that my residency would be held against me.

Greeneway spent time carefully looking through the material I gave him.

"Who edits your writing?" he finally asked, looking up from one of the subcommittee reports I had authored.

"No one edits my writing. I edit the writing of other members of the staff. That's why I was hired. As a writer, I mean. The general counsel thought the committee needed someone who could take the lawyers' technical writing and turn it into plain English," I said, smiling pleasantly so as not to seem defensive.

"What about this?" he said, his eyes narrowing. He handed me a copy of the speech Judiciary Committee Chairman Peter Rodino delivered on the floor of the House when he cast his vote against Gerald Ford for vice president to replace Spiro Agnew, who had resigned in disgrace.

"I wrote it in close consultation with Mr. Rodino," I said. "The chairman is very particular about his speeches. He has certain phrases he likes to use. We went through several drafts on this speech because it was so momentous. He had voted to report out Vice President Ford's name from the committee, but then he believed he had an obligation to his own constituents to oppose it on the floor when he was acting as an individual congressman, not as committee chairman," I said, trying to explain the elaborate reasoning Rodino had been so adamant that I capture in the speech itself.

"So then this speech was edited," Greeneway said, jumping on what he perceived was an inconsistency in what I had told him.

"I would say it was a collaborative process," I answered.

"It has been my experience that Mexican Americans have difficulty writing. The fellow who was in this job before couldn't write worth a damn," he added, to my amazement.

"As you can see, I was an English major. I have no difficulty writing," I tried not to sound angry, but my blood was boiling, and I could feel my face flushing.

"Let me think about it. I'll get back to you in a couple days," he said.

What was it with these liberals, I thought as I left the office. They were dying to hire minorities, though they apparently didn't think much of their skills. What they didn't like was a minority who didn't fit their neat little stereotypes. Greeneway's response wasn't all that different from the Ford Foundation's. In their minds, a well-spoken Mexican American who could actually write a coherent paragraph in English was automatically suspect.

When Greeneway didn't call after a couple of weeks, I called him. I was surprised that he took the call.

"Is there anybody at the committee who can verify that you wrote this material," he asked me.

I couldn't believe my ears. He was still at it.

"You can call Alan Parker," who had become subcommittee general counsel when Zeifman was promoted to general counsel for the full committee. "Or, better yet, Jerry Zeifman. He's the one who hired me in the first place," I added, knowing that Zeifman's name would carry some weight, since he was currently one of the most important people on Capitol Hill because of his role in the impeachment process.

But Greeneway never called either man, and I didn't get the job. I suspect that it was easier for him to believe that I was lying to him than to accept that someone with my background could actually string two sentences together. Or perhaps I was just too uppity for him. I was beginning to think affirmative action was poisonous for me. When I finally left Judiciary for a job as a lobbyist for the National Education Association, I became convinced of it. I lasted less than a year at the NEA, feeling pigeonholed the entire time. Although I initially thought the NEA hired me because of my Hill experience, it became obvious on my first day at work that the organization needed me to round out their "rainbow lobby." Of the five lobbyists on staff, one was black, one was American Indian, two were white men, and I provided them with a "two-fer," filling two affirmative action slots as both a woman and a Mexican American. The NEA prided itself on its racial, ethnic, and gender quotas. The bylaws of the organization mandated that its elected leaders mirror the racial composition of the population and that half the elected slots go to women. Race, ethnicity, and sex were destiny at the NEA; everyone was defined in terms of his or her group. Consequently, they assigned me to attend the NEA's Chicano caucus meetings and to follow civil rights legislation—a responsibility I shared with my black and Indian colleagues—and bilingual education.

I found the whole thing offensive—if not downright illegal. The civil rights laws themselves forbade employers to discriminate on the basis of race, sex, national origin, color, or religion. They didn't say anything about granting a certain number of slots to minorities or women to make up for past discrimination those groups had faced. In fact, Title VII of the 1964 Civil Rights Act expressly said that nothing in the law should be interpreted "to require preferences" on the basis of race or sex. Hubert Humphrey, the chief sponsor of the act, had promised that if anyone could find any language which provides that an employer will have to hire on the basis of percentage or quota related to color, race, religion, or national origin, he would start eating the pages one after another, because that was not in there.[12]

Yet the supporters of affirmative action everywhere seemed to believe that the only way to eliminate racial discrimination against blacks, Latinos, and women was to discriminate against white men. By 1975, racial, ethnic, and gender preferences were pervasive in public employment, dictating the hiring of police officers, firefighters, and teachers, and in public contracting, setting aside a certain percentage of government work for minority firms. Colleges and universities routinely admitted minority students under less stringent requirements than white students and gave preference to women in fields in which they had been excluded in the past. I found the trend troubling. My own experience suggested that double standards cast a pall on the qualifications of all minorities and women, even those who were highly qualified. And they caused deep resentment among those who were denied jobs, promotions, or admission to college because they happened to be white men.

After my years teaching in affirmative action programs and working in politics, I was beginning to despair that I would ever find a job where my employers shared my views on race, ethnicity, and gender. I believed fervently that no one should be discriminated against because of his or her color or sex—and that included white males. I also knew that affirmative action programs were creating new kinds of prejudices that all blacks, Latinos, or women who succeeded got there because they had benefited from preferential treatment. And, perversely, affirmative action had become the excuse every time a white man did not get a job or promotion, which simply perpetuated old-fashioned racial bigotry and sex-based stereotypes. I was desperate to work for an organization that believed in equal opportunity but eschewed quotas, preferences, and double standards. I finally found it at the NEA's rival, the American Federation of Teachers, where I would remain for eight years, with a brief interruption to go into the government. Although I would find my years at the AFT among the most rewarding of my career, I would also come to realize that I was slowly drifting to the right politically. On a whole host of issues, I found myself agreeing more often with conservatives than liberals. My views on the Vietnam War, affirmative action, and feminism were only a precursor of what was becoming increasingly apparent. I was no longer a liberal Democrat, much less a socialist, though it would take almost a decade longer for my political transformation to be complete.

5

The Evolution of a Neoconservative

Any man who is not a socialist at age 20 has no heart. Any
man who is still a socialist at age 40 has no head.

—Attributed to George Clemenceau,
Benjamin Disraeli, Winston Churchill,
among others

MY EIGHT YEARS at the American Federation of Teachers transformed me both
politically and intellectually, and the person most responsible for that transformation was Al Shanker, the president of the American Federation of Teachers.
Although Shanker never fully adopted neoconservatism himself, at least not in
his public positions, he was clearly attracted to neoconservative ideas and to the
men and women who espoused them. His weekly column "Where We Stand,"
which ran as a paid advertisement for twenty-seven years in the Sunday *New
York Times*, introduced a broad audience to ideas he often culled from neoconservative journals, such as *Commentary* magazine and *The Public Interest*. He'd
pass on articles to his staff as well, scribbling in the corners of pages torn from
some neocon journal a list of names he'd want the piece sent to. During the
years I spent at the AFT, I became a frequent recipient of these intellectual tid-
bits, which helped form my own attitudes and ideas. Ironically, the ideas planted seemed to take firmer hold in the pupil than the mentor. Shanker held neoconservative positions on foreign policy and defense and on some social issues,
but he remained a trade union liberal on much else from minimum wage to
government spending to privatization,[1] whereas I came to embrace conservative
attitudes across the board. But it took nearly a decade for this process to be complete, and nothing in my earliest years at the AFT would have predicted this
turn of events.

I was a little nervous about meeting Shanker for the first time in 1975. I had
seen him on television during the Ocean Hill–Brownsville teacher strike in
1968, when he had led a walkout that shut down the New York City schools

rather than allow black radicals to take control of a city school district.[2] Shanker looked like a very tall Woody Allen—which may be why Allen included a comic reference to him in his 1973 movie *Sleeper* about a man who wakes up the lone human survivor one hundred years after a nuclear holocaust and learns that civilization was destroyed after "a man named Albert Shanker got hold of the bomb." Indeed, Shanker's reputation as both a cold warrior and a take-no-prisoners union negotiator was well deserved. He was widely regarded as one of the most effective union leaders in the nation. Admired for his brilliant and original thinking, even by his critics, Shanker almost single-handedly transformed the United Federation of Teachers into one of the most powerful union locals in the country, wielding enormous political clout in both the city and state of New York. In 1974, Shanker became president of the national union, the American Federation of Teachers, which at the time represented nearly 500,000 members. Although the AFT was small in comparison to the NEA, which had nearly 1.5 million members by the mid-1970s, once Shanker took the helm, the AFT, too, became an important political force.

Joining the AFT, I felt like I was being hired into the family business. Almost all the leadership positions on staff were held by Yipsels, many of them my closest friends, brought in by Shanker when he took over the national union a year earlier. Shanker expected two things from his employees: that they be smart and that they have "good politics," which consisted chiefly of being pro-union, anti-communist, and opposed to racial quotas. On the day he interviewed me, after I'd been recommended for a job in the legislative department, Shanker was more interested in testing my political views than in finding out what I knew about Capitol Hill. He asked me a few questions about my view of affirmative action. I told him briefly about my experiences at CU and UCLA, throwing in the fact that I had been an AFT member when I taught at UCLA—something I hadn't revealed to my employers at NEA, who never thought to ask.

But despite passing the quotas test, I had been warned that I had two strikes against me: I had worked for the Democratic National Committee when George McGovern was nominated, and I'd worked for Don Edwards, whom Shanker regarded as a "shmuck," a word he applied liberally to any New Politics Democrat. If I was to get the job, I needed to demonstrate that I was politically reliable. So I brought along a movie review of the Robert Altman film *Nashville*, which was about to be published in *New America*, the monthly newspaper of the Young People's Socialist League.[3] It was the first thing I'd ever published under my own name, and I was very proud of the piece, especially since it took on one of the most popular and acclaimed figures in Hollywood for his New Left anti-American bias. "Altman attempts to indict the political/cultural values of contemporary America and instead delivers a most telling indictment of his own talents as a director," I wrote, excoriating Altman both for his elitist views and his disjointed filmmaking. "Altman uses Nashville as a convenient symbol for what he perceives to be American decadence . . . while Altman's characters lecture us on the Kennedy assassinations and hand-gun ownership," I complained. After skimming the piece, Shanker gave a char-acteristic grunt of approval and then spent the rest of the interview talking about movies. I soon came to recognize that this was his way of showing approval. If he liked you, Shanker could spend hours talking about stereos or books or wine, subjects that engaged him every bit as much as politics or edu-cation. And if he really liked you, he'd take you along on one of his afternoon jaunts to a local bookstore or help you set up a stereo system in your home. You could pretty much tell where you ranked in the AFT pecking order by how many Shanker "finds" from used bookstores lined your shelves or how many Shanker-inspired stereo components you owned. I knew I had finally entered the inner sanctum of the AFT when Shanker took me to Kramer's Bookstore in Dupont Circle to buy the anti-communist classic *The God That Failed* and he sold me an "Ampzilla"—an ugly, 200-watt-per-channel, monster amplifier he insisted I needed to power my huge stereo speakers—plus a tuner he had built himself from a kit.

I became an AFT lobbyist when Gerald Ford was president and spent much of my time lobbying to overturn vetoed spending bills. I hated being a lobby-ist, hanging out in the corridors of the Capitol trying to buttonhole senators and congressmen. It was demeaning. Even when I had great success, as I did, for example, when I was able to get my former boss, Don Edwards, to include language in a bankruptcy bill that protected the UFT's pension funds during New York City's fiscal crisis, the sense of accomplishment was ephemeral.[4] My successes were never my own but depended on the clout of the union I repre-sented. Worse, I often felt like a political hack. Congress was filled with back-slappers who would do anything the labor unions asked, so long as they could be guaranteed a campaign contribution and a few union members to man the phone banks before Election Day. I especially hated the congressional recep-tions I was expected to attend. All the lobbyists stood around over limp cru-dités, hoping to catch a few minutes with a senator and ended up talking to each other all evening. I was bored and alienated. My feet ached and my back hurt, and it got worse once I became pregnant with my second child.

It had been almost eight years since my son David was born. He had grown into a handsome and sweet child who talked a mile a minute and loved to draw intricate pictures of his favorite birds. But he was lonely, despite his friends at school and in the neighborhood, and constantly begged for a baby brother or sister. We had just moved into another house in Shepherd Park—a large, clapboard, four-bedroom house on Geranium Street with a huge wraparound porch, built in 1908 when it must have stood among farms just six miles from the White House. Here was a house much like the elegant old homes that had been turned into apartments in which I had lived as a child. But now the entire house was mine, not just some tiny basement or attic space.

The extra rooms cried out to be filled, and I became pregnant right after we moved into the new house. I became sick immediately and stayed that way for nine months, as I had during my previous pregnancy. So long as I took my Bendectin pills, I could manage through the day without vomiting. But if I took the pills even a few hours late, I'd be doubled over, throwing up, no matter where I happened to be at the time. Once when I was returning from the Hill in a taxi, I barely made it out of the cab before I threw up all over the street, leaving me weak and humiliated several blocks from my office on Dupont Circle. I worried constantly that the same thing would happen to me when I was on the Hill and carefully mapped out every ladies' room in all the Senate and House office buildings, including those that had couches where I could lie down and rest my swollen legs. I envied other women who talked of how robust and healthy they felt during their pregnancies. To me, pregnancy was an extremely difficult and unpleasant time, to be endured because the reward at the end was so great.

As with my earlier pregnancy, I worked until the day before I delivered. I stayed in the hospital two nights and came home on Christmas eve with my new son, Pablo Chavez Gersten, dressed in a red snowsuit, looking like a very tiny Santa. I managed to stay home four whole weeks, although I had to fight for every day. The AFT's policy allowed employees to take one week paid leave for the birth or adoption of a child. But when I notified Shanker's assistant, Al Lowenthal, that I intended to take that week plus three weeks combined sick leave and vacation I'd accumulated, he balked.

"The union contract only covers fathers taking off so that they can help their wives," he informed me, sitting in his office next to Shanker's.

"That's odd," I said. "The contract provision refers to 'parental leave' not 'paternal leave.' Is that a typo?" I asked, but Lowenthal missed my sarcasm.

"We wrote that provision into the contract for Dave Elsila when his wife had twins and needed him to help out," he offered, as if that somehow explained everything.

"You can't discriminate between men and women in benefits," I said, incredulous that he actually intended to push this line of reasoning. "It's illegal. It's forbidden by Title VII of the 1964 Civil Rights Act. If you don't believe me, ask Larry Poltrock," I said, referring to the union's general counsel.

"I'm sure the *Washington Post* would love to learn that the AFT is lobbying to pass the Pregnancy Discrimination Act to force employers to let pregnant women use sick leave for the birth of their babies but won't allow its own staff the same right," I added in a barely veiled threat.

Lowenthal's face turned beet red, but he wouldn't back down. Everyone in the AFT regarded him as a tyrant, but hardly anyone was willing to take him on. I refused to be intimidated, and after I sent him a series of blistering memos, he relented. I got my four weeks—one week of parental and the rest as sick and vacation leave.

The month went by quickly, much of it spent hunting for a full-time baby-sitter. I had already hired and lost three different sitters before the baby even arrived, none of them lasting more than a few weeks. One turned out to be pregnant herself, another decided to go home to Brazil to get married, and a third left to open a Chinese restaurant in Kansas City. I put yet another ad in the paper right after I brought Pablo home from the hospital, and, happily, a Salvadoran woman named Margarita Mejia applied. She seemed to fall in love with Pablo the minute she laid eyes on him, and I hired her almost on the spot. Her English was great—a not insignificant qualification in a field in which most applicants spoke little English. She was clearly smart, and in a strange coincidence, it turned out that she, too, had worked for Raul Yzaguirre briefly as a secretary.[5] I was able to return to work confident that both Pablo and David would be in good hands—for the next seven and a half years.

Back at the AFT, I found myself once again being offered a job for which I hadn't applied, this time by the new Carter administration. I couldn't bring myself to vote for Jimmy Carter in 1976, but the thought of voting for a Republican never entered my mind. So I stayed home from the polls—the only time in my life that I sat out an election. But I had lots of friends and acquaintances in the new administration, including the new assistant secretary for legislation at the Department of Health, Education, and Welfare, Dick Warden.[6] Dick and I had spent many hours standing outside the Senate chambers in the Capitol when he was chief lobbyist for the United Auto Workers union, and he offered me a job soon after I got back from maternity leave. Despite my dislike of Carter, I respected Dick and thought it would be a great experience to work in the executive branch. The job also paid more than the AFT, and I was eager to get out of lobbying, so I accepted. By the end of the first week, I knew I'd made a terrible mistake.

The federal government was not at all what I expected. Nothing—and almost no one—worked. I showed up the first day to find that no one had any idea where to put me or what I was to do. Most of the other political appointees weren't in place yet, including the deputy assistant secretary to whom I was supposed to report. And the physical surroundings were more dreary than any place I'd ever worked. The new HEW building—a concrete monstrosity on Independence Avenue across the street from my old Judiciary Committee office in the Rayburn Building—was built during the open-space architectural fad. A few precious offices lined the outer walls, and the rest of the staff were expected to sit in open spaces, separated only by ugly, gray modular screens. Of course no one could work under such conditions, so walls had sprung up around the desks of anyone who had enough clout to order one built, leaving the place a warren of temporary cubicles, broken up by an occasional out-of-place wall. I sat in a semi-open area, outside the empty deputy assistant secretary's office, with nothing to do. On my second day, a fellow pushing a mail cart came around passing out dozens of copies of the newly promulgated regulations for the Federal Paperwork Reduction Act. It was nearly two inches thick. Sitting alone in my little cubbyhole, I laughed out loud: How thick would it have been if Congress hadn't passed a law to reduce paperwork, I wondered.

My secretary, whose desk sat just a few feet from my own, was a surly twenty-year veteran. When the phone rang, she'd wait until the tenth ring, lift the receiver a half an inch, and drop it back into its cradle, disconnecting the caller. If the person was persistent enough, she might deign to answer the call on the third or fourth round.

"You can answer the phone your own damn self if you don't like it. I'm busy," she told me when I confronted her on her little trick, which was pretty much her response for most things. It was never clear what she was busy doing, but it certainly wasn't the work she was assigned. Congressional letters would sit on her desk for weeks without being typed.

"Senator Byrd is a very important man to this agency," I tried to explain, when I found a response to an inquiry from Robert Byrd, one of the most influential men in the U.S. Senate, untyped days after I'd put it in her inbox. "When he has a question for us, we need to be responsive. If I can draft an answer in less than an hour, I don't see why it should take more than a week for the letter to be typed. From now on, every senator or congressman who writes this office will receive a reply within one week."

I thought I'd solved the problem, but I quickly learned who had real power in the department, and it wasn't me. In response to my complaint, the woman

hauled the union in to inform me that I'd violated the union contract by setting time limits for the completion of work. Dick wasn't interested in a conflict
with the government employees union, so members of Congress would just
have to wait.

But if the career employees goofed off a good deal of the time, the political
appointees believed that it was their duty to put in twelve-hour days. Dick
Warden was there before I arrived at 8:30 in the morning and always hung
around his office until eight o'clock at night. And Buddy Blakey, the new
deputy assistant secretary to whom I'd finally been assigned as special assistant,
usually hung out with him. There was no way I was going to join them. I was
still nursing Pablo and needed to get home, plus I wanted to have dinner with
Chris and David—even if it was take-out chicken from a nearby fast-food joint.
A few minutes before six, I'd stick my head in Buddy's door and say good night.
He never said anything about my leaving early, but he always looked up at the
big clock on his wall as I bid goodbye. On the nights I actually stayed late, I'd
find him in Dick's office, both of them with their feet propped on Dick's desk,
shooting the breeze. It was a pattern I saw repeated nearly everywhere in political Washington. No one wanted to be the first to leave the office. The men
especially would stay late every night just for the privilege of being invited into
the boss's office. In Buddy's case, he hoped Dick would invite him up to his
suite. And I imagined Dick himself was hanging around to see if Joe Califano,
the HEW secretary, might call him upstairs for a chat. I never minded working long hours so long as there was actual work that needed doing, but I had
no interest in hanging around for its own sake while my husband and two kids
waited anxiously for me to come home.

There was more to my unhappiness at HEW than being caught between the
workaholic political appointees and the indolent career staff, however. At
twenty-nine, I was a GS 15 in the federal government—the highest rank outside the executive service. It was a position that others probably envied, but I
felt like a failure. I hated my work. I was a very tiny cog in a gargantuan
machine. I felt that my work was virtually meaningless. I felt more worthless
than I did when I was a lobbyist. There was no substance to my job. I had nothing to show for my efforts each day, and the work itself offered little intellectual challenge. I wanted a job where I made a difference, where I could make
my own mark, where I would actually produce something. At the end of the
day, I wanted to be able to look back at what I'd done during my hours at work
and know that it was important that I'd been there. I certainly didn't have that
feeling in the federal government, so I decided to explore returning to the AFT
if I could do something besides lobby.

Shanker had launched a new quarterly magazine at the AFT about the time I left. The *American Educator* was to be a journal of ideas, unlike the *American Teacher*, the AFT's monthly newspaper, which covered union business. Both publications came under the direction of Larry Sibelman, the man who had replaced my nemesis, Al Lowenthal, who had since died. I had heard through the grapevine, however, that Shanker was unhappy with the magazine. It was pedestrian, consisting mostly of reprints from other publications, with nothing to make it stand out among the dozens of similar education and trade association magazines. Shanker decided to turn over the magazine to his trusted assistant Eugenia Kemble, who had always served as his alter ego among the staff. Gene Kemble didn't want to edit the magazine herself, but she didn't want to keep the current editor, who routinely published the magazine late and over budget. At my urging, Gene decided to propose me for the job. Shanker bought the idea, and I was on my way back to the AFT, but not before a short detour at the Office of Management and Budget. While I was waiting for Shanker to make up his mind, an old friend from my days on the Hill, Jeffrey Miller, persuaded me to join him and his boss, Howard Glickstein, the former staff director of the U.S. Commission on Civil Rights, at the President's Reorganization Project at OMB. They were writing a plan to reorganize civil rights enforcement among various federal agencies and departments. The assignment would last only a couple of months, just long enough for Shanker to ease Sibelman out of responsibility for the magazine and pave the way for me to become editor. I returned to the AFT in September, having lasted in the government barely six months.

However short my tenure, the experience profoundly changed my views about the role of government. I had gone into HEW believing that the federal government could solve problems better than the private sector. I came out thinking that federal government created as many problems as it solved, perhaps more. I saw earnest but often clueless bureaucrats writing government regulations with no real sense of how those regulations would affect the people who would have to abide by them. Most of the federal employees I encountered had spent their entire lives working for government. How could they possibly know how the rest of the world operated? I had always assumed government was at least as efficient as business, with a greater stake in promoting the common good. But a few months at HEW quickly disabused me of any notion of government efficiency and shook my confidence in the idea that any group of people was capable of defining what was good for others. These were certainly not the views of a socialist. I wasn't sure how to characterize them, but I knew that the way I'd defined my politics in the past no longer fit.

Meanwhile, I was excited about my new duties at the AFT. Although I'd never so much as worked on my high school newspaper, I figured I would easily learn the mechanics of putting out a quarterly magazine. My only problem was that I had to turn out two issues in the time I would normally have had for one. The magazine was so far behind schedule that it was in danger of losing its non-profit mailing permit, which would have cost the union tens of thousands of dollars. I could not have gotten through the first few months without the help of the magazine's art director, Andrew Bornstein, who taught me about galleys and page proofs and led me gently through the process of putting out a magazine. But I enjoyed the challenge, and despite my inexperience, I had definite ideas about what I wanted to do with the magazine's look and content. I immersed myself in serious magazines and journals, poring through old issues of the *New Republic, Atlantic Monthly, American Scholar, Foreign Policy, Commentary, Public Interest,* and others, looking for models on which to base *American Educator.*

I also began reading books on political philosophy, a subject I'd barely explored in college, and then only in literature classes. I started by reading Jean-Jacques Rousseau, John Locke, and Edmund Burke, but it was when I discovered Adam Smith that I felt I had found my true philosophical soul mate. Smith's description of the "invisible hand," which operates through the accumulated free choices of individuals to produce the best outcome for society, struck home. "By pursuing his own interest he frequently promotes that of the society more effectually than when he really intends to promote it," Smith wrote in *The Wealth of Nations.* "I have never known much good done by those who affected to trade for the public good."[7] That had certainly been my experience in government; when the few tried to make decisions for the many based on some abstract notions of the public good, they often ended up making matters worse.

A few years earlier, Chris had tried to introduce me to political philosophy by encouraging me to read Marx for a Yipsel discussion group we attended, but I found the assigned readings nearly indecipherable, with their abstruse language and convoluted economic theories. About the same time, Chris abandoned Marxist economics when he concluded that the declining price of color television sets proved Marx wrong. According to Marx, capitalism was supposed to lead to an ever greater concentration of capital, creating monopolies that would arbitrarily drive prices constantly upward and out of reach of ordinary working people. In 1972, we bought a 25-inch Motorola Quasar—the largest set made at the time—for five hundred dollars. Under Marx's theory, the price of color televisions should have risen constantly. But instead of becoming more expensive in subsequent years, the price of a color TVs continued to go down year after year, while the size and quality of the sets went up—and both Chris and I became free market enthusiasts.

I had been back with the AFT less than a year when I became pregnant again, with my third child in 1978. That July the heat and humidity were particularly unbearable as I entered my sixth month. Our house was big, but it lacked central air conditioning, and I sometimes crept downstairs to sleep on the couch so as not to keep Chris awake with my tossing and turning. In the early morning hours of July 15, as I slept on the living room couch, I awoke suddenly to see a mouse on its hind legs in the middle of the Persian rug just inches from my face. It seemed to be staring at me. I lay very still, terrified of the tiny creature, as I had been afraid of mice all my life.

The sight of the rodent brought back memories of my childhood when we had lived in cramped, basement apartments infested with mice. At one point my parents brought home a kitten from the Humane Society to keep them under control. But instead of killing the mice outright, she would catch them and drop them, still squirming, at my feet or on the bed if I happened to be sleeping. One time I awoke to a mouse, twitching on my pillow, and let out a blood-curdling scream. Although my screams failed to bring my father, who had slipped out of the apartment to the corner bar after my sister and I had fallen asleep, they did attract the police. I lied to the policeman and told him that my father had just gone out to the drugstore and would be right back. He wanted to stay until my father returned, but I convinced him that it would just be a few minutes and my sister and I were perfectly fine, even though I was afraid to go back into the bedroom with the half-dead mouse still on my bed. The incident had happened twenty years earlier, but I remembered it again as I watched the mouse on my rug. My father, thousands of miles away was still a huge presence in my life. As always, I was filled with pangs of guilt when I thought of him. I had succeeded where he had not, despite his obvious intelligence and talent. I lived in an elegant house I owned, when he had never been able to afford to buy a home after we lost the one my grandfather had given us when I was six. He never overcame the demons of his childhood, while I had mostly left behind the sadness of my own. I was unable to fall back to sleep. Just after dawn, I heard a knock at the door.

A young policewoman stood outside on my porch.

"May I help you," I asked quietly so as not to wake Chris or the boys, still asleep upstairs.

"Ma'am, it's important that you call your mother right away," she said awkwardly. "She's been trying to get through to you. Your phone is out."

"My phone is out? No, that can't be. It's fine," I said, trying to close the door on the woman. I had a terrible foreboding about what she was telling me and did not want to listen further.

"Do you understand? You must call home. Your mother needs to talk to you. Call this operator," she said, handing me a piece of paper through the small crack in the door. "Is there a neighbor, can you call from a neighbor's?" she asked. There was something wrong with the way the woman was looking at me. Her face was full of pity. I wanted her to go away.

I took the piece of paper from her and shut the door. It was my father. I knew it; something had happened to my father. He and my mother had moved back to Albuquerque from Denver just a year before. I walked into the kitchen and picked up the phone. It was dead, just as the policewoman said. I went upstairs into our bedroom and quietly put on my clothes. I didn't want to wake Chris, but he stirred as I sat on the bed tying my tennis shoes.

"What's up?" he said, groggily.

"Something's happened to my father. I have to go down the street to call."

"What are you talking about?" he said, sitting upright now. "What's wrong with you?"

"I said I have to go use the pay phone. Something's happened. A police-woman was just here. Our phones are out."

"Do you want me to go with you?"

"No, I'll be all right. I gotta go," I said.

The filling station two blocks from the house had a phone booth. I drove there, clutching the scrap of paper with the operator's number scribbled on it. Before I'd even dialed the number, I knew my father was dead. I knew that he'd been killed in a car accident. He'd had so many accidents all my life, banged up, bones broken, laid up in the hospital for weeks at a time— always alone, never anyone else in the car, never any other car involved in the accident.

"He's gone, honey. Daddy's gone." My mother's voice sounded oddly calm when the operator put her through. "It happened last night. He went to the races in Santa Fe. His tire blew out on the interstate coming home. He died instantly. He didn't suffer at all," she said.

"I knew it. I knew this would happen someday. Was he drinking?"

"I don't know. They didn't say anything like that. He was on the exit. The guy driving the car behind him said it looked like the tire exploded. He lost control. The car rolled over. He died instantly."

"I'll come right away, Momma. I'll come home today," I said. I felt numb. All my life I had expected this call. Whenever the phone would ring late at night, I'd grab for it, terrified. But it would always be my father's voice, boozy, his words slurred, calling to tell me that he missed me.

"Call me tomorrow, Daddy," I'd say. "It's too late now. I've got to go to work in the morning."

"Don't hang up," he'd plead, his normally deep voice now almost a whimper.

But I couldn't listen. It was as if he was reaching through the phone lines dragging me back to everything I had escaped. And now I would never have another phone call from him. I was filled with anger, as well as sadness. How could he have done this to me, to my mother? How could he have abandoned us like this? And with me pregnant. How was I going to get through this? I drove back home. Chris was waiting for me, taking me in his arms before I was able to say a word.

It was difficult to comprehend that my father was dead. All my life, he had been both my protector and my greatest source of insecurity. He was big and strong and fearless, and when I was with him I felt absolutely safe. But he would disappear for days at a time, and then I would be left feeling scared and abandoned. And it never changed. I continued to feel the torment of his drinking even 1,800 miles away when I was grown, with children of my own. I loved him more than anything, and I always knew he loved me. I couldn't bear to think that I would never hear his voice again or see his handsome smile. But I also felt a guilty sense of peace when he died. It was as if I had been waiting so long for the worst to happen, and now that it finally had, the anxiety that always gnawed at me was gone.

I flew to Albuquerque that afternoon in a stupor. Margarita took eighteen-month-old Pablo home to her house to care for him. Chris took a separate flight, after putting David, now almost eight, on a plane to North Carolina where he was to begin summer camp at a nature preserve. It was a terrible mistake not to bring him with us, even though we thought we were doing what was best for him. He and his grandfather had been especially close. David would accompany his Grandpa Rudy to the golf course or spend the day with him as he painted houses whenever we'd visit. I don't know how we could possibly have thought David would still be able to enjoy the camp even though his beloved Grandpa had died. Instead he lay in his bunk bed each night crying himself to sleep.

Chris took over making all the arrangements for the funeral when he arrived. My aunt Elsie and my uncle Pete, two of my father's siblings, still lived in Albuquerque. My aunt Irene flew in from Chicago, and several old friends came in from out of town to be pallbearers. It had been almost twenty years since I had seen many of my father's old friends, a group of men who had grown up together, gone to war in the South Pacific together, and who were a constant presence in my early childhood. Jimmy, who had become a heroin addict during the war, still lived at home with his mother and worked off and on as a housepainter. Charlie was a successful building contractor, who'd become rich enough to own homes in several cities but whose mottled face bore the tell-tale signs of his heavy drinking. My uncle Pete, whose mental illness prevented him from ever holding down a steady job, supported himself somehow on his disability pension and peddling used furniture and other odds and ends. Sammy had worked for my father off and on over the years, even in Denver, where he would sometimes share our cramped apartment, sleeping in a tiny space off the boiler room. Ramon, a distant cousin and the only one of the pallbearers I didn't remember from my childhood, was a tall, silver-haired man who bore an uncanny resemblance to my father. My dad was the first among this group of hardscrabble boyhood friends to die, too young, at sixty.

The funeral mass was held at San Felipe de Niri, a beautiful eighteenth-century adobe church in Old Town, which my father's family had helped build more than 250 years earlier and where they had attended services ever since. But the priest had never met my father, and his words were generic. They captured none of my father's spirit, his intelligence, his humor, his warmth. Afterward, we rode in Charlie's new white Cadillac to Santa Fe, where my father was laid to rest in the National Cemetery in the foothills of the Sangre de Cristos, while a scratchy recording of "Taps" played in the background. I rode back to Albuquerque holding on tightly to the folded American flag that had draped his coffin, unspeakably sad.

Back in my mother's living room, I was suddenly confronted with the realization that it would now be my responsibility to take care of her. She had quit work when they moved back to Albuquerque, and her mother had moved in with them, sharing a two-bedroom house on the east side of Albuquerque, with a fine view of my father's beloved Sandia Mountains. My father had no life insurance and only a tiny veteran's survivor benefit and, at fifty-seven, my mother was not yet eligible for Social Security. I wasn't sure how she was going to survive on her own. I could help her financially, but I could never make up for the loneliness she would feel. She had always been so totally fused with my father that I could not imagine how she would live without him. My father's sister Elsie offered to have my mother move into a small apartment attached to her house, which would save some money. Besides, my mother did not want to stay in the house where she had lived with my father for so short a time. Susie would go to live with her other daughter, Mary, in Sun City, Arizona.

"You better call Pamela," Elsie said as we sat discussing my mother's future. I was stunned.

"You know where she is?" I asked, incredulous. For years, whenever I brought up my sister's name, I was told that no one knew what had happened to her.

"She's married with a bunch of kids, the last I heard," my mother said, as if she were talking about some old acquaintance. "I'll call Ann and tell her," she said walking over to her address book.

"Who's Ann?" I asked, my heart racing.

"Ann Murphy. You know the Murphys, the people who adopted her."

It was a favorite technique my mother used whenever she revealed some long-hidden information. Pretend that I knew it all along.

"No, I don't know. I didn't know you knew how to reach her. I'd like to talk to Pamela. I'd like to see her again. She's my only sister now, you know."

"That's not a good idea. I don't think Pamela's husband knows about your daddy. He's very prejudiced, and I don't think Pamela wants him to know she's part Spanish," she said. "It would be better if you didn't try to contact her," she said with a finality I recognized.

As always, when she wanted to shut the door to certain information, she just clammed up. I knew better than to press the matter; I wouldn't get anywhere anyway. She made the call to Ann Murphy, which lasted only a couple of minutes. I could hear her telling Pamela's adoptive mother about me, but she didn't mention that I was expecting my third child or much else about my personal life. It didn't seem right that she had waited to notify Pamela's mother until after the funeral. What if Pamela had wanted to come? But then that is probably why she didn't make the call earlier.

Later, after Elsie had left, my mother suddenly brought up Pamela again.

"I don't think she was really your father's child. She didn't even look like him," she said out of nowhere.

I knew she would never have said such a thing if my father were still alive. Perhaps she wanted to believe that Pamela was not my father's daughter, but he certainly believed she was, and there was never any evidence to the contrary. I was angry at my mother for suggesting otherwise. Not only did it demean my father's relationship to Pamela, but it diminished my own as well. Next to losing my sister Wendy, giving up Pamela was the hardest thing my father ever went through, and it had affected me deeply, too. I wanted to ask my mother for Ann Murphy's phone number, but I was afraid to. When I finally did ask her some time later, she said she didn't have it and didn't know where they lived, somewhere in southeastern New Mexico on a ranch was all she could remember. Once again, I'd hit a stone wall in getting any information about my sister.

In October I gave birth to another baby boy. I named him Rudolph Chavez Gersten, after my father, who would have been very proud of his chubby, green-eyed namesake. I stayed home only three weeks after Rudy's birth, not nearly long enough to recuperate. I was much more tired throughout my pregnancy than I had been with either David or Pablo, no doubt because I had a toddler to chase after when I came home from a full day's work. Plus, I was taking on new responsibilities at the AFT. After little more than a year editing *American Educator*, I was about to become editor of the union's monthly newspaper *American Teacher* and the weekly newsletter as well. With the new responsibilities I would become a full department director and inherit additional staff, which would be a mixed blessing since it entailed more management duties. My rise at the AFT had been very quick, earning me as many enemies as allies, even among some people whom I considered good friends. I soon earned the reputation of being "ambitious," a highly suspicious trait in an organization in which most people remained in the same job their entire career. But Shanker's support was firm. Little by little, he included me in his inner circle—the "schmendreks," the Yiddish word for jerks, as one envious staffer dubbed the group. Gene Kemble, who had been my supervisor, left to work for the AFL-CIO in Europe, and I soon joined the elite ranks of "assistant to the president."

Although Shanker was a traditional liberal Democrat on economic and labor issues, his positions on many other issues were more unconventional. He took surprisingly conservative stands on occasion, especially on affirmative action, foreign policy, and defense. In 1977, for example, when the Supreme Court was about to hear the landmark *Bakke* case, challenging an affirmative action program that relied on racial quotas at the University of California at Davis Medical School, Shanker blasted the Carter administration for defending the university. "There is no issue in American society today that is as divisive as preferential treatment along racial and ethnic lines—no issue more guaranteed to keep race relations in this country in a state of conflict. Unless the Supreme Court declares once and for all that the Constitution demands equal treatment for all Americans and bars race as a consideration, we are in for endless lawsuits, mistrust and resentment," he wrote in his weekly column in the Week in Review section of the Sunday *New York Times*.[8] He also abhorred the anti-corporate left and once admonished me when I ran an article in *American Teacher* about a boycott of Nestlé Corporation over its sales of infant formula in the Third World, despite the fact that the boycott had been endorsed by the AFT itself at its annual convention. And he was an early and vocal advocate of improving education standards and tougher testing for both students and teachers, endorsing the idea of a national teachers exam. "Teaching will never be a profession unless we have the equivalent of the bar or medical exam," he frequently told audiences.[9]

Shanker gave me virtually a free hand with *American Educator*. I could commission articles without prior clearance from anyone, once Gene Kemble left. And Shanker saw the magazine when everyone else did—after it was printed. I relished my intellectual freedom, which I knew was a rare commodity in a political job. Shanker picked his top staff carefully but then left them alone to function autonomously—which made the AFT an often unruly place but created an environment in which I thrived. Shanker wanted me to produce a journal that would earn him respect in certain intellectual circles. As long as he got positive feedback on the magazine from those he respected, I could take on controversial issues in its pages without interference.

"The *American Educator* should be the kind of journal that *Commentary* writers would want to write for," he told me.[10] I followed the suggestion literally and began recruiting *Commentary* authors to write articles for *American Educator* on topics that had a certain edge to them, not the usual bland fare customary in most education or union publications. Many of the writers were largely unknown at the time, outside a small circle of intellectuals, but would become household names in a few years: William J. Bennett, Jeane J. Kirkpatrick, Robert Bork, as well as Thomas Sowell, Diane Ravitch, Admiral James Stockdale, and others—hardly the lineup one would expect from a union publication.[11]

Bennett's first article for me in the Fall 1978 issue was on the subject of homosexual teachers. I originally had asked *Commentary* author Midge Decter to write the piece after I'd read a controversial article on homosexuals she'd written for *Commentary*.

"I've said all I have to say on the subject already," she demurred. "Why don't you give Bill Bennett a call down at the National Humanities Center in North Carolina. He's a very bright fellow, and I think he'd do a fine job on the piece."

I took her advice and Bennett agreed to tackle the thorny question of whether there should be any restrictions on homosexuals in the classroom. He came to the office in person to hand in the piece. Wearing jeans and a blue work shirt with the sleeves rolled up, he looked more like an ex-Notre Dame linebacker than a scholar.

"I believe that homosexuals who are overt and self-declared about their homosexuality," Bennett wrote, "who have an interest in arguing for homosexuality as a lifestyle, and who make efforts to change student values about homosexuality in ways fundamentally inconsistent with values that the school and community affirm, should not be teaching in the public schools." The piece pulled no punches, but neither was it a jeremiad against homosexual teachers, acknowledging that many fine teachers were, in fact, homosexuals. If it came down to choosing between two candidates for a teaching position, one of which was "a discreet homosexual who is a responsible teacher" and the other a "straight model of heterosexual normality who tries to get away with as little preparation as he can," Bennett argued, "the choice of the homosexual teacher" is the right one "for reasons that have to do precisely with his values and the positive effect on students' values his presence in the classroom implies."[12] The issue was whether a teacher—of whatever sexual orientation—insisted on making his or her sex life the subject of classroom discussion. The article drew less fire than I expected, though I expect today it would raise an uproar.

Bennett and I came from similar working-class backgrounds, had both attended strict 1950s Catholic schools, and were both registered Democrats grown dissatisfied with many of the stands our party had taken in recent years. We hit it off immediately and ended up spending hours talking on the phone each week. Bennett became a regular contributor to *American Educator*, and we soon hatched a plan to use the magazine to promote moral education in the classroom—a subject Bennett wrote on frequently and about which we were both passionate.

The 1970s became the decade of values-neutral education. A whole movement had sprung up to strip public schools of their function of teaching right from wrong. Instead of inculcating universal values, schools began encouraging students to develop their own value systems. Influenced by the work of philosopher Lawrence Kohlberg and others, teachers promoted "values clarification," presenting students with "moral dilemmas," which were supposed to help them sort out their own individual ethical codes, depending on the specific situation.

One famous values clarification exercise used in many school programs involved a lifeboat scenario in which students were asked to pick which person to throw overboard in a situation in which the rules dictated that not everyone could survive. The students were not allowed to come up with alternative scenarios to permit all passengers to stay onboard. These situational ethics lessons were supposed to teach children that there was no such thing as absolute right and wrong. Deciding what was right and wrong always depended on the specific situation and the "values" of the individual making the decision.

Sometimes it was right to lie, steal, cheat, even kill—and students spent more time deciding when such behavior was permissible than when it was not.

School systems around the country were rushing to adopt values clarification programs in the name of promoting values education, even in traditionally conservative areas in the South and Midwest. I was appalled when I witnessed AFT teachers using the lifeboat exercise in classrooms I visited in Vermont and Pennsylvania. The kids themselves often resisted the directions they were given. "Why can't we figure out a way to lighten the load or stretch the food and water supply instead?" they'd ask plaintively, only to be told it was their duty to pick a candidate to throw overboard. The teachers didn't seem any more comfortable with the exercise than the students—but it was part of the lesson plan and they followed blindly. I persuaded Shanker that the AFT should try to do something to educate its members on the dangers of the values clarification movement, which I believed not only corrupted personal morality but had subtly corrosive political effects as well. If all values were "relative," so too were all political systems. The United States was no different from the Soviet Union; democracy no better than communism. There could be no such thing as unalienable rights. Universal human rights could not exist, and our government could not expect other countries to respect them. Indeed many of the textbooks of the era promoted precisely these views. Shanker was enthusiastic and suggested that I invite Bill Bennett to put together a small meeting of like-minded people to explore ways the AFT might take on values clarification with its members. I set up a day-and-a-half session at the Ritz Carlton Hotel, which included Bennett and a group of about a dozen scholars and educators he had worked with on this issue. Over the course of the meetings we hammered out a proposal for a series of teacher's guides on specific virtues that we believed were fundamentally important to a democratic society.

We settled on five specific virtues: honesty, courage, loyalty, compassion, and responsibility. Bennett agreed to write the introduction to the series, and Steven Tigner, a young philosophy professor from the University of Toledo, agreed to gather the materials to be included, which I then supplemented. Over the course of the next couple of years, from its Winter 1981 to its Spring 1983 issues, the *American Educator* ran special teaching supplements on these virtues drawing from literature, history, journalism, art, popular culture, law, and religion—using classical and contemporary illustrations. There were selections from the Bible, the Mishnah, the Boy Scouts Manual, Plato, Homer, Jean-Jacques Rousseau, John Steinbeck, Maya Angelou, Ogden Nash, newspaper accounts, court decisions, and popular songs and movies. Each supplement included a long bibliography of additional materials that could be used by teachers in preparing lesson plans. The series was radical for its time and place—in a union publication—but drew mostly accolades from teachers and made me new friends in some unusual quarters. Supreme Court Chief Justice Warren Burger invited me to lecture the interns in his office on the issue. Bennett later expanded his work on moral education, eventually publishing a best-selling compilation, *The Book of Virtues.*

It was clear that under my direction the *American Educator* had become a conservative journal of ideas. Not only did we promote Shanker's hard-line anti-communist views with articles critical of China, Cuba, and the Soviet Union, but we also took on affirmative action, ethnic studies, radical feminism, including the feminist assault on language (in an article titled "To Err Is Huperson"), and the "nuclear freeze" movement. I was particularly interested in tackling the nuclear freeze issue, which was at the height of its popularity after Ronald Reagan became president and had started to rebuild America's defenses in the wake of the Carter administration's four-year neglect. President Reagan's decision to place nuclear-armed Pershing missiles in Europe to counteract the growing Soviet threat sparked a huge international anti-nuclear movement aimed at "freezing" nuclear weapons production and deployment, with protest marches, sit-ins, and demonstrations at American military bases in both Europe and the United States.

I met with James Woolsey, a defense expert who would later become director of the Central Intelligence Agency in the Clinton administration, to discuss the issue, and he brought to my attention a study guide on nuclear arms being widely disseminated to high school students around the country. The National Education Association, the AFT's rival, had produced the study guide, in conjunction with the left-wing Union of Concerned Scientists. The *Washington Post* described the guide as "political indoctrination," saying it was "not teaching in any normally accepted—or for that matter, acceptable—sense."[13] Shanker was enthusiastic about my addressing the guide, which went beyond advocating merely "freezing" nuclear weapons to push for unilateral nuclear disarmament by the United States in the guise of promoting a "peaceful and secure future for the United States and the world." I spent weeks poring over the NEA guide, talking to defense experts and reading analyses in foreign policy journals. It was what I loved best about my job: the opportunity to explore almost any issue that caught my fancy, to spend my days reading, writing, and editing. At the end of the day, I could look back on what I'd done and have a real sense of accomplishment and satisfaction, and when the magazine came out, I could hold in my hands the fruits of my labor. It reminded me of my father's attitude toward his work. On Sunday afternoons, we'd drive around Denver, and he'd point out this house or that building he'd painted, with a sense of pride in a job well done. Being an editor or a writer, I discovered, was not all that different from being a skilled craftsman.

Although I was happier at the AFT than I had ever been in any job, I occasionally ran into trouble—usually because I'd misjudged how far I could go on some issue, pushing Shanker farther than he liked. I hit a raw nerve once in writing about the effects of divorce on the academic performance of children from broken families. Shanker himself was divorced and remarried, as were a large portion of union members—like most Americans. The conventional wisdom of the era, backed up by much of the social science of the 1970s, reassured couples that children were better off living with one parent than in two-parent households in which there was conflict between the adults. In an unsigned article I wrote for *American Educator,* I suggested otherwise, citing a new and controversial study on the topic. "One-parent children show lower achievement in school than their two-parent peers. . . . Students from one-parent families are consistently more likely to be late, truant, and subject to disciplinary action than two-parent students. . . . One-parent students are more than twice as likely as two-parent children to drop out of school," I wrote.[14] As if the topic itself were not controversial enough, I decided to illustrate the cover with a provocative photograph, a family portrait printed on shattered glass with the words "The American Family: The Shattered Dream," which I tried to mitigate slightly by placing a question mark at the end of the title. When the magazine came out, Shanker called me into his office to complain.

"Don't you think this is a little harsh?" he asked.

"No, I'd say it's visually dramatic. It makes you want to open the magazine and see what's inside," I said, defending myself.

He peered out over the top of his glasses, still skeptical.

"Our members are affected by what's happened to family life in the United States," I continued, hoping to persuade him that I'd used good judgment. "The whole point of my piece is that kids are harmed by divorce and it, in turn, hurts their school performance. Divorce makes our members' jobs more difficult. It's as plain as that."

Never one to use his power as president of the union to win an argument, Shanker seemed mollified, but he continued to leaf through the magazine.

"What about this?" he asked, pointing to another Bennett piece, this one on sex education.

In the article, Bennett blasted the sex education programs that were popular in many school systems around the country.[15] Bennett warned against explicit sex education courses that went beyond biology lessons, "watching chickens come from eggs and answering [children's] questions about the process. . . . I do not see any reason for initiating or inciting interest in sex in the young, which these materials do, before the young come to this interest on their own," Bennett wrote. "And when they do come to this interest, as they inevitably will, I would recommend the individual counsel of parents, priests, ministers, rabbis, and of teachers, of adults who know the child and who will take the time and offer the advice needed to *that* child."

"The guy sounds like a prig," Shanker said. Although I had tried to foster a relationship between the two men, both of whom I admired, Shanker disliked Bennett. When Bennett later went into the Reagan administration, Shanker found him a useful ally, but he never warmed to Bennett. Whenever the two men disagreed on a policy issue, however, I found that my position was closer to Bennett's.

By 1980, I realized that I was to the right of Al Shanker and everyone else at the AFT on many issues. Nevertheless, I continued to enjoy my job and the chance to influence opinions through the union's publications, which a half million teachers and others received regularly. Occasionally, however, I was called on to promote views with which I personally disagreed, though never to such an extent that I felt intellectually dishonest doing so. Part of my job consisted of preparing the *American Teacher* election guides, which the union not only disseminated to its members but gave to candidates to use in their campaigns—a widespread, if illegal, practice popular among labor unions, which continues to this day. In the spring of 1980, I prepared a special issue of *American Teacher* endorsing Ted Kennedy for president in his uphill battle against incumbent President Jimmy Carter for the Democratic nomination. I was still friendly with Kennedy's former legislative assistant, Mark Schneider, who now worked on Kennedy's presidential campaign, and after the pro-Kennedy *American Teacher* supplement was printed, I had thousands of extra copies shipped to him at Kennedy's headquarters. Although Shanker was under no illusion that Ted Kennedy was an anti-communist hawk, he believed that it was important to oppose President Carter and that Kennedy was the best vehicle for doing so, at least in the primaries.

Shanker was very unhappy with the Carter administration, as much over Carter's inept handling of foreign affairs as anything else. Carter had watched idly while country after country fell to communist insurgencies in Central America, Africa, and Asia, and only when the Soviet Union invaded Afghanistan did Carter profess to understand the nature of the communist threat: "The action of the Soviets has made a more dramatic change in my own opinion of what the Soviets' ultimate goals are than anything they've done in the previous time I've been in office," Carter told ABC News on December 31, 1979.[16] What's more, the taking of American hostages by Ayatollah Khomeini and his radical Islamic followers, after the fall of the Shah of Iran, had deeply shaken all Americans' confidence in their president. Carter had also made deep cuts in defense spending, which Shanker opposed.

Shanker had some education policy disagreements with Carter as well, including a major dispute over the course of bilingual education. Just before the 1980 election, Carter's newly formed Department of Education promulgated regulations that would have mandated Spanish-language instruction as the only acceptable method to teach non-English-speaking Hispanic children, despite considerable evidence that misnamed "bilingual education" programs didn't work well. Shanker and the AFT helped lead the fight against the regulations, which were eventually withdrawn—but only after President Reagan took office.

On Election Day 1980, I did something I had never imagined I could do: I voted for a Republican for president. Shanker and the AFT had fallen back in line after Kennedy failed to win the Democratic nomination, but I detested Carter—much as I had despised Richard Nixon. Carter was a national embarrassment. I dutifully prepared the fall election issue of *American Teacher*, which endorsed Carter in the general election, but when I went into the polling booth, I cast my vote for Ronald Reagan. I liked Reagan's style, and I agreed with his positions on the issues I considered most important: defense, foreign policy, and affirmative action. Still, it was difficult emotionally to pull the Republican lever. From my youngest years, I had thought of myself as a Democrat. I remembered my father watching the 1952 election returns on our first television set and crying when Adlai Stevenson lost. But my father hadn't liked Carter very much, and I consoled myself with the thought that had he lived, he probably would have voted for Reagan. And Chris—whose opinion on politics I trusted more than my own—was enthusiastically supporting Reagan. And when I went out to lunch with a group of my AFT coworkers on Election Day, I was surprised to learn that several of them had voted for Reagan, too. I knew then that Reagan would win in a landslide.

Although I thought of Shanker as my intellectual mentor—and he both influenced me and encouraged me to explore my own instincts on issues—I realized that many of my views had been shaped much earlier, primarily by my religious training and education.

On most issues, I was still the Catholic schoolgirl, respectful of authority, more comfortable with a fixed moral code, and with a reverence for tradition

My paternal grandfather's parents, Eduardo Chavez and Excelsa Armijo, came from two prominent families of wool traders and merchants who emigrated from Spain and Mexico in the early 1600s and 1700s. As a child, I loved to look at this wedding photograph (about 1889) and imagine what life might have been like had my grandfather not gone to prison for bootlegging, plunging the family into poverty.

My mother, Velma Lou McKenna, was a glamorous blond divorcee from Wyoming when she met my father, Rudolph Chavez, in Albuquerque after World War II. Although he was an incredibly bright man and loving father, the legacy of his own troubled childhood took its toll. My father took this self-portrait and the photo of my mother when he studied photography on the G.I.

My mother gave up her two sons from a previous marriage. Dickie (left) was killed in a car accident at 15, and Michael (right) died in 1997.

My sister Pamela (right), my father's daughter from his first marriage, was given up for adoption a couple of years after this picture of us was taken. We found each other again forty-seven years later through the Internet.

My father snapped this picture of my sister Wendy (left) and me on Easter 1959. A few months later, Wendy died from kidney disease, which made me draw further inward from the pain of losing those close to me.

Chris and I were married on June 15, 1967, at Temple Emmanuel in Denver. I agreed to convert to Judaism, a decision that was to become an issue in my 1986 Senate campaign. I later returned to my Catholic faith, and our marriage was blessed by the Church in 1994.

Although most Americans know me as a conservative Republican, I traveled mostly in liberal Democratic circles in my early career in the 1970s. Here I am shaking hands with NAACP president Roy Wilkins,

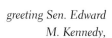

greeting Sen. Edward M. Kennedy,

and with my former boss, American Federation of Teachers president Albert Shanker, who is standing next to me at a reception in Costa Rica. Credit: (Wilkins) National Education Association Publishing, Joe Di Dio; (Kennedy) Rick Fleming/NYSUT.

On November 30, 1984,
President Reagan signs
the bill reauthorizing the
U.S. Commission on
Civil Rights, passed after
a fierce battle on Capitol
Hill, while Chairman
Clarence Pendleton and
I look on. Credit: White
House Official Photo.

Pat Buchanan and I
enjoy a light moment
with President
Reagan in the Oval
Office in 1985.
Credit: White House
Official Photo.

I present President
Reagan with a political
"yard sign" for the
White House lawn at
a fundraiser for my
1986 Maryland U.S.
Senate campaign.
Credit: White House
Official Photo.

I am surrounded by my large, and growing, family on Thanksgiving Day 1999. Back row: my son David, husband Chris, sons Rudy and Pablo. Front row: Granddaughter Phoebe and David's wife, Sandi, next to Pablo's wife, Bella, who is pregnant with granddaughter Abigail. Not pictured are David's son Liam and Pablo's daughter Liliana, born later.

Flanked by Benson Bui (left) and Josh Reyes (right), two people I'd taken into my home over the years, I address questions about my decision to allow an illegal alien to live with me in the early 1990s, which prompted my withdrawal as President George W. Bush's first labor secretary nominee in January 2001. Credit: AP Photo/Doug Mills.

and decorum. No matter how far I had strayed from the religion of my youth, I had carried it inside me, and it shaped my views on everything—family, popular culture, even politics. I didn't need books like *The God That Failed* or *The Yogi and the Commissar* or *Darkness at Noon*, copies of which Shanker had given me to read, to convince me of the evils of communism. I'd learned my anti-communism, literally, in elementary school. But on other matters, I had begun to feel out of step, not just with the broader popular culture, but with the largely Jewish, agnostic group of friends around me. Most of my friends lived entirely secular lives, even if they were nominally Jewish or Christian. Hardly any of my friends attended church or synagogue on a regular basis, and no one seemed to miss religion in their lives. I, on the other hand, felt a hole in my life, as if something fundamental to my being was missing. I was happy in my job, I loved my family, but there was an emptiness at my core that greatly troubled me. And it got worse around the holidays. In December 1981, those feelings came to a head.

David turned thirteen in October of that year, the time when most Jewish boys have their bar mitzvah. But since Chris did not belong to a synagogue, David did not take the usual religious classes with boys his age, which would have led to a bar mitzvah. Nonetheless, Chris just assumed that David would have a bar mitzvah when he turned thirteen and, belatedly, hired a young religious Jew to give David Hebrew lessons and prepare him for a private bar mitzvah ceremony in a rented Reform synagogue. The ceremony took place during Chanukah, just days before Christmas.

As the day approached, I found myself feeling increasingly bitter—not so much because David would be raised in the Jewish faith but because I knew that the decision to raise him in his father's religion would mean that he would get no religious upbringing at all. Chris had never practiced his religion beyond occasionally going to high holy day services, and I didn't see how I could transmit a religion that I didn't observe beyond lighting Chanukah candles and cooking a Passover meal once a year. I missed going to mass, and I resented that I was being deprived of raising the children in the religion that I understood and still believed in. I felt like a coward for not insisting that the boys be raised in the Catholic faith.[17]

Chris's argument was always the same when we discussed the issue: There are more than a billion Catholics in the world and only 12 million Jews. It was as if the future of the Jewish people rested on my shoulders. The conflict caused one of the biggest strains in our married life and created a profound personal crisis for me. But we got through it, with some compromises. David had his bar mitzvah, and I even lit the Chanukah candles during the ceremony, and Chris encouraged me to start going to mass again. Even if I was deprived of receiving the sacraments, going to mass gave me some peace. It would be more than a decade, however, before I fully returned to the Catholic Church.

Other changes were taking place in my life as well. Having worked for Al Shanker for nearly eight years, I had become increasingly restless, despite moving up the ranks in the AFT to become one of Shanker's top assistants. Soon I would leave the AFT to work for the man I'd voted for in 1980: Ronald Reagan. The leap from Al Shanker's inner circle to the upper reaches of the Reagan administration was not as unlikely as it might seem, however. Other former liberals also found places in the new administration, including Jeane J. Kirkpatrick and William Bennett whose work had appeared in *American Educator*. Although my transition from labor union liberal to neoconservative was now complete, I remained friends with Al Shanker until his death in 1997, having lunch with him regularly over the years, until he became too ill from cancer to travel to Washington from his home in New York. I feel privileged to have known and worked with a man who was clearly one of the great public intellectuals of our time.

6

Battling the Civil Rights Establishment

I will eat the pages *of the civil rights bill if anyone can find in it language which provides that an employer will have to hire on the basis of percentage or quota relating to color.*

—attributed to Senator Hubert H. Humphrey
during Senate debate on the
1964 Civil Rights Act

I WAS ALONE IN MY OFFICE on January 15, 1983, when the phone rang. It was Martin Luther King's birthday, and the AFT office was officially closed, but I had come downtown to catch up on some work.

"Hi, Linda. This is Dennis Patrick at White House Personnel. Do you think you could come over here this afternoon? I have something I'd like to talk to you about," he said.

I had met Patrick the previous year when he had interviewed me for a spot on the Consumer Product Safety Commission. Bill Bennett, who became director of the National Endowment for Humanities soon after President Reagan took office, was asked to recommend some like-minded Democrats for slots on commissions requiring bipartisan representation, and he'd given the White House my name. The consumer protection job went to another Democrat, but Patrick and I liked each other, and I thought he might approach me again at some point. I had also done some consulting work for the Reagan administration in the previous year, with Shanker's permission. Tom Pauken, the director of Action, a federal agency that then incorporated both the Peace Corps and some remnants of War on Poverty programs left over from the Kennedy-Johnson era, hired me to review and make recommendations on some community action programs in 1982, again at Bennett's suggestion. So I was not entirely unknown in the Reagan ranks.

"Do you know anything about the Civil Rights Commission?" Dennis asked after we'd exchanged pleasantries in his cramped West Wing office. Created in 1957, the U.S. Commission on Civil Rights was primarily an advisory body whose job it was to study discrimination, monitor the enforcement of civil rights laws by federal agencies, and make recommendations to the president and Congress. The commission had no enforcement powers, but it did have a kind of moral authority. The staff saw themselves as advocates, and there probably wasn't a soul in the place who'd voted for Ronald Reagan.

"A lot, actually. I worked closely with the commission when I was on the Hill in Don Edwards's office," I said.

"Don Edwards. Don't remind me." Patrick interrupted. "I'm not sure how we'll ever get you cleared," he joked. It was what I liked about him; he wasn't at all the stuffy, uptight conservative I imagined most Republicans to be, but a thirty-something Rolling Stones fan with a keen sense of humor.

"We're thinking of making some changes over there," he explained. "You know the commission has six commissioners, three Republicans and three Democrats, all appointed by the president and confirmed by the Senate?" he asked.

"And a full-time staff director," I added. "That's where the real power is, in the staff director's position."

"Really? Why?" he seemed genuinely surprised and began leafing through the "Plum Book," the list of political appointee slots available to every incoming administration. "Here it is. Staff Director, PAS, Level V," he said referring to the arcane designation, which identified the job of staff director as a presidential appointment requiring Senate confirmation, with pay set one step below that of an assistant secretary or commissioner.

"The commissioners are part-time appointees. They come into town once a month for meetings, but the staff director runs the place. The commissioners have very little say in the studies and reports the commission issues, which is the heart of the agency's work. The staff director is also the only full-time presidential appointment in the agency. I worked for Howard Glickstein, who was staff director for years, when he headed Carter's civil rights reorganization project," I reminded him. "The staff director hires everybody and directs all the commission's work. He's like the CEO, and the commissioners are the board of directors," I added, picking an analogy I thought Patrick would identify with.

"I was considering recommending you for a commissioner slot. The president wants to replace all three Democrats. Every one of them is pro-quota. They're a really bad lot."

I knew two of the Democrats: Blandina "Bambi" Cardenas Ramirez, a Mexican American educator from Texas, and Mary Frances Berry, a Carter appointee whom I'd known since my own days in the Carter administration, who would later become chairman of the Commission on Civil Rights, a post she still holds today. Berry was an abrasive woman and a real leftist. I disliked her intensely. A few years earlier when she was Carter's assistant secretary for higher education, she had gotten into a very public feud with Al Shanker. After returning from an official visit to China, Berry delivered a speech at the University of Illinois in which she praised the Chinese education system and attacked the U.S. press for publishing "false" reports on the Chinese system. Shanker wrote her a letter, which he made public, saying he was deeply disturbed that she returned from her trip "so enamored of the results of a totalitarian educational system. . . . Your willingness to chastise the American free press for misreporting what is going on in China hardly inspires confidence when it comes from one who has been spoon-fed Chinese propaganda on a highly controlled trip." Berry responded that she hoped "we have moved far enough from the anti-communist crusade of the 1950s to feel secure enough to consider ideas, whatever their country of origin."[1] I certainly understood why President Reagan wanted to get rid of her.

"But I'm not sure the Republicans are much better," I added. One thing Republicans wanted to forget was that their man Richard Nixon, not LBJ or JFK, was the father of quotas.

"You're right, but I don't think we'll do anything with them," Patrick said. Mary Louise Smith, one of the Republicans and a former cochairman of the Republican National Committee, was a nice, ineffectual, gray-haired patrician who basically did whatever Berry wanted her to do. Jill Ruckleshaus, another Republican commissioner, was the wife of Bill Ruckleshaus, whom President Reagan had just recently appointed to head the Environmental Protection Agency.

"But the chairman's a great guy," Patrick added. "I'd like you to meet him at some point." Clarence Pendleton, a black businessman from San Diego appointed by Reagan in 1982, had been much in the news lately. Penny, as everyone called him, was a jovial, blunt-spoken, ex-high school coach who had no use for racial quotas.

"I'd be more interested in the staff director position than one of the commissioner slots," I reiterated. "I don't think it would be tenable to stay in my current job and be a member of the Reagan administration," I added.

"I would have thought there'd be no problem," he said. "Shanker seems like a pretty level-headed type."

Shanker was less a fan of the Reagan administration than someone like Patrick might have assumed. Shanker was first and foremost a labor union leader, and he'd been at the front of the march of some 100,000 union officials from around the country who protested President Reagan's firing of federal air traffic controllers when they went out on strike. Shanker supported Reagan's defense buildup and approved of his stand against racial quotas,[2] but he opposed much of the Reagan domestic agenda, and I knew I would find it difficult to work for Al Shanker and Ronald Reagan at the same time.

"I want you to meet a couple of other folks here at the White House," Patrick said as he picked up the phone. "Mike, do you have a couple of minutes to talk to Linda Chavez?" he said into the phone. Michael Horowitz was general counsel of the Office of Management and Budget, but his portfolio consisted of pretty much anything he wanted to stick his nose into, which was just about everything. Horowitz was an anomaly in the button-down Reagan White House. A Jew—and a former Democrat and Marine enlisted man—his style was intense, sometimes to the point of being bombastic. But he was also smart and intensely loyal, and he quickly became my champion. After I'd been in his office half an hour, he, too, picked up the phone.

"Dennis, you've got to hire this woman," he told Dennis Patrick, who didn't need much persuading. I made two more stops that day, to meet Michael Uhlmann, who worked in the domestic policy office, and Ken Cribb, an assistant to Edwin Meese, a longtime Reagan aide who was now counselor to the president. By the time I left the Old Executive Office Building after my round of meetings, I was confident that Patrick would recommend me as the new staff director of the U.S. Commission on Civil Rights. But I had no idea how long or arduous the process would be—or what a tremendous challenge and opportunity it would offer.

It took months for the White House to announce its new appointees for the Commission on Civil Rights: three commissioners, Morris B. Abram, former president of Brandeis University and a veteran civil rights attorney; John H. Bunzell, former president of San Jose State University; and Robert B. Destro, a Catholic University Law School professor—and me as staff director. White House officials expected a firestorm because they were replacing existing commissioners, something that had been done only once, when Richard Nixon was president. However, they hoped that I would provide some cover. Although all of us were registered, active Democrats, I was also a union official, a female, and a Hispanic—which meant that the White House expected that I'd be treated more favorably than the three white men. Instead, I was largely ignored—assumed to be the token minority female—when the story hit the front pages of the *New York Times, Washington Post,* and every other major newspaper in the country on May 26, 1983.

One reporter, NBC's Chris Wallace, actually asked if I would step out of the picture while he questioned the other three nominees, during a session in the

Roosevelt Room of the White House where we were introduced to the press corps—and the nation. But presidential assistant David Gergen, who stage-managed the event, had carefully put me in between Abram and Bunzel, to avoid any photos or camera shots depicting only the three white male civil rights nominees. Meanwhile, Mary Frances Berry, the commission's most forceful member and former vice chairman, persuaded the existing commissioners to send a letter to the president questioning whether I had "sufficient managerial experience" to become staff director. My blood boiled. I'd spent a lifetime being underestimated by others. But I'd always proven myself, and I would again at the Commission on Civil Rights—in spades.

The reaction to the appointments was swift and predictable. It didn't matter that all of us were Democrats in good standing, that we'd been active in civil rights causes for years—in the case of Abram, going back to his days as a young lawyer in Atlanta, where he'd once got the Reverend Martin Luther King out of jail, who'd been sent there on trumped-up charges. We were all adamantly opposed to racial quotas, and that was enough to make us public enemies in the eyes of many civil rights organizations and the Democrats in Congress. The civil rights debate was no longer between those who opposed racial discrimination and those who favored it, as it had been in the early days of the civil rights movement. Public opinion polls showed that by 1972, 97 percent of Americans believed in nondiscrimination in employment.[3] The debate now was whether blacks and other minorities deserved special treatment to make up for past discrimination, even if it meant discriminating against other groups in the process. Abram, Bunzell, Destro, and I considered ourselves every bit as supportive of civil rights as the civil rights leaders who were opposing our nominations. We disagreed with them about means, not ends, but they treated us like apostates—more treacherous and indeed more dangerous because we could not easily be caricatured as anti–civil rights. It was clear from the near hysteria provoked by our nominations that none of us would be confirmed easily—and the White House braced for a fight. Our opponents couched their attacks carefully, blaming the Reagan administration for what they said was an abysmal record on civil rights and claiming that the president had no authority to fire sitting commissioners. It was a ludicrous claim, but one the Democrats intended to push—and the editorial pages of liberal newspapers around the country picked up the theme. "Not Even Symbolism on Civil Rights," the *New York Times* editors whined; "Another Blunder on Civil Rights," criticized the usually sensible Edwin Yoder in the *Washington Post.*

The hearings were set for early July. In the meantime I had a lot of work to do. Aside from Mary Berry, who was trying to convince everyone I wasn't qualified for the job of staff director, my chief critics were on the Right, not the Left. The people at the National Right to Work Committee were incensed that President Reagan was naming a union official to a top job and were threatening to raise trouble—and a number of conservative senators had voiced concerns, especially Senator Jesse Helms. In the weeks before the hearings, I made the rounds of Senate offices, meeting with skeptical senators and others who might be willing to help. Nancy Kennedy, a tough, brassy White House lobbyist, accompanied me on all my visits, picking me up at the AFT in a White House limousine and ferrying me to the Hill.

"We're going up to Helms's office," Nancy informed me when I got in the car. "We're meeting with Dr. Jim Lucere. He's Helms's top assistant, and it'll take all your charm to win this guy over," she warned. Senator Jesse Helms was the bête noir of American liberalism, and he had some of the best staff on the Hill. Lucere was known primarily for his foreign policy acumen, but Helms trusted him on all issues.

Lucere invited us into a small, stark office in the Russell Building and invited me to sit down in a hard, wooden chair facing him. The sun was streaming into the room, nearly blinding me. I felt like I was being held in an interrogation room, being given the third degree. Lucere wasted no time.

"Tell me, Mrs. Gersten, which Linda Chavez are you, the one who edits this magazine," he said—holding up a copy of the *American Educator* with a cover that read "Values: Education and Morality"—"or are you the editor of this rag?" he said waving a copy of *American Teacher* ominously in front of my face. He had picked his examples well. The magazine not only had nothing in it that he—or Senator Helms—could object to, it came pretty close to what a conservative might write on the subject. But the *American Teacher* was another matter. He happened to pick the May 1982 issue, with a huge caricature of Ronald Reagan on the front cover, with the headline "Headed for Disaster." And the inside of the newspaper was worse. One particularly nasty drawing by Vint Lawrence, illustrating an article on the New Federalism, depicted President and Nancy Reagan looking like Louis XVI and Marie Antoinette, with the caption "When Reagan passes the buck, you'll foot the bill." The contrast could not have been more stark, nor Lucere's meaning more obvious. Was I some kind of poseur, a liberal who feigned conservative positions when it suited me, who used my Spanish maiden name instead of my less politically useful married name? In fact, I had consistently held the same views on matters of race my entire career. I was opposed to any discrimination on the basis of color. I hadn't changed; rather the debate on racial preferences had transformed what was once a liberal position into a conservative one. And as for my name, my decision to use my maiden name had little to do with ethnic pride or feminism. I was emotionally attached to the Chavez name, my father's family name, which had been carried down through ten generations in New Mexico. But since no sons were born in my generation, the Chavez name in our particular branch of the family would die out. I intended to keep the name going for at least one more generation and had given my younger two sons "Chavez" as their middle names as well.

I chose to ignore Lucere's sarcasm.

"The publications have different purposes and different audiences, and I have more leeway with *American Educator* than *American Teacher*. The magazine is a professional journal. It's supposed to be more thoughtful. I have much more discretion about what articles I can publish. Shanker has given me free rein with *American Educator*. But *American Teacher* is the official publication of the union. It represents the union's position—not mine. Sometimes I agree with those positions. Sometimes I don't, but I'm not free to substitute my views for the organization's," I said. I was embarrassed by the cruelty of the *American Teacher* drawings, but there was no question that they were effective propaganda and that they reflected the union's position, which was what I was paid to do.

Lucere seemed unpersuaded. After several more testy questions, he ended the interview. I hadn't succeeded in charming him, but he hadn't managed to intimidate me either.

"The chairman can see us for a few minutes," Nancy Kennedy informed me as we left Lucere's office. "He'll be a lot nicer to you," she promised.

Strom Thurmond, the chairman of the Judiciary Committee, was eighty-one years old in 1983; he'd originally been elected as a Democrat in 1956, run for president on the segregationist States Right Democrat ticket in 1948, and switched to the Republican Party in 1964 to support Republican presidential candidate Barry Goldwater. He was also known to have an eye for the ladies, and many a young Hill staffer had tales to tell of encounters on the elevator when Strom Thurmond was onboard.

"You know I have children about the same age as yours," Thurmond said, leaning over to me, our knees almost touching, after Nancy explained why we were there. His meaning was obvious—he might be old, but he was still virile. In fact, he had remarried late in life, to a former Miss South Carolina, and they did indeed have young children.

"I know, Mr. Chairman," I smiled, catching Nancy's twinkling eyes. She looked like she was about to burst. This was going a little too well. We talked briefly about the role of the Civil Rights Commission, I explained my position on several issues, and then the old rascal did something that almost knocked me off my chair.

"You're not all that dark," he said, putting his hand next to mine for comparison. I could just see the wheels turning—would it be miscegenation if he managed to have his way with me?

"I think your next appointment is here, Mr. Chairman," his assistant intervened before things got too out of hand.

Thurmond leaned back in his chair. "It's been a real delight, Mrs. Chavez," he said, smiling. I'd have no problems with his vote.

"The old codger doesn't miss a trick," I said when we stepped outside into the hall.

Thurmond proved a strong ally to all the nominees, when the hearing was finally scheduled for July 13. Opening the session in a crowded committee room, with every seat taken, and the television lights glaring, Thurmond read from a letter from Martin Luther King Sr., the martyred civil rights leader's father: "'I do not believe that many Southern white people have had a longer experience in support of civil rights than Mr. Abram,'" Thurmond read. The irony could not have been missed by many in the room. Here was a former staunch advocate of racial segregation invoking the venerable name of Martin Luther King Jr. in defense of a Jewish civil rights lawyer appointed by a conservative Republican president.

But the Democrats were having none of it.

"I don't have any argument with you, but I'm going to vote against all of you," Senator Joseph Biden, the ranking Democrat on the committee announced at the outset.[4]

"The Civil Rights Commission must feel free to act on the basis of their moral judgments without fear of being fired for political purposes," the vituperative Senator Howard Metzenbaum announced. Known as one of the most partisan members of Congress, his admonition sounded hollow, especially since the commission itself had often acted in highly partisan fashion. "Regardless of the merits of the new appointees, the issue before us relates directly to the independence of the commission. . . . Nothing they can say or do or have done has any relevance. These appointments carry with them the president's anti–civil rights firings."

It was clear to me that the Democrats were not going to confirm us, no matter what. In addition to the denunciations by Senate Democrats, a group of 157 House members—all but one of them Democrats—also signed a letter opposing our appointments, ostensibly because they believed the president had no right to appoint new commissioners.

Their claim was outrageous on its face. Article II, Section 2 of the U.S. Constitution says that the president "shall nominate and by and with the Advice and Consent of the Senate, shall appoint Ambassadors, other public Ministers and Consuls, Judges of the supreme Court, and all other Officers of the United States, whose Appointments are not herein provided for, and which shall be established by Law; but the Congress may by Law vest the Appointment of such inferior Officers, as they think proper, in the President alone, in the Courts of Law, or in the Heads of Departments." The law that created the Commission on Civil Rights in 1957 provided that the president would name six commissioners, no more than three from a single political party, and a full-time staff director, all of whom were subject to Senate confirmation. But the Congress did not set terms of office for the commissioners, as it sometimes did for independent agencies that had quasi-judicial or legislative functions, such as the Federal Communications Commission or the Federal Trade Commission. The civil rights commissioners served—as all political appointees do—"at the pleasure of the president," which meant that he could remove them for any reason he chose. To suggest otherwise was a constitutional travesty, regardless of what the Democrats said.

Besides Senator Thurmond, only Senator Hatch stood up for us, taking over the chairman's seat when he tired after the first hour, with the other Republicans acting sheepish about the entire proceeding. When Thurmond agreed the next week to delay the vote on our nominations in committee as a courtesy to the Democrats, I knew our fate had been sealed. The White House continued to reassure us, but I had little confidence in their ability to get any of us confirmed. Ironically, I would easily have made it through, if I had been willing to be considered separately, despite Mary Berry's effort to question my qualifications. Al Shanker testified on my behalf, dispelling any misgivings about my managerial capabilities, noting that he had recently promoted me to oversee the work of the entire Washington-based professional staff of the union. But I had cast my lot with the other nominees, and for the time being, I was willing to be patient. Meanwhile, I began to marshal the forces to defend our nominations, enlisting opinion writers, rounding up organizations to lobby the Senate, and making sure the White House staff did not leave us twisting in the wind. In an unfortunate confluence of events, however, the legislation authorizing the commission was about to expire.

Originally created as a temporary agency, the commission had been reauthorized several times and was due for another extension in September. The Senate's delay in scheduling a confirmation vote on our appointments, coupled with the expiring legislation, made our prospects look even dimmer.

When Congress went out for its August recess, Dennis Patrick called me to tell me that the president had agreed to give me a recess appointment. The Constitution provided that "the President shall have Power to fill up all Vacancies that may happen during the Recess of the Senate, by granting Commissions which shall expire at the End of their next Session." By precedent, presidents used recess appointments sparingly and then usually only after the Senate had failed to act on a noncontroversial appointee who had been nominated formally. The Senate hated recess appointments and often punished those who received them (and the president who appointed the officials) by refusing to extend the appointment after it expired.

"How about Jack and Morris—and Bob?" I asked of the other nominees, almost forgetting Bob Destro the youngest of the three nominees and the one I knew least well.

"No deal. We'd take too much flap and it would be a pyrrhic victory. They'd never make it through when we resubmitted their names," Patrick said.

"It doesn't look like they're going to make it through anyway," I added.

"You always said the staff director had the real power in the agency; now let's see what you and Penny can do," Patrick teased. "The president will sign the papers tomorrow."

I couldn't believe it. After almost three months of guerrilla warfare against the Democrats, I was about to achieve victory, at least for myself. The White House announced my recess appointment on August 16, which merited no more than a three-paragraph mention in the B section of the *New York Times*. Ken Cribb, Ed Meese's assistant at the White House, offered to round up someone at the White House to swear me into my new post, so that I could assume my new duties at the Civil Rights Commission. But I got a better offer. Mark Cannon, Supreme Court Chief Justice Warren Burger's assistant, whom I'd worked with at *American Educator*, called me around noon.

"Congratulations, Linda. I read that the president gave you a recess appointment. You must be very relieved," he said.

"I feel terrible about my colleagues, but I think I might be able to help more from inside," I said.

"Do you have any plans for being sworn in?" he asked.

"Ken Cribb has offered to round up someone this afternoon. It'll be a really informal affair," I said guiltily, knowing I wouldn't be able to invite people like Mark who had helped me over the years and given moral support over the last several months.

"I think I might be able to do a little better than that. The Chief Justice has some time open on his schedule this afternoon. What do you say, four o'clock?"

I couldn't believe it. Short of being elected president some day, I was not likely ever again to have a Chief Justice of the United States swear me into office.

Burger's wood-paneled study in the Supreme Court building was warm and comfortable, with large, leather-bound volumes of law books lining the wall. Chris stood at my side as I stood with my hand on the Bible, while the Chief Justice, wearing his official robes with tan suede Hush Puppies peeking out beneath, administered the oath. We took a few pictures, shook hands, and the ceremony—one of the most thrilling events in my life, presided over by a man whom I admired deeply for reining in some of the activist excesses of the Court—was over in minutes.

It was late in the day, but I decided to drop by my new offices on 14th and Vermont at Logan Circle afterward. The building, a nondescript, wedge-shaped modern structure housed several small government and nongovernment offices. I took the elevator to the eighth floor and walked into the corner suite, where the staff director's office was located.

The young woman sitting at the reception desk looked startled when I entered the office.

"I'm Linda Chavez, the new staff director," I said.

"Just a moment, I'll get Mr. Buggs," she said, and walked into the acting staff director's outer office. John Buggs, a career official, had been acting staff director since President Reagan assumed office in January 1981 and failed to name a political appointee to replace him. A middle-aged, soft-spoken man, Buggs was surprised to see me, but courteous.

"We didn't expect you until later this week," he apologized. "I'm just cleaning out my office, I mean, *your* office," he stuttered.

"No hurry. You can find me a temporary place to sit and take your time. I won't move my things in until later in the week," I said. It was awkward all around. The staff of the Civil Rights Commission were not happy that I'd been appointed. They wouldn't have been happy with any Reagan appointee. Clarence Pendleton, whom I'd gotten to know since being nominated, warned me that the place was a viper's den. Although Penny was the chairman, Mary Berry ran the show. She maintained a permanent office at the commission, with a full-time assistant, even though Penny had no such luxuries. Penny still lived in San Diego, where he operated his own business, and came into Washington once a month for commission meetings. His assistant, Sydney Novell, worked part-time for him on commission business and part-time for his company. When they came into town, Penny and Sydney sat in a small conference room next to the staff director's office, where they were provided with nothing more than the use of a telephone.

I had no intention of letting the career staff bully me, and I set out early on to establish my authority. I soon found out that many of the staff considered it a game of sorts: They would never outright lie to me, but I had to make sure that I always asked precisely the right question and that I listened carefully to the answer I was given. When I inquired whether the agency maintained a car that could transport me or the chairman to the Hill or elsewhere for meetings, the head of the office of administration, Bert Silver, replied casually, "There's no car available for the staff director's or commissioners' use." I should have listened to his answer more carefully. He didn't say the commission didn't have a car, just not one "available" for my use or for the commissioners. I quickly put the conversation out of my mind and continued to take taxis, drive my beat-up Volvo, or walk—if the distance was short—even though an agency car would have saved time and been more convenient. Then one day, when I was stuck in traffic about a block from my office, I looked up and noticed a placard in the back window of the car in front of me.

"Official Use," the sign read, "U.S. Commission on Civil Rights." The car—a shiny, black Lincoln Town Car—pulled away as soon as the light turned, but I followed it into the garage in the commission's building and noted that the driver, someone I thought I recognized, parked it in a space marked "USCCR."

"You won't believe what I just saw," I told my assistant Nancy Watson, one of the few political appointees I'd been able to hire. "Remember when I asked if the commission had a car?"

"Yeah, Bert told you they didn't."

"That's what he said, but I just saw a car marked 'U.S. Commission on Civil Rights' drive into the garage downstairs," I said.

"Well that explains why his office has a gasoline credit card, which we are expected to pay, and Bert said they used it on rental cars when staff traveled," Nancy said, as I stood shaking my head.

"That's very interesting. How about you copy the bills and call Mr. Silver upstairs for a chat with me?" I said.

He must have known something was up when he came in. Perhaps the driver alerted him that I had seen the car.

"I guess you're wondering about the Town Car. It's not ours," he said.

"So the commission doesn't own a car?" I asked.

"We don't own that car. We're just using it temporarily," he replied.

"Let me get this straight. The commission doesn't own the car I just followed into the garage? The one with a sign in the rear window that says for official use of the U.S. Commission on Civil Rights? Does the commission own *any* car?" I asked, trying to cover more possibilities.

"Oh yes, the commission owns a little Ford Escort," he said, as if this was something he'd simply forgotten to mention earlier. "But it wouldn't be suitable to transport you or the chairman around town. It's just a little station wagon we use to take materials to and from the warehouse, that sort of thing. But if you want a car, we can certainly buy one. We could probably buy one just like the Town Car you saw," he added.

"Yes, I think that would look very good on the Federal Page of the *Washington Post*: 'New Civil Rights Commission Staff Director Demands Limo.' Thanks, but a Ford Escort will do just fine."

"We don't have a regular driver. We'll have to hire one," he said.

"Who drives it now?" I asked.

"Whoever needs to deliver something."

"I'll look into it," I said, dismissing him.

Nancy suggested that we hire a young man she had worked with at the President's Commission on Industrial Competitiveness, who would serve as both a messenger and a driver and do whatever other odd jobs needed doing around the agency. I gave the go-ahead and began using the agency's car whenever I had official business, being scrupulous about never using it for personal appointments or for transportation to or from home, which is prohibited except for cabinet secretaries and a handful of other high-ranking officials.[5]

The power struggles in the agency were not just about petty matters, however. Of the six commissioners, only the chairman had been appointed by President Reagan, and the others, including the Republicans, were either hostile to the new administration or too timid to resist Mary Berry's efforts to embarrass and attack the administration at every turn. And the commission had strayed far beyond its legislatively defined mission to study discrimination on the basis of race, color, religion, sex, age, handicap, or national origin and submit reports, findings, and recommendations to the president and Congress.[6] At the time the commission was created, there were few institutions in the government or private sector that focused exclusively on civil rights issues, and the commission served a valuable role in studying race and ethnicity and issuing scholarly reports. But those days were long past, and in their place the commission had begun to produce shoddy, biased studies by third-rate researchers, most of them on the commission's own staff. I hoped to change this by enlisting preeminent authorities to contribute their expertise and to oversee the work of the commission staff—but I would have to wait until the president was able to replace some of the existing commissioners. In the meantime, I could still make waves when necessary.

Barely a month after I became staff director, I decided to challenge the commissioners directly over their backing of race-based quotas. The

Supreme Court was scheduled to hear a case involving a racial quota system in the Memphis, Tennessee, Fire Department. The case involved a 1980 court-ordered consent decree in which the fire department agreed to hire a certain number of black firefighters in order to settle a discrimination suit against the department. The problem developed when the department later had to lay off some of its employees in response to budget cutbacks and had done so under the terms of its union contract seniority system, which required the last persons hired to be the first laid off—in this case mostly black employees. The black firefighters sued, and the case was now before the Supreme Court on appeal. The Civil Rights Division of the Reagan Justice Department—headed by William Bradford Reynolds, an implacable foe of quotas—filed its own brief in the case opposing the quota system and defending the union's seniority system, which infuriated Mary Berry. The commission's acting general counsel prepared a seventeen-page legal analysis critical of the Justice Department position, and the commission was scheduled to issue its own report defending racial quotas. On the eve of the commission meeting, I sent out my own memorandum urging the commission not to defend racial quotas.

Within hours of my sending out the memo to the commissioners, reporters were on the phone asking me questions. Someone—probably Mary Berry—had leaked my memo, which made headlines the following day. "New U.S. Rights Aide Backs Whites for Jobs in Memphis," the *New York Times* reported hysterically.[7] In fact, all I'd done was reiterate what the 1964 Civil Rights Act had to say about seniority systems and urge the commissioners not to attack the Justice Department for following the law. The Justice Department's position, I wrote, "appears to be a rather straightforward interpretation of Title VII" of the Civil Rights Act. "The issue as I see it," I wrote, "is whether or not the Civil Rights Commission . . . wishes to ignore the provision of the Civil Rights Act protecting bona fide seniority systems and endorse instead an employment practice that allows individuals to be laid off or demoted based on the color of their skins."[8]

I felt passionately about this issue. The whole civil rights struggle had been to take race out of the equation when it came to deciding who would be hired or fired, but in recent years that principle had been turned on its head. Civil rights proponents had deserted the high moral ground. They were no longer insisting that blacks be treated the same as everyone else, required to follow the same rules, be subject to the same standards, which had been the goal of the civil rights movement for decades. Now, civil rights groups routinely argued that blacks—and increasingly Hispanics, too—be given special preferences to increase their numbers in colleges or certain professions. Racial balance became the goal, even if it meant picking a less-qualified black or Hispanic over a better-qualified white or Asian—or, as in the Memphis firefighter case, laying off whites first, regardless of seniority.

But making headlines was not the same thing as making policy, and the commission rebuffed my recommendation, with only the chairman, Clarence Pendleton, voting for it. "This whole incident shows that we have good reason to be concerned about the independence of the commission being eroded," Mary Berry huffed.[9] But it was precisely the commission's independence—from Berry's domination—that I was fighting for, and would soon win. The Supreme Court ultimately vindicated my position—and the Reagan Justice Department's—by a 6–3 decision. Writing for the majority, Justice Byron White said, "Title VII protects bona fide seniority systems, and it is inappropriate to deny an innocent employee the benefits of his seniority in order to provide a remedy in a pattern or practice suit such as this."[10]

With September drawing to a close, the commission's authorization was about to expire, and Congress had yet to pass legislation to reauthorize the agency. If Congress failed to act, the Civil Rights Commission would close its doors for good on November 29. Several proposals were floating about to prevent the commission's demise, but their main purpose was not just to keep the agency in business but to ensure that President Reagan would not be able to appoint new commissioners. Some of the bills offered lifetime appointments to commissioners, a move that provoked even the liberal *Washington Post* to protest: "The House of Representatives may not have realized, as it was hurrying toward adjournment, what an extraordinary thing it was doing when it in effect voted lifetime tenure for members of the Civil Rights Commission. The Constitution gives lifetime tenure to federal judges 'during good behavior,' but no presidential appointee has ever had a lifetime job. . . . Lifetime tenure makes sense if what you want is continued cheerleading for the points of view of certain organizations and reassurance that they need not change any of their views and priorities. But if you think there's a need for an organization within government that examines carefully and critically racial and other impermissible discrimination in a changing America, then it's better to have some turnover from time to time in the Civil Rights Commission," the *Post* editors wrote.[11]

But even the Republican-controlled Senate seemed to have no stomach for a fight on civil rights issues, and I was beginning to despair that I would ever gain any allies on the commission. Furthermore, several of the proposed bills would deprive me of my position as staff director by making the staff director appointment one that would require the approval of a majority of the commissioners, which I could never win from the existing members. I spent hours each week on the telephone with Abrams, Bunzell, and Destro, and they, too, were pessimistic about the future. I was also in constant communication with the White House, not—as my critics charged—getting my marching orders but rather urging Ken Cribb on Ed Meese's staff to make sure the White House stood firm on the commission appointments. My greatest fear was that some of the more pragmatic members of the president's staff—mainly in chief of staff James Baker's office—would talk the president into accepting a compromise that would abandon Abrams, Bunzell, and Destro. Cribb became my chief ally.

"Meese has persuaded the president to fire Mary Berry and company," Cribb informed me one morning in late October. "The lawyers in the counsel's office tell us that we have to hand deliver letters informing them of their removal and that the chief administrative officer of the agency—in other words, you—can receive them on their behalf. It'll happen sometime after five o'clock. You just wait in your office until I call you," he said.

In the meantime I had a session at the Old Executive Office Building scheduled from 1:00 to 4:00 P.M. The Harvard Business School was running executive training sessions for presidential appointees, and I was looking forward to the seminar, which was being conducted in the Situation Room of the OEOB. I had never been in the super-secret Situation Room, which was one of two White House offices where important overseas or military "situations" were managed and directed, the other smaller Situation Room being in the basement of the West Wing. Equipped with sophisticated monitoring and satellite communications capability, as well as secure telephones, the larger OEOB Situation Room was guarded by a Marine but looked much like any other conference room in the building, except for several clocks on the walls, each showing the time in a different city with the name printed underneath. As I sat around the huge conference table, I noted the clocks, one with Washington time, another with Greenwich mean time, another with Beirut time—which made sense because a military barracks housing U.S. Marines had been bombed only two days before, killing more than 200 servicemen. But the fourth clock had the name St. Georges printed beneath. I wondered where St. Georges was and why it was up there, but I didn't think any more about it until the next day. After the seminar I returned to my office to await Cribb's call.

My office was cold and spooky as I waited for the phone to ring. The building heat went off at five-thirty, and I put on my coat and gloves to keep warm. Cribb called around seven to make sure I was still there.

"You hanging in there?" he asked quietly. I could hear voices in the background. "We're in with the president. It won't be long now." Finally, I got the call telling me that the letters were on the way. I went downstairs to retrieve them from the messenger and went home. The next morning I discovered where St. Georges was. In the predawn hours of October 26, an American force of almost two thousand Marines and Army Rangers invaded the small Caribbean island of Grenada, whose capital was St. Georges. President Reagan ordered the attack to rescue some eight hundred American medical students on the island, who he feared would become hostages in an increasingly anarchic environment on the island, following two communist coups. "Grenada, we were told, was a friendly island paradise for tourism. Well, it wasn't," Reagan informed the nation the evening of the invasion. "It was a Soviet-Cuban colony being readied as a major military bastion to export terror and undermine democracy," he said in a televised speech.[12]

"So, you guys kicked the commies out of Grenada and the Civil Rights Commission, all on the same night," I joked with Cribb the next morning. Although I didn't believe Mary Berry was actually a member of the Communist Party, she was certainly more than a garden-variety liberal. Her pro-Soviet and pro-Maoist views were well known in Washington and to me personally. My first run-in with her occurred in 1977 when I was still editor of the *American Educator* and she was an assistant secretary of education in the Carter administration. I interviewed her about the comments she'd recently made praising the Maoist Chinese education system. After Al Shanker had publicly criticized her remarks, I decided to interview her for the magazine to give AFT members a firsthand look at her views. She not only reiterated her praise for the Chinese education system for using students as laborers as a form of "productive work while they are learning other things," she also used the occasion to defend racial quotas in higher education. "[I]t was refreshing to see them sit down and say unabashedly, 'Well, we're instituting quotas because there are economic reasons.' . . . To sit in a discussion where people were talking about quotas without getting involved in whether we should have quotas or goals or whatever, but rather 'yes, we have quotas and this is why we have them'—I found that refreshing."[13] Nor were her sympathies only for the Chinese communists. In a book she coauthored in 1982, Berry explained why blacks "remained cool to the Communists": "Subjected to a massive barrage of propaganda from the American news media, few of them knew about Russia's constitutional safeguards for minorities, the extent of the equality of opportunity, or the equal provision of social services to its citizens."[14] Cribb may not have known Berry's full history as I did, but he loved the joke and repeated it at every opportunity afterward.

"Hey, by the way, you should let the folks at the National Security Council know that somebody left St. Georges up on the wall clocks when the Harvard guys were conducting their seminar in the Situation Room yesterday. Thank goodness none of us knew where St. Georges was or we might have blown the whole sneak attack," I chided him.

The timing of Berry's firing, along with the two other Democrats on the commission, Rabbi Murray Saltzman and Blandina Cardenas Ramirez, was perfect. With the Grenada invasion taking up the entire front page, the commission firings story got bumped inside most newspapers and was barely mentioned on the evening news—unlike the blast of publicity surrounding the nominations of Abram, Bunzell, and Destro months earlier. Rabbi Saltzman took his dismissal with characteristic grace, but Berry and Ramirez refused to go quietly. So I ordered the locks on Berry's door changed, which drew howls of protest. "They cleaned out Mary Berry's office last Friday; packed her things in crates and hauled them away. It was an ignominious end to her tenure as a member of the U.S. Commission on Civil Rights, and it might have marked, just as ignominiously, an end to the commission itself," wrote *Washington Post* columnist William Raspberry.[15]

Berry, however, was in court within forty-eight hours seeking a temporary restraining order, alleging that the president did not have the authority to remove a sitting commissioner, despite the fact that the document appointing her said clearly that she served "during the pleasure of the president for the time being." A liberal judge, appointed by Democratic President Jimmy Carter, issued a temporary injunction barring Berry's removal, and within hours she was in my office with her attorney, Elaine Jones. All sweetness and light, I handed over new keys and welcomed Berry back onboard, offering to sweep out her office myself if it wasn't properly cleaned. Berry took to referring to me as a "honey-tongued viper" to others, but we managed to remain civil to each other face-to-face on most occasions.

With the clock ticking on the commission's legal authority, the Senate was trying to fashion a compromise, which would give President Reagan the right to appoint at least two new commissioners—with Abram and Bunzell being the favored candidates—and would allow Berry, Ramirez, and the others to keep their existing jobs in an expanded eight-member commission. Ralph Neas, executive director of the Leadership Conference on Civil Rights, was brokering the deal on behalf of civil rights groups, with Senate Majority Leader Howard Baker and Senator Bob Dole representing the Republicans. "The U.S. Civil Rights Commission apparently was reconstituted, saving it from oblivion, just before midnight last night," the *Washington Post* reported on November 11.[16] However, the compromise would make my appointment and the chairman's subject to approval by the newly reconstituted commission, and I didn't have the votes, nor did Clarence Pendleton. I was furious and called Cribb immediately.

"Don't worry. We're taking care of it," Cribb promised. "We have no intention of reappointing Mary Louise Smith or Jill Ruckleshaus, unless they agree to vote for you and Penny, which I doubt they will. You have Ed Meese's word on it," he said.

Over the next two and a half weeks, I waited patiently. On November 29, the day the commission was due to go out of business, I informed the White House that I would have to shut down the agency unless the president signed the new legislation. But the Justice Department was unhappy with the new structure—a hybrid that gave the president authority to appoint some members and Congress the authority to appoint others and restricted the president's right to remove sitting commissioners.

"The Office of Legal Counsel at DOJ thinks the bill is unconstitutional," Cribb informed me. "But the president will sign it anyway, with a strong statement of reservation." Nonetheless, I packed up my things at the end of the day and turned in my keys. The next day, Clarence Pendleton and I went to the White House to meet with President Reagan and to witness his official signing of the new legislation, at the same time he signed the papers reappointing me and Penny. I had met the president on two other occasions, very briefly, but this was my first time in the Oval Office. The president welcomed us into the room, inviting Penny to sit opposite him in one of the two Queen Anne chairs in front of the fireplace, where a cheery fire burned brightly. I sat on one of the two facing couches, and we chatted briefly about civil rights issues and how civil rights groups had come to define support for racial quotas as synonymous with being pro–civil rights. Penny recounted his favorite Civil Rights Act anecdote.

"You know, Mr. President, Hubert Humphrey promised he would eat the pages of the bill if the Civil Rights Act was ever used to require racial quotas," Penny told the president.

"Well, he'd have a pretty bad case of indigestion if he were around today," President Reagan shot back.[17] Reagan's wit was legendary, but somehow I never imagined he could be so quick.

When it was time for us to leave, the president's aide, Fred Ryan, whispered into his ear, and Reagan stood up to shake our hands and present us with the pens he'd used to sign the new legislation reauthorizing the U.S. Commission on Civil Rights, a memento that I framed with a copy of the bill and the photos taken in the Oval Office and that still hangs in my office today as one of my most treasured possessions. Though I was to meet with President Reagan dozens of times in the Oval Office and elsewhere over the next few years, that first visit remains my favorite.

Two days later, the commission was back in the headlines. "Aides Doubt Reagan Is Planning to Rename Rights Panel Member," Robert Pear reported in the *New York Times*, noting that the president was not likely to reappoint Mary Louise Smith and complaining that I was back on the job. "Linda Chavez, a Reagan appointee, started work today as acting staff director of the new agency without waiting for the approval of the commission members," Pear wrote.[18] "Democrat members of the old commission asserted that Miss Chavez had tried to soften criticism of the Reagan Administration and compromised the commission's independence by working closely with the White House," he said. They were right about my working closely with the White House, which was nothing new for the Commission on Civil Rights. During the presidency of John F. Kennedy, the commission staff director, Berl Bernhard, was actually assigned to a White House office and met regularly with staff from the Democratic National Committee.[19] My purpose was never "to soften criticism of the Reagan administration," however, but to restore some sense of balance and fairness to the commission's work. My old boss Don Edwards apparently didn't see it that way, however. The *New York Times* article said that Edwards, chairman of the House Judiciary subcommittee with oversight of the commission, had intended that Bert Silver, the man who'd been so duplicitous about the agency car, act as staff director "until the new commissioners could concur in the appointment of someone else." I was ruining all their plans—and it was about to get much worse.

Over the next few weeks, President Reagan named three additional persons to join Clarence Pendleton as his four appointees to the Civil Rights Commission under the new law, which provided for an eight-member commission: Morris Abram and John Bunzell, who were among the original nominees, and Esther Gonzalez-Arroyo Buckley, a high school science teacher from Laredo, Texas. Robert Destro, who had originally been nominated by President Reagan, was appointed by the Speaker of the House, on the recommendation of the House Minority Leader Robert Michel. The House Speaker, Democrat Thomas "Tip" O'Neill, also appointed Mary Frances Berry. The Senate Majority Leader, Howard Baker, appointed Francis S. Guess, the secretary of labor from his home state of Tennessee, and Bambi Ramirez, who was the choice of the Senate Democrats. Berry and Ramirez were back on the commission, even though the Court of Appeals had dismissed their lawsuit. "This is the time for re-evaluation of the policies of the old commission," I told the *New York Times*. "Busing and quotas will be on the agenda for re-examination," I said, noting that there was "a majority of five for the President's position" against busing as a remedy for school segregation and against quotas.[20] And I quickly set to work to put together an agenda for the first meeting of the newly reconstituted commission. Finally, I had the opportunity to be more than a gadfly in an agency I didn't really control. With my new allies on the commission—as it turned out six, not five, all but the two holdovers—I was about to steer the commission toward a drastically different course.

Our first meeting was scheduled for January 16, 1984. I had decided that we should have a retreat, held away from Washington, where we might be able to do our work without the glare of the national press. In advance of the meeting, I met with my staff, including Max Green, former national secretary of the Young People's Socialist League, whom I'd hired from the United Federation of Teachers in New York, and Mark Disler, my new general counsel, whom I had recruited from the Justice Department where he had served as one of Brad Reynolds's special assistants in the civil rights division. We discussed several options for new studies, including one on the effect of affirmative action programs on the quality of higher education.

That evening, I sat down at my dining room table and drafted a short memorandum to the commissioners, outlining proposed changes in commission policy, including which studies in progress should be dropped and which new studies initiated. I had my assistant, Nancy Watson, type the memo for distribution in advance of the meeting and then decided to make a phone call, to Robert Pear of the *New York Times*. Pear had impressed me as the fairest of the reporters who covered the Civil Rights Commission. He generally got his facts straight and usually included both sides' views when he wrote on a controversial issue. I told him that I was sending the commissioners a memorandum that would outline proposed changes and offered to give him an exclusive, advance copy—the proverbial Washington leak.

We met at a deli across the street from the agency where I handed him the document in a plain, brown wrapper. It is how the game is played in Washington. If you want halfway decent press, you curry favor with reporters by leaking them information in advance. I felt a little guilty about doing it, since I was giving Pear the memorandum before the commissioners had a chance to read it. But I knew that if I waited, someone else—Mary Berry, for example—would leak it first, with her spin. And the reporter, no matter how much he might wish to remain objective, would generally be kind to his leaker, so as not to cut off the source of future valuable information in the cutthroat competition to be first with an important story.

The next morning, a Friday, there it was: Page one, *New York Times*, "New Director of U.S. Rights Panel Calls for Major Change of Course."[21] Pear accurately described my proposals, with a minimum of editorializing.

> Miss Chavez . . . recommended cancellation of three projects, including a study of how cutbacks in student financial aid affected colleges at which most of the students were black or Hispanic. . . . Miss Chavez also recommended "a major study of affirmative action" in college hiring and admissions. "A general decline in academic standards coincided with the advent of affirmative action in higher education," she said, but she added that there had been no "empirical assessment" of whether these two developments were related. . . . At the elementary and secondary school level, Miss Chavez said, the commission should give special attention to the role of bilingual programs in increasing the segregation and "isolation" of Hispanic students. The old commission supported busing as a means of school desegregation. Miss Chavez said the agency could reassess this policy in a study of voluntary methods. . . . She also urged the commission to investigate the legal theory that employers should set equal pay for jobs of comparable value, as measured by such criteria as skills and responsibility.

By the time I reached my office, the phone was ringing off the hook, with more reporters calling for interviews and demanding copies of the memo. I agreed to give copies to Juan Williams of the *Washington Post* and met briefly with him at the same deli where I'd met with Pear.

I liked Williams, a talented young black reporter clearly on his way up at the *Post*, but I had mixed feelings about his story, which appeared the next day. On the one hand, his article covered more subtle points than Pear's. "Chavez said she is concerned not only that affirmative action may have damaged academic standards but that minority students unprepared to do college-level work are later forced from school without obtaining degrees,"[22] he wrote after our on-the-record interview. He also got the point of my recommendation that the commission drop its study of the effect of Reagan budget cuts on predominantly black colleges. I had no quarrel with the idea that this might be a legitimate inquiry into public policy. The only question was whether the U.S. Commission on Civil Rights had any jurisdiction to study the issue. "The jurisdiction of the Commission," Williams quoted from my memorandum, "is to study discrimination on the basis of race, color, national origin, religion, sex, age, and handicap. Unless the Commission wishes to establish that federal student financial aid is a civil right guaranteed to members of minority groups, this project would appear clearly beyond our jurisdiction." For years, the commission had wandered far from its legal mandate to study racial, ethnic, sex, and other forms of discrimination covered by federal statutes. It was my intent to bring the commission back to its original purpose—the only one it was authorized by Congress to undertake.

But then Williams made a serious error of fact in his story, one that caused me considerable problems at the time and for years afterward. "She also asked the Commission to begin a study of whether equal pay should be given for equal work," he wrote. He then quoted directly from my memo: "'The principle that underlies comparable worth is a fundamentally radical one that would alter our existing marketplace economy,' she wrote." Williams had made it seem as if I were against equal pay for equal work—that men and women doing the same job should be paid the same wages—a principle that has been enshrined in law since 1963, a year before race discrimination was outlawed. Comparable worth, however, was just what I said it was—a radical idea that would transform our economy.

The idea behind comparable worth was that wages should be set according to abstract notions of intrinsic value, based on the level of education required in a given job, the responsibility it entailed, and to a less extent, the working conditions involved. Under the theory, all jobs in a given company or government agency would be evaluated by a set of criteria that embodied these factors and would be assigned points; jobs receiving comparable points would be assigned equal pay. If, for example, an employer, such as a municipal government, hired both electricians, who were most often men, and librarians, who were most often women, the employer would have to rate these jobs according to their "worth" as measured by education, effort, responsibility, and working conditions. If librarians scored higher, which they would under a system that valued education above all other factors, then their pay would go up, and theoretically anyway, the electricians' pay would go down.

The problem with the theory, of course, is that in a free market economy, wages—like prices—are set primarily by the forces of supply and demand. Diamonds are more valuable than water because diamonds are rare and water is plentiful, relative to the demand. Similarly, professional basketball players earn more than teachers, because the skills of the former are in relatively short supply and the demand for their services high, while there are millions of people trained as teachers. Even though water is necessary to survival and teachers are more important to society than basketball players, the price of a commodity or service doesn't depend on moral or inherent values. No matter how many years a person has invested in education, if there is little demand for the particular skills that person has acquired—or a great many people have the same skills and are looking for work—the pay in that profession will be low, or at least lower than some might think fair. If, however, someone has skills that are much in demand—or there are few people willing to do a particular job because it's risky or dangerous or unpleasant—the pay in that profession will be higher. This is why electricians often earn more than librarians, and tree trimmers earn more than day care workers.

Feminists have assumed these disparities are the result of sex discrimination and have wanted to force employers to pay according to what they believe a job is worth based on arbitrary criteria weighted to favor the characteristics women are more likely to possess. Their theories would require a complete restructuring of the way that wages—and ultimately prices—are set, relying on government to enforce the standards. In the end, the system would become even more arbitrary and unfair than the free market. I believed that the concept was a particularly dangerous one—and argued that "comparable worth" would become the most important civil rights issue of the eighties.

On Monday morning, two days after Williams's *Post* article ran, James Baker III, President Reagan's White House chief of staff, was on the phone with me.

"What's this I read that you are opposed to equal pay for equal work?" Baker said.

"You read it all right, but it's not true, sir," I said to a man I knew only by reputation, although I had dealt with members of his staff periodically. "The reporter covering the story didn't understand the difference between the 1963 Equal Pay Act, which of course I support, and comparable worth, which as you know is a very different concept and one that I oppose. I believe the president does as well. I've asked for a *Post* retraction, which I've been assured will be issued," I said.

Baker was not as enthusiastic about my stewardship of the commission as Meese and some others in the White House were. Known as a pragmatist, not an ideologue, Baker was concerned about the president's standing with women, the so-called gender gap, and I had just made matters worse in his eyes. With the president facing re-election later in the year, Baker did not want some loose cannon in the administration that could cost female votes. In all my dealings with the White House over the previous month, contrary to Mary Berry's assumptions, this was the first time that I'd ever felt pressure on any issue—and I wasn't about to back down. Baker's call gave me the opportunity to show my independence from the White House. Whether the White House—or more accurately, the moderates on the president's staff—liked it or not, I intended to make comparable worth a major focus of the commission's new agenda. As it happened, my proposal to take on the comparable worth issue became not only one of the most controversial decisions I made but one of my proudest achievements.

When the commission met a week later, all my recommendations passed easily, by six-to-two votes, with only Mary Berry and Bambi Ramirez opposing the change in agenda. The media went into a frenzy. The commission meeting was the lead item on the network news and once again on the front page of the major newspapers. "The Civil Rights Commission As Parrot," the *New York Times'* editorial harrumphed: "For a generation, the United States Commission on Civil Rights has served as something like a rooster, trying to waken the nation to racial discrimination and the need to extend equal protection to all citizens. . . . The new Commission sounded a lot like a parrot of the Reagan Administration's views when it began with a 6-to–2 majority's statement criticizing racial quotas in employment as 'another form of unjustified discrimination.'"[23] However, public opinion supported our point of view—by wide margins. Most Americans, including a plurality of blacks, disliked quotas and opposed the idea that minorities should be held to different—lower—standards than whites. The *Washington Post* reflected this more measured approach:

> At the heart of the argument on and over the Commission lies a large, politically unresolved question. It is whether civil rights activity on the part of the government should be viewed quite strictly as a matter of providing and guaranteeing equal opportunity to all citizens or of providing and guaranteeing them not just equal opportunity but in fact equal results—that is, a definite share of society's monetary and other rewards.[24]

The *Post* gave us credit for bringing new clarity to the debate. "Thus, the new staff director of the Commission, Linda Chavez, and the new majority variously speak of such things as the need to stop viewing economic programs as civil rights imperatives, the anti–civil rights implications of numerical quotas, the fact that all disadvantage is not a function of discrimination," the *Post* editors said. "Intellectually—in theory—much of what they say is right," but they weren't sure we would go about our jobs seriously. "The Commission itself will have to choose whether its accomplishments are to be political and transitory or moral and enduring."

I intended to prove that the new commission could produce first-rate studies that would bring new vigor to the debate on race and civil rights, but that required a major overhaul of the institution itself. I brought in new staff, including a new director of research, June O'Neill, a talented economist from the liberal Urban Institute, who would go on to become director of the Congressional Budget Office in the 1990s. I put together advisory panels of outside experts to oversee all the commission's studies, including some of the leading academics in the country at the time: Columbia University economist Jacob Mincer, University of Chicago sociologist William Julius Wilson, Harvard University economist Glenn Loury, University of Pennsylvania economist Claudia Goldin, Harvard historian Stephan Thernstrom, Northwestern University sociologist Christopher Jencks, and others, many of whom did not agree with me on issues such as racial quotas. It had been many years since the Civil Rights Commission had recruited such a distinguished group of advisors.

We were engaged in more studies of higher quality than our predecessors had even dreamed of, and we were conducting our work with more balance than the commission was accustomed to, making sure that opponents of the commission's majority view were well represented in commission hearings and public forums. When it came time to schedule hearings on the comparable worth issue,[25] I made sure that the witness list included the most prominent advocates in favor of comparable worth, as well as those who were critics. Only one prominent advocate turned us down—because we were unable to pay her $10,000 for her testimony, a fee far above the standard government rate. Of the sixteen witnesses, half favored comparable worth, and half were opposed; the witness list was absolutely fair and balanced. The effort began to show some dividends. The *Washington Post*'s Bill Raspberry took the occasion to compliment me: "Linda Chavez Is Right," he titled his column on comparable worth.[26] "Any woman who's out in the working world has encountered sex discrimination at some point," Raspberry quoted me saying. "The question is how to remedy it. My view is that you remedy it not by trying to force employers to pay higher wages for so-called women's work but by better enforcement of the laws that are already on the books: making sure that employers don't pay women less for doing the same jobs as men, and by making sure that women have access to whatever jobs they are qualified for, regardless of their gender." Raspberry agreed: "That strikes me as reasonable," he wrote. I was finally gaining some respect.

But it couldn't last—not in Washington's highly partisan environment. Our critics in the civil rights organizations—and more importantly, among the Democrats in Congress—only became more strident in their attacks on everything we did. And the commission chairman occasionally gave them help, if inadvertently. Penny was a lightning rod. He was often provocative for its own sake. A warm, generous man with a deep hearty laugh, he loved the limelight and knew exactly how to get it, even if it meant undermining the commission's legitimacy. On the day we were to release the papers that had been presented at our comparable worth hearing, he came into my office, beaming.

"I know what I'm going to say at the press conference," he said, an impish grin on his face, which signaled trouble. "I'm going to say comparable worth is the looniest idea since Looney Tunes came on the screen."

I was crestfallen. After all my hard work to build respectability for the commission's work on comparable worth, Penny was about to destroy it in a single sentence.

"If you say that, it will be the lead on the evening news," I said, trying to reason with him. "And then no one will even listen to the careful arguments we've mustered." But I could see I was getting nowhere. And once again, the commission was back in the news, and Mary Berry was getting another chance to take potshots. "'This is a political preemptive strike' to support the Reagan administration's opposition to comparable worth 'and deep-six the issue before it has a fair hearing,'" the *Washington Post* quoted Berry.[27] It was no such thing. If anything, the commission was leading the charge against comparable worth in the administration, not the other way around. But it didn't matter. Once Penny uttered his memorable line, no one would bother to look at the serious work we'd done on the issue—no one that is until Judge Anthony Kennedy, later to become a U.S. Supreme Court Justice but at the time a member of the Ninth Circuit Court of Appeals, quoted our study in his opinion reversing a pro–comparable worth decision in the state of Washington, which was the beginning of the end for comparable worth as a legal doctrine.[28] Nonetheless, Penny's comments gave our adversaries more ammunition against us.

The Democrats in the House were so enraged that they began a campaign of continual harassment, launching congressional audits of the agency, filing numerous requests for information that took tremendous time and resources to respond to, and holding a series of oversight hearings. What seemed to irritate them most was my ability to criticize affirmative action programs, comparable worth, and other examples of liberal social engineering without sounding like a right-wing bigot. I was their worst nightmare: an articulate female and a minority who didn't buy into their patronizing agenda. They much preferred dealing with Reagan's white male appointees, such as assistant attorney general Brad Reynolds, whom they could caricature—even if unfairly—as an unfeeling, rich white guy who simply wanted to protect white privilege. Or with Penny, whom they nastily caricatured as a buffoon who simply parroted the GOP line. Hoping to catch Penny in a faux pas, the House Democrats wouldn't allow me to testify when they called us up for hearings, insisting that only the chairman could represent the agency, even though the staff director—

the chief executive officer—had been representing the commission in congressional testimony for nearly thirty years with no objection. In a fit of pique, the Democrat-controlled House Appropriations Committee slashed our funding in half, from more than $12 million a year to barely $6 million, and then divided it into several individual appropriations, so that I could not move money between programs within the agency, and the Republicans in the Senate wouldn't fight to restore or consolidate the funds.

But it was a pyrrhic victory for the Democrats. I wanted nothing more than to get rid of the dead wood at the agency—and couldn't because of civil service rules and protections that made it nearly impossible to fire anyone. The only person I'd been able to dismiss was an employee I caught stealing from the agency—and even that took a battle of wills, with the solicitor of the agency recommending that I simply issue a written reprimand instead. But with the agency's budget halved, I was able to cut more than half the staff, reorganize the agency without objection, and eliminate programs I thought were worthless. To this day, the commission has not regained its former budget nor been able to hire as large a staff as the one I inherited—which is just as well since the agency has become almost completely irrelevant in the intervening years.

In little more than a year, I'd successfully turned around a government agency, reversing policies of at least a decade, and along with a handful of other Reagan appointees, helped redefine the terms of debate on affirmative action, and challenged the dubious concept of equal pay for so-called comparable worth. And I'd done so without making any gaffes or breaking any rules, as so many other Reagan appointees had, such as Department of Interior secretary James Watt and Environmental Protection Agency administrator Anne Burford.[29] My ability to traverse the treacherous territory of race without embarrassing myself or the president made me a particularly dangerous—and hated—foe to my liberal adversaries. In the process, I earned both fierce critics and loyal fans—among the latter, President Reagan himself, who one day called to give me a verbal pat on the back.

"Miss Chavez," the female voice said when I answered the phone one Saturday morning, still groggy and half-asleep, "It's the White House operator. I have the President on the line."

"Hello, Linda, I hope I'm not interrupting." The familiar voice sounded bright and cheerful.

"No, Mr. President, I'm just watching a little Saturday morning television," I said, not wishing to admit I was still in bed at almost ten o'clock.

"I was watching a little television myself earlier this morning in the gym—and guess who I happened to see?" I'd forgotten that a show I'd taped earlier in the week was airing that morning. "You did a terrific job. You really handled yourself well under fire," he said. I could barely believe I was having this conversation. We chatted a few more minutes, mostly about Ed Meese, whom the president had nominated to be his new attorney general. Meese was meeting intense opposition, and for a time, it appeared he might not be confirmed.

"You know they're really mad at me, but they take it out on Ed," the president commiserated. "He's one of the most decent men I've ever known," he said, with real affection.

"He certainly stood by me and the others at the commission when we were under fire. I wouldn't be in this position if it weren't for Ed," I told the president. We spoke for a few minutes longer, and then, in characteristic humility, he signed off with, "Well, I better let you get back to what you were doing before I interrupted you."

In early 1985, after months of continuous battle with the Hill, the difficulties of holding together a sometimes tenuous majority of commissioners—who weren't always happy with the amount of publicity the chairman and I managed to attract, leaving little attention for the other members of the commission—and a sense that if I didn't move on, I would be pigeon-holed as a civil rights appointee forever, I decided to cast about for a new role. I settled on two that interested me: assistant secretary for human rights at the State Department—a role held by Elliott Abrams, who was moving on to become assistant secretary for Latin America—and director of public liaison at the White House, a job being vacated by Faith Whittlesey, who had recently been appointed ambassador to Switzerland. The White House job was the more glamorous of the two; at the time, it was the highest-ranking job held by any woman on the White House staff, and it had been held by Elizabeth Dole before Whittlesey. With lots of encouragement from Chris, I decided to go after it. It wouldn't be easy, especially since both Ed Meese and Ken Cribb, my two best contacts in the White House, were now at the Justice Department. Nonetheless, I decided to mount a campaign on my own behalf, a decision that nearly backfired.

An ally on Capitol Hill—Don Eberly, a young staffer for Congressman Newt Gingrich's Conservative Opportunity Society, an informal caucus of conservative House members—began putting together a list of some one hundred House Republicans who signed a letter to the president backing me for the job. By the end of January, my name was regularly being mentioned in the press, "Rights Panel Director Eyed for Liaison Post," the *Washington Post* reported,[30] but I had plenty of competition, including prominent Republican women, while I still maintained my Democratic Party registration.

My biggest problem, however, was Don Regan, the new chief of staff at the White House. Regan, who had been secretary of the Treasury Department in the first term of the Reagan administration, had recently switched jobs with Jim Baker, who moved from the position of White House chief of staff to become Treasury secretary. Regan didn't want to be lobbied and took particular offense when I showed up at the National Prayer Breakfast, an annual event attended by most Washington conservatives, seated at his table. Veteran political reporters Rowland Evans and Robert Novak wrote in their syndicated column that Regan did not want me for the job, noting I'd "gained no points with Regan by confronting him at social events." I was humiliated. I had never confronted the man anywhere, barely speaking to him at the Prayer Breakfast—it just wasn't my style, as I was always a bit shy in social settings. Finally after months of speculation with no one yet picked for the job, I decided to take the bull by the horns and put in a call to Regan's office. I figured I had nothing to lose, since I probably wasn't going to get the job, but I was tired of waiting to find out.

The young woman who answered the phone seem startled when I gave my name and told her I'd like to talk to Don Regan. She put me on hold for what seemed like forever and then came back on the line.

"Mr. Regan can see you tomorrow at five o'clock. Come to the Northwest gate and give them your name," she said, to my utter amazement.

When I was ushered into his office the next afternoon, I expected Regan to be gruff and annoyed. Instead, he was charming. I noticed the computer on his desk—still a relative rarity in 1985—and asked him if he used it much. He walked me over to the machine and showed me his index-finger pecking style while he called up stock quotes on the screen. The former CEO of Merrill Lynch, Regan apparently still followed the market closely. I sat in one of two identical chairs in front of the fireplace, while his two staff assistants took seats on the couch.

"So you want to be director of public liaison. Tell me why," he launched into the interview almost immediately.

I'd already thought through my answer to what was a predictable question and told him that I thought the job was very important to marshaling support for the president's agenda. I knew that he was unhappy with Whittlesey's tenure from the same Evans and Novak article that said he didn't want me for the job. Regan, while certainly a conservative on economic issues, was viewed as indifferent, maybe even hostile, to the conservative social agenda, which Whittlesey had aggressively pushed during her years as director of public liaison. I needed to convey that I had no particular agenda of my own but saw my role as one of facilitating his and the president's priorities.

"You know this job has always been the top White House job for Republican women. I expect I'd get a lot of criticism if I appointed a Democrat in the position," he said.

"I had wanted to change my party affiliation last year, before the election," I told him, truthfully. "But during the campaign, there was a lot of effort to identify 'Reagan Democrats' like Jeane Kirkpatrick [the U.N. ambassador who delivered the keynote address at the Republican Convention in Dallas] and Bill Bennett [my old friend and fellow Democrat who moved up from the National Endowment for Humanities to be secretary of education in the Reagan administration]. It was you guys who talked me out of switching. I was more useful to you where I was," I said.

"If you don't get this job, is there anything else you're interested in," Regan asked.

"Assistant secretary for human rights at State," I told him.

"Well that's an interesting possibility. We'll be in touch," he said, and with that I left the office. I doubted seriously that I would get the White House job, but I felt better having forced the issue. Now I could quit worrying about it.

A couple of weeks later, while I was having lunch with my friend Andy Bornstein at Duke Zeibert's on Connecticut Avenue, a popular restaurant with lobbyists and media types, the maître d' approached our table to tell me that I had a call from the White House. It was Don Regan, calling from the Reagan ranch in California, where the president was vacationing over the Easter break.

"The job's your if you want it, on two conditions," Regan said without much ceremony. "You have to change your party affiliation, which you said was no problem, and you have to accept Linda Arey as your deputy. She was the Federation of Republican Women's candidate. You'll get along fine with her. She's a very nice lady," he said.

"I accept," I said, surprised and elated. My chutzpah had apparently paid off.

My last official duty at the Civil Rights Commission was to usher through the next commission meeting a position paper with findings and recommendations on comparable worth. We wrote,

> The wage gap between female and male earnings in America results, at
> least in significant part, from a variety of things having nothing to do
> with discrimination by employers, including job expectations resulting
> from socialization beginning in the home, educational choices of
> women who anticipate performing child-bearing and child-rearing func-
> tions in the family and who wish to prepare for participation in the

labor force in a manner that accommodates the performance of those functions, the desire of a number of women to work in the kinds of jobs that accommodate their family roles, and the intermittency of women's labor force participation.[31]

After a 6–2 vote, we stated: "We recommend that the federal civil rights enforcement agencies, including the Equal Employment Opportunity Commission, reject comparable worth and rely instead on the principle of equal pay for equal work." Although the commission's work became a scholarly reference point for much that was written later on comparable worth, Penny's characterization—that comparable worth was the looniest thing since Looney Tunes—was what was remembered most.

My decision to change party affiliation brought predictable criticism when my appointment was announced. "From childhood in the Hispanic section of Albuquerque, N.M., to the White House, from the Democratic Party to the Republican, from the Carter administration to the Reagan administration, Linda Chavez's story is a study in contrasts," the Associated Press reported in a story detailing the reaction to my appointment.[32] "'I don't see how you can explain traversing the course she has traversed other than by sheer personal ambition,' said William Blakey, who was her boss as assistant secretary of HEW in charge of legislation on education." Practically the only person who had anything nice to say other than my old boss Al Shanker, who defended me against charges of opportunism, was Congressman Don Edwards. "'All I am prepared to say is that she is a very competent administrator and I respect her. I am sorry she is on Reagan's side. I wish she were on our side,' he said." The harshest attack came, predictably, from Mary Berry: "'I would give her very high marks for effectively destroying the mission of the Civil Rights Commission,' said Mary Frances Berry. . . . 'She is the first director in the history of the commission to so ingratiate herself with the administration that she has ended up getting a plum job.'" I'm not sure how much my old nemesis's comments reflected sour grapes, but my plum, too, was about to turn sour. In the months that followed, I kept remembering the old saying "Be careful what you wish for, you just might get it."

7

A Woman's Place
in the Reagan White House

But since I ... clambered up the towers of ambition and pride, a thousand woes, a thousand torments, and four thousand tribulations have haunted and worried my soul.

— Miguel Cervantes, *Don Quixote*

I ARRIVED AT THE WHITE HOUSE in April 1985 in the middle of a political firestorm. President Reagan was scheduled to travel to Germany in early May to meet with West German Chancellor Helmut Kohl, a staunch Reagan ally in the defense buildup against the Soviets, as part of a ten-day European visit. Now the entire trip was in jeopardy. Months earlier, Kohl had made a personal request to the president to participate in a "ceremony of reconciliation" at a cemetery near a U.S. Air Force base in Bitburg, Germany, commemorating the German soldiers who had been killed in World War II. Kohl told Reagan that French President François Mitterrand had participated in a similar ceremony at Verdun honoring World War I soldiers at Kohl's request, and the sight of old enemies now united had been deeply appreciated by the Germans.[1] Reagan was happy to accommodate his ally and friend, but the decision cost him dearly. Though the president didn't know it at the time he made the commitment, it turned out that in addition to the hundreds of common soldiers buried at Bitburg, forty-nine members of the Waffen-SS corps were also buried there. The Waffen-SS were the elite combat arm of the SS, who carried out Hitler's "Final Solution" against Europe's Jews.

The decision offended both Jewish and American veteran groups deeply. "Honoring German war dead, while ignoring the thousands of Allied war dead who fought there and the millions of European Jews who were the victims of the Third Reich, has nothing to do with reconciliation," the American Legion said in its official statement. "I think it's a tragic error. It's a historic kind of mistake," said Mark Talisman, Washington director of the Council of Jewish Federations. What made matters worse, Talisman told the *Los Angeles Times*, was that the decision to go to Bitburg was announced during the Jewish Passover holidays.[2] As the newly appointed director of public liaison, I was in charge of outreach to these groups, among others, and my first assignment, even before I was officially on the job, was to reach out to individual Jews and Jewish organizations that might help the president resolve his predicament. I was in a very awkward position, not least because I thought the decision itself was a disaster, compounded when the White House announced that the president would not visit the Nazi death camp at Dachau in addition to the Bitburg cemetery. My husband was also the new, founding director of a Jewish Republican organization, the National Jewish Coalition (NJC), having recently left his job as political director of the American Israel Public Affairs Committee. Chris's new role gave me great access to Jewish leaders but also complicated my job, since many of them saw me as their conduit to the White House. Worse, I was in no real position to influence decisions, which were being made way above my pay grade, and I had the feeling that my superiors in the White House—including Pat Buchanan, my immediate boss—merely wanted me to gather together a group of prominent Jews who could be persuaded to defend the president's decision.

It was an impossible task. Nevertheless, I helped put together a small group of Jewish leaders, mostly Republicans from the NJC, to meet with Don Regan and Pat Buchanan in Regan's office. I also polled a number of leaders on how this was playing in the Jewish community. Morris Abram, a member on the Civil Rights Commission, told me that he would not criticize the president, but he suggested that I have the officials in the White House watch the 1961 film *Judgment at Nuremberg* if they needed a reminder of who the Waffen-SS were and why this issue had so inflamed Jewish passions.[3] The film might actually have influenced the president's feelings, if anyone had been willing to heed the suggestion, but I couldn't see Don Regan marching the president down to the White House theater for a private viewing. Abram also told me that Gordy Zachs, one of the cochairman of the NJC and a strong supporter of the president, was "violently opposed" to the decision to go to Bitburg and that Nathan Perlmutter, the executive director of the Anti-Defamation League, had a constituency to appease even if he personally might be more sympathetic to the president's bind. However, Abram said, Elie Wiesel—a Holocaust survivor and one of the most outspoken critics of the president's action—might be mollified if we could get the president to announce his decision to visit a concentration camp to honor Jewish victims on the German visit during a special White House ceremony scheduled for the coming week in which Wiesel was being awarded the Congressional Gold Medal of Achievement for his role as chairman of the United States Holocaust Memorial Council.

Wiesel was a real problem for the White House. He had survived the Auschwitz and Buchenwald camps as a teenager and had written several best-selling books on his experience, becoming one of the most widely recognized Holocaust survivors in the world. I learned prior to the Congressional Medal ceremony that Wiesel was threatening to resign from the Holocaust Memorial Council if the president would not cancel his Bitburg visit, as was Abe Foxman of the Anti-Defamation League. Wiesel had agreed, however, "not to blow off" the ceremony. Regan decided to bring Wiesel in for a private twenty-minute session with the president before the East Room ceremony in which he would be presented with the Congressional Medal.

Whatever words transpired in that private meeting, it wasn't enough to keep Wiesel from scolding the president publicly. "That place, Mr. President, is not your place," Wiesel admonished the president, while the television cameras packing the room recorded what had suddenly become a major story. "Your place is with the victims of the SS."[4] Even though the president agreed to go to Bergen-Belsen to honor Jewish victims of the Holocaust, as Wiesel had wanted, he had made a terrible gaffe the day before the Wiesel ceremony when he'd said that the German soldiers buried at Bitburg were "victims of Nazism just as surely as the victims of concentration camps." Wiesel later told the *New York Times* that he'd heard Reagan's remarks on the radio while riding in his car. "I heard the comments and I couldn't believe it,"[5] he said, and Wiesel then considered resigning from the Holocaust Memorial council and refusing the medal. Instead, Wiesel rewrote his speech, adding the harsh rebuke. "This medal is the American people's medal, not the president's medal," he told the *Times*, turning the knife further.

When I met with Wiesel a few weeks later to discuss the Holocaust Memorial Council, he said that it was time for "reconciliation," promising there would be no resignations at the council meeting scheduled for the next week, and he urged me to try to expedite the selection of an executive director for the council. As he left my office, Wiesel took my hand in his and squeezed it so hard I winced in pain. I've never been sure whether he was merely being overly enthusiastic or taking his revenge on me.[6]

The Bitburg fiasco not only hurt Reagan, who despite being one of the most pro-Israel presidents in history never earned majority support in the Jewish community, but also further enhanced the accusations that Pat Buchanan was an anti-Semite. The blame that Buchanan took on the Bitburg affair was undeserved, however. Mike Deaver, not Buchanan, originally picked Bitburg as the site for the president's visit to commemorate the German war dead, not knowing at the time that SS men were buried there as well. And Don Regan—and the president himself—dug in their heels once the original decision was made. Buchanan—with whom I worked closely, spending hours each week in his office—certainly supported their judgment, but he was not the driving force by any means.

At the time, Buchanan was mistrusted by many Jews largely because he had written a series of inflammatory articles defending John Demjanjuk, a Cleveland autoworker who was accused of being the infamous Treblinka death camp guard, Ivan the Terrible. The Justice Department deported Demjanjuk, who immigrated to the United States from the Ukraine after World War II, and sent him to Israel for trial. The Israeli Supreme Court eventually freed him in 1993, when it found there was insufficient evidence to prove that he was indeed Ivan.[7] Nonetheless, Buchanan seemed overly zealous in his defense of almost anyone accused by the U.S. Justice Department's Office of Special Investigations, which tracked down Nazis and other war criminals living in the United States. A few years later, Buchanan's sympathies would become the source of great consternation within the conservative movement itself. In a lengthy essay in *National Review* magazine, William F. Buckley wrote, "If you ask, do I think Pat Buchanan is an anti-Semite, my answer is he is not one. But I think he's said some anti-Semitic things"—among them, calling the United States Congress "Israeli-occupied" territory. But when we worked together in the White House, Buchanan was not yet the bitter foe of Israel he would one day become.

To the contrary, Buchanan often supported Israel and was regarded by many of the Jewish organizations that worked with the White House as an ally, a fact that no doubt would shock both his critics and some of his supporters today.[8] On the morning after Israel bombed Yasser Arafat's Palestine Liberation Organization headquarters in Tunis, Tunisia, on October 1, 1985, I received a courtesy call from my contact in the Israeli embassy informing me what had occurred and telling me that Buchanan, too, as another "friend in the White House," would be getting a call from the ambassador. When we all gathered at the morning staff meeting a short while later, Buchanan was enthusiastic about the strike. Larry Speakes, the White House press spokesman, went over the official reaction to the incident, which everyone agreed would be that the bombing was a "legitimate act of self-defense against terrorists," since it occurred in response to the PLO's assassination of three Israelis in Cyprus a few days earlier. "But is it a violation of the Export Control Act?"—which forbids governments to whom the U.S. sells arms from using them except for self-defense—Speakes wanted to know, since the Israelis used American-built planes in the attack. National Security Adviser Robert "Bud" McFarlane said no, and the rest of the conversation focused on how to express concern for the Tunisian and Soviet victims of the bombing while condemning terrorism. As we walked back to his office after the meeting, Buchanan seemed under-whelmed by the lack of enthusiasm expressed by our colleagues for what the Israelis had done. "You've got to admire those Israelis," he said. "They don't mess around."

Israel wasn't the only issue on which Buchanan did an about-face from his years in the White House, and I, inadvertently, may have played a small role in one major policy shift. Ever since his first run for president in the Republican primaries against (the first) President George Bush in 1992, Buchanan has been known as a protectionist, favoring tariffs on imported goods and opposing free trade. "If you take the great nations that have risen to pre-eminence, they did so with protectionism," Buchanan told reporter Bob Davis in 1996.[9] But he took exactly the opposite position—at least on trade—when we were in the White House.

The Reagan administration and most Republicans in Congress were free traders, whereas many Democrats had become protectionists—a dramatic shift in partisan views on this issue from early in the century when the two parties' positions were flipped. When the Democrats proposed a bill that would have put a 25 percent surcharge on textile imports from Japan, Taiwan, and several other nations unless they cut their trade surpluses with the United States, Buchanan was one of the most outspoken critics of the proposal. In one sen-ior staff meeting one morning, Buchanan even delivered a short history lesson on the Smoot-Hawley Tariff Act of 1930, which raised import duties on foreign goods to their highest levels just as Europe's economies were collapsing. "Smoot-Hawley caused the Great Depression," Buchanan opined, by setting off a trade war with Europe at the very time economies on both sides of the Atlantic could least afford it.

However, that was before Buchanan met Sir James Goldsmith, a flamboyant Anglo-French financier to whom I introduced him in October 1985. Roy Godson, the president of the National Strategy Information Center and a con-sultant to the National Security Council, who was an old friend from my days at the AFT, suggested that I bring in Sir James, along with media tycoon Rupert Murdoch, to meet with Pat. I set up special NSC briefings for both men, and the four of us had lunch in the Executive Dining Room in the White House basement. As we walked down the hall past a photo of the nine Supreme Court justices, the Australian-born Murdoch, who had recently become a U.S. citizen in order to acquire several American television stations, quipped that he "could have used a copy of that picture," when he took his citizenship test, on which he apparently missed a question concerning the number of justices. Buchanan hit it off with both men, but it was Goldsmith with whom he developed a close friendship—and one that had lasting impact on Buchanan's views. In later years, Buchanan acknowledged that Goldsmith—who once wrote that free trade "will provoke a disaster unparalleled in the history of mankind"—was a major influence on his thinking about trade.[10]

Putting people together, in groups large and small, was what I did every day. Sometimes I would assemble a friendly audience to be briefed on aid to the Contras, usually run by a dashing young Marine lieutenant colonel named Ollie North, who worked at the NSC. Other times I put together groups of corporate CEOs in the Cabinet Room to meet with President Reagan to discuss budget priorities or to meet with Secretary of State George Schultz in the Situation Room to hear firsthand the administration's position on economic sanctions against South Africa, one of the most controversial issues of the day. The goal was usually to enlist our guests' help in reversing public opinion on a controversial issue, but I also helped outside organizations plead their case to the policymakers in the White House. Although Don Regan had reduced my staff to twenty-four people, it was still one of the largest offices in the White House. Every constituency had its point of contact in public liaison: Jews, Catholics, and Evangelicals; the business community and labor unions; veterans; women, blacks, and Hispanics. Although I picked new staff members when someone moved on—voluntarily or involuntarily—most of the staff was made up of my predecessor's holdovers, who had no personal loyalty to me and operated their own small fiefdoms. Since they were able to dispense favors to constituent groups, they had independent power bases, making it a difficult office to manage.

It was neither a collegial environment nor one, in my view, that best served the interests of the White House, so I decided to restructure the office, with Don Regan's blessing. I tried creating departments within public liaison that mirrored the White House policy councils that had been set up in the president's second term: one for economic issues, another for noneconomic domestic issues, and a third for foreign policy and defense issues, getting rid of the Jewish liaison, the Hispanic liaison, and the women's liaison. "The reorganization accomplishes two goals: more effective communication with groups on the issues of importance to the Administration," I wrote in a memo to Dennis Thomas, Regan's right-hand man, and "better policy input from outside organizations to the White House." But it never really worked. The old system was too ingrained, and both the individual staff members and the constituent groups liked the system the way it was. When I assigned Mona Charon, a former speechwriter for Nancy Reagan who later became a nationally syndicated columnist, to deal with the Eastern European groups as part of her domestic policy portfolio, several of the groups protested loudly to Pat Buchanan because Charon was a Jew. Meanwhile, Don Regan—still smarting from the Bitburg imbroglio—was adamant about not assigning a Jew to deal with Jewish groups, since we were ostensibly eliminating all the ethnic liaisons, though he eventually relented and let me hire Max Green, who came over from the Civil Rights Commission.

The fuss, predictably, made it into the Jewish press, "How Much Access Do Jews Have to the White House, and Which Jews Have It? A Deaf Ear," a long article in the *Palm Beach Jewish World* asked, though I was given high marks.[11] "Chavez . . . is pictured by most Jewish leaders, even those who disagree with her conservative politics, as being closely attuned to the Jewish community and understanding its concerns"—hardly surprising since my husband was the head of a Jewish organization. Even Hyman Bookbinder, the longtime lobby- ist for the American Jewish Committee and a committed liberal, was opti- mistic about my role: "There could be a major change, because she is in a key spot," he told the *Jewish World*. "We disagree with her on affirmative action since she is opposed to the use of quotas, but she is very charismatic and could turn out to be our direct line to the president," he said.

Yes, I saw the president frequently, but usually in passing when I introduced him at the beginning of a meeting I'd arranged. He always made the same joke as he stepped to the podium in the Old Executive Office Building, "We've got to stop meeting this way, Linda," he'd whisper. Even in the small groups I put together in the Cabinet or Roosevelt Room, he'd give his prepared remarks, writ- ten on three-by-five-inch cards, and then engage his guests. My only opportuni- ty to influence his thinking was in drawing up the guest list itself. In Washington, everyone pretends to have more access and be more important than they really are. It was how the game was played—and it was a dangerous one.

It was why, during the Iran-Contra scandal, for example, so many people thought President Reagan had to know what Ollie North was up to when it was discovered that North was funneling money to the Contras, the U.S.-backed guerrilla group trying to overthrow the communist regime in Nicaragua. At briefings and in meetings with supporters, North often gave the impression that he had a direct line into the Oval Office, but I doubt that he ever met private- ly with the president and probably had fewer visits in the Oval Office than I did. He did spend a lot of time with Pat Buchanan, who shared North's passion about ousting the Sandinista government, but Pat didn't spend time alone with the president either. I often ran into North as I was leaving Pat's office at the end of the day, and I'm sure he had access to Bud McFarlane—but North's contact with President Reagan, I am convinced, was mostly through indirect channels.

North was an enigma. Good-looking, with bright blue eyes and a gap-toothed, ready smile, he was terrific in front of an audience. He had a way of making you believe everything he said. I used him frequently to brief audiences on the cruelty of the Sandinistas, the threat of communism spreading in Central America, and the need for Congress to renew support for the Nicaraguan rebels, since they had recently cut off funding the Contras. Overthrowing the Sandinistas was a top Reagan administration priority, one that I supported enthusiastically. North, however, was a bit too conspiratorial for my tastes. He seemed to be carrying around a big secret; of course, it turned out that he really was, but he also enjoyed playing the part.

On the face of it, being the top-ranked woman in the White House would seem to be the pinnacle of my career. I had a West Wing office, but only after a fight to obtain the coveted space; ate my meals in the exclusive Executive Dining Room in the basement of the West Wing, right next to the super-secret Situation Room; attended the senior staff meeting in the Roosevelt Room every morning at 8:00 A.M., after yet another fight to be included; and saw President Reagan a few times a week. But the job was not at all what I imagined.

I had fantasized that here I would have real opportunities to influence policy in a variety of areas, not just civil rights. I now had a place at the table, where I would take part in the most important discussions affecting the nation—or so I imagined. In fact, I felt like little more than a high-status hostess, whose job it was to arrange meetings between outside organizations or individuals and the president, in a job with very little real substance. Sure, it was an honor to share the platform with the president of the United States on a regular basis, to sit in on Oval Office meetings, to meet everyone from the president of General Motors to Mother Teresa, but I found myself missing the intellectual challenge of running the Civil Rights Commission, or even editing *American Educator*.

Much of my time—and nearly all of my energy—was absorbed by petty bureaucratic infighting. The fiercest struggles in the White House were not over policy but over whether you got invited to the right meetings. Your worth wasn't measured by whether you contributed anything substantive but by which car you traveled in on the presidential motorcade. Don Regan had reshaped the White House staff along a more corporate model, more hierarchical, with few competing centers of power, and his imperious style soon earned him the moniker "the Prime Minister."

Under Don Regan's stewardship, the White House power structure changed dramatically. Regan insisted on being the single gatekeeper to the Oval Office, keeping out even Bud McFarlane, unless Regan himself was present for the meeting. The strained relationship between McFarlane and Regan had become the subject of frequent Washington gossip. You could feel the tensions at the daily senior staff meeting in which the two men sat, Regan, presiding at one end of the long mahogany table in the intimate Roosevelt Room in the West Wing, and McFarlane at the other end. Regan's temperament was mercurial. He seemed to relish biting off subordinates' heads in public, which only made the small group of young male aides around him—dubbed "the mice"—all the more obsequious. McFarlane, on the other hand, seemed perpetually in a slow burn, never quite erupting but dangerous nonetheless.

The staff weren't the only ones in the White House with volatile tempers, as I discovered when I found myself on the receiving end of Maureen Reagan's notorious temper a few months after I became director of public liaison. I didn't know the president's daughter well. We'd been in a few meetings together over the years but had no close relationship, so I was surprised when she called me personally one day to invite me to be on the official U.S. delegation to the United Nations "Decade on Women" Conference in Nairobi, Kenya.

Maureen was a controversial figure in the White House. She held no formal position in the administration, but she obviously had some influence—though exactly how much was in dispute. She was known as an outspoken feminist, pro-choice, in favor of the Equal Rights Amendment and affirmative action for women—views that differed from her father's and made her anathema to conservatives. She was also prone to tirades against those she viewed as subordinates, but warm and loyal to her friends.

"I'm very flattered to be asked," I told Maureen when she invited me to Nairobi, "but I'm not sure I can take the time off," I said.

"Oh, you can take the time off," she shot back, her voice suddenly turning icy. I realized immediately that I had offended her.

"Of course," I said, "I just need to clear it with Regan."

"If Don Regan gives you any trouble, just have him call me," she said, letting me know who had the most power, at least in her mind.

The Nairobi Women's Conference, with 10,000 feminists gathered from around the world, was about the last place in the world I wanted to be. But the idea of going to Kenya was appealing, even if I couldn't stay for the safari that Maureen had planned for the two dozen women and one man in the delegation—Alan Keyes, who had recently moved to the United Nations as one of Ambassador Jeane Kirkpatrick's deputies. We traveled by Air Force jet, landing first in Dublin, then in Cairo, where we were hosted by the Egyptians at the airport, an awkward moment since they served us Cokes with ice, which all of us were afraid of drinking for fear we'd get ill. As it was, I was too sick to enjoy much of anything, having come down with a strange set of symptoms the day before we left. My complexion was green, I had terrible headaches and nausea, and I thought about canceling the trip. By the time I landed in Nairobi, I could barely walk. Thankfully, the alert medical aid at the U.S. embassy in Nairobi quickly recognized that I had overdosed on my anti-malaria pills from a faulty set of instructions on the prescription bottle supplied by the White House physician's office. As soon as I stopped taking so many anti-malaria pills, I improved dramatically, well enough to be called into action when it came time for the United States to make its first serious reply to an accusation made by one of the other delegations.

The huge hall at the Kenyatta Conference Center where the U.N. was hosting the formal proceedings was filled with thousands of delegates, most—but not all—women. The Iranian women wore the traditional head-to-toe black chador required by the radical Islamic government that overthrew the Shah of Iran in 1979, much as Afghan women were required to cover themselves under the Taliban more than a decade later. The Iranian women were accompanied everywhere by bearded male guards, who also dressed in black. Several countries, including the Soviet Union, sent official delegations made up of females but also sent males along to direct what the women could and could not say. Iran and Iraq were engaged in a decade-long, bloody war at the time, which made things particularly awkward since the two delegations were seated next to each other at the front of the huge stadium-like structure where the meetings took place. On the first day, the Iranian women displayed a small photo of their leader, the Ayatollah Khomeini—whose face was indelibly ingrained in Americans' minds as a result of the U.S. hostage crisis, during which the radical Islamic government had held fifty-two hostages for 444 days. Each day at the Nairobi conference when the delegates returned from lunch, the Iraqis displayed a somewhat larger picture of their leader, Saddam Hussein, then largely unknown (to Americans anyway). At each new session, the two warring delegations returned with ever bigger photographs of their respective leaders, until both had huge six-foot-high posters that virtually obscured the stage, at which point the conference organizers decided to ban photos altogether.

As usual in any gathering of representatives from Third World countries, the United States was the favorite target on which to heap scorn and blame for all the world's ills. The U.S. policy at such U.N. forums was not to respond to generalized attacks, but if the allegations were distinct and the United States was named specifically, we would answer them. Both the delegations of Vietnam and Afghanistan delivered fiery, tendentious speeches. Nguyen Thi Binh, the head of the communist Vietnamese delegation, accused the United States of promoting an arms race: "In Asia and the Pacific, the United States persists in its policy of maintaining and broadening their military bases," she said, calling the policy "United States imperialism," one of the favorite catchphrases of the day.[12]

Maureen decided that I should deliver the U.S. response. It would be an incremental approach. As a senior White House official, if I delivered the speech, it would be taken very seriously—though not as ominously as if Maureen, the president's daughter and head of the delegation, delivered it. The subtle signals worked. As I moved into position in front of the microphone at our table, the female Soviet delegation sitting next to us—including former Soviet cosmonaut Valentina Tereshkova, the first woman ever to make a space flight—stepped back, while several dour-faced men took their places. Things were apparently getting serious, and the Soviet diplomats couldn't trust a bunch of female amateurs to counter whatever charges I might level.

In my most stentorian voice, I assailed first the Vietnamese, then the Afghan delegation: "I would simply point out that today there are millions of refugees in Southeast Asia, the majority of whom are women and children, who are in that tragic condition as a direct result of Vietnam's brutal military occupation of Cambodia," I said.[13] As for Afghanistan's accusations, I countered that they were "particularly absurd coming from a delegation whose government is at war with its own people," referring to the Soviet-backed regime of Babrak Karmal. The Karmal government, which the U.S. was trying to oust by giving military aid to the anti-Soviet mujahadin forces, stayed in power only with the help of more than 100,000 Soviet troops who had invaded the country in 1980.

It was the most fun I'd had since joining the White House staff. After I finished speaking, without ever attacking the Soviet Union by name, the Russian men returned to their seats behind the female delegates. I left the conference early to return to Washington soon after giving my speech, but I continued to play a role—my most important one—behind the scenes.

The most controversial item on the conference agenda was a resolution to include virulently anti-Semitic "Zionism equals racism" language aimed at Israel in the final document, a feature that had become de rigueur for U.N. meetings ever since similar language had been adopted in a U.N. resolution in 1975. The U.S. delegation was committed to walking out if the final document included the offending language, and most of the attention of the State Department officials traveling with the delegation was on avoiding this embarrassment. However, there was another issue on the agenda that promised to cause problems for the United States, especially since the head of the delegation, Maureen Reagan, supported a stance on the issue that was in direct opposition to the official administration position, and no one in Washington seemed to be paying attention.

Maureen favored the concept of comparable worth—the proposal I had fought so hard against at the Civil Rights Commission. She had agreed in committee meetings to support language in the final report that called for "equal pay for work of equal value." Alan Keyes alerted me by phone that Maureen had broken with administration policy by supporting comparable worth. He was in an awkward position, defending Maureen's action publicly: "In the interest of compromise and consensus, we were willing to go along," he told the press.[14] But behind the scenes he hoped I might get Maureen to pull back. I was particularly worried since comparable worth proponents on Capitol Hill were using Maureen's position in Nairobi to try to jump-start their proposed legislation in the House. I decided to go to Don Regan on it, whom I was scheduled to brief about the conference anyway. Regan asked me to draft a short memo describing the administration's opposition to comparable worth and insisting that the U.S. delegation oppose any language in the final document that incorporated it.

Regan took my language and shot off a cable to Maureen. "We should make it very clear that the U.S. delegation opposes the concept of equal pay for work of equal value. Language that differs cannot be accepted by the U.S. on consensus, and you should be prepared to protest its inclusion and vote against it," Regan wrote Maureen on July 23. It worked. Maureen had to pull back and eventually opposed the comparable worth language in the final draft, but she was not happy about it.

"How dare you go behind my back to Don Regan!" Maureen screamed at me on the phone when she got back to the White House. "I was humiliated," she said, her voice still shrill.

"Maureen, it was my duty to tell Regan that the delegation was about to do something that could prove extremely embarrassing to the administration," I said in defense.

"I don't know who you think you are, but you wouldn't even have been on that delegation if it weren't for me," she shouted.

"I appreciate that," I said, "I'm grateful, truly. But this was a serious matter that could have caused us real problems on the Hill. And with all due respect, Maureen, I work for your father, not you, and it's his position I have to protect," I said.

"Anybody could have gotten ahold of that damn cable. The Russians, anybody. He didn't even bother to send it through secure channels," she said, still yelling at me as if I were an underling.

"I'm sorry," I said, now getting angry myself, "but I can't continue to talk to you if you're going to keep screaming at me," I said, at which point she hung up on me. It isn't every day that a member of the president's family yells at, much less hangs up on, you. I was sure that I'd get a call from someone reprimanding me, maybe even firing me. But it never happened, though the fracas did eventually make it into a Robert Novak column. The next time I saw Maureen, several months later, she was all sweetness and light, as if nothing had ever transpired.

Although I scored one minor victory on a public policy issue I cared deeply about, I struck out completely when I joined with other administration conservatives to try to persuade the president to eliminate racial quotas in federal contracting. It was an idea that had been kicking about since President Reagan's first term. There was nothing in the Civil Rights Act of 1964 requiring "affirmative action." Moreover, the act said explicitly that nothing in it required "preferential treatment" because of an "imbalance" in the work force. The term "affirmative action" was first used in the civil rights context in an executive order signed by President John F. Kennedy in 1961. The Kennedy order was later revised and extended by President Lyndon Johnson in 1965 in Executive Order 11246, which mandated that federal contractors "take affirmative action to ensure that applicants are employed, and that employees are treated during their employment, without regard to their race."[15] The Johnson order didn't mandate racial quotas or preferential treatment, either. But in 1970, the Department of Labor, which enforced the Executive Order through its Office of Federal Contract Compliance Programs (OFCCP), issued an implementing regulation that directed federal contractors to ensure that "the rate of minority applicants recruited should approximate or equal the ratio of minorities to the applicant population in each location."[16] The order thus established recruiting quotas for companies that hoped to do business with the federal government, covering roughly one-fourth of the entire American workforce.

Assistant Attorney General for Civil Rights Brad Reynolds had been arguing against racial quotas in the courts for four years, and the president himself was on record vigorously opposing quotas, so it was especially galling that the administration's own Department of Labor was using a pre-existing presidential executive order to continue to press for the euphemistically dubbed "goals and timetables" for federal contractors. Several of us believed that it was time for the president to issue a new executive order banning quotas, but our first battle was to get the proposal on his desk. We were sure that if President Reagan were presented with an option to wipe out federally mandated racial quotas with a stroke of his pen, he'd seize the opportunity. But with Ed Meese gone from the White House—although in an arguably more powerful role as attorney general—there was no one inside who could press the case directly, and there were plenty of staff who would argue against it on political grounds.

Conservatives within the administration began planning in earnest over the summer, lining up support among cabinet officers and plotting how best to get Don Regan on our side. We knew that without his acquiescence we'd have a difficult time getting the new executive order to the president. I wrote up a memo to Regan describing the issue and the politics and urged Pat Buchanan to get an agreement from Regan to take the issue to the president before the Congress came back from its August recess. But nothing happened. Meanwhile, Brad Reynolds and Ken Cribb in Attorney General Meese's office continued to work on draft language and talking points, and all of us called potential allies within the departments to line up support in anticipation of a Domestic Policy Council meeting at the White House sometime in the fall.

Regan's staff was not eager for my participation, however. Alfred Kingon, the presidential assistant responsible for overseeing cabinet meetings, seemed particularly keen to keep me out. Kingon, a former editor-in-chief of *Saturday Review* who had been one of Regan's closest aides at the Department of the Treasury, put together the invitation list for all internal White House meetings—deciding who could attend and who could not—a powerful position in the status-obsessed environment of the White House. He tried to keep me off the invitation list for the planning sessions on the executive order revisions, but I cornered him outside the White House mess one afternoon.

"There's no one in this building who knows more about civil rights than I do, Al," I said, making the case for why I should be at the meeting.

"I'd love to talk to you about this, Linda," he said, literally backing into the men's room, "but not now." It was the first time anyone had ever ducked into a bathroom to avoid me. In the end, Kingon relented and invited me to the meeting held on October 22.

The Roosevelt Room was packed for the 2:00 P.M. meeting, with seven cabinet members in attendance including Attorney General Ed Meese, Labor Secretary Bill Brock, Transportation Secretary Elizabeth Dole, who also happened to be the wife of Senate Majority Leader Bob Dole, and Housing and Urban Development Secretary Sam Pierce, the only black in the Reagan cabinet. Two other black appointees were also present, Clarence Thomas, the head of the Equal Employment Opportunity Commission, and my old colleague Clarence Pendleton—both of whom were expected to support revising the executive order. I knew Penny could be counted on, but I was worried about Clarence Thomas. He had never been one to make waves. He was opposed to racial quotas, but at the Department of Education, where he'd served as the head of the Office for Civil Rights, and at the EEOC, he took a low-key approach to the fight against racial preferences. Once, when I was still at the Civil Rights Commission, Thomas called me to complain about my style.

"You and Penny like to be lightning rods. You go out and issue statements about how you're going to reverse the policies of the last twenty years, and then the press and the civil rights groups have a field day. I just do my business, without making a big deal about it," he said, chiding me. Years later, in his fight to become a Supreme Court justice, Thomas was vilified as a right-wing extremist by most of the civil rights establishment, but when he was head of the EEOC, the most common complaint among many conservatives was that he was soft on the issue of racial preferences.

To my relief, Thomas came through during the meeting, after Brad Reynolds made a well-thought-out brief for why it was important for the president to issue a new executive order immediately.

"We've already endured the criticism on this issue," Thomas said in his deep baritone voice. "Now's the time to do what's right."[17]

"This meeting is four and half years late," Penny chimed in. "It's time for President Reagan to lead blacks off the plantation," he said in characteristically provocative language.

Still, Brock, who was responsible for implementing the executive order, was unconvinced. He was especially worried about how the business community would react.

"The business community is comfortable with the way things are now," he argued. "I think we can accomplish our goals managerially, without bringing the president into what will be characterized by the media as the gutting of affirmative action programs," he said.

"Some business groups might oppose us," I said, "but others, like the Chamber of Commerce, will be on our side," I argued. "And massaging the regulations won't help. Most Americans believe 'goals' are the same thing as quotas," I asserted. I shot a look at my friend Mike Horowitz, who was sitting across the room.

Horowitz, the general counsel at OMB and the man who had told presidential personnel to hire me when I first interviewed for the Civil Rights Commission more than two years earlier, was now on the other side in this fight. He believed—naively, I thought—that it was foolish to push a new executive order when Brock could simply rewrite the existing regulations to accomplish the same goal. Horowitz had been meeting secretly for weeks with one of Brock's top assistants, Michael Baroody, to craft a compromise. I saw Horowitz's fingerprints all over Brock's assertion that he could do what was necessary to stem the abuses through the regulatory process.

After more than an hour of intense debate, Meese agreed that a decision document for the president would be drawn up that would include three options: do nothing, which would leave the existing executive order in place; issue the proposed new language, which would prohibit preferences and quotas but, under new compromise language, would allow voluntary goals and timetables if contractors wished to continue to use them; or reissue the existing executive order, which would put the president on record as favoring goals and timetables, the least attractive option. With these as the alternatives, I knew we had lost. We simply didn't have the votes, and Brock wasn't going to back down.

Although discussions on the issue continued for the next several weeks, by mid-December the revised executive order was dead. Sixty-two senators, many of them Republicans, wrote the president urging him to retain the existing language, and the civil rights groups mounted a vigorous public relations campaign to portray the proposed new executive order as one more example of the Reagan administration's hostility toward blacks. "There's nothing happening on it now," an anonymous White House official—I suspected it was Al Kingon—told reporters. "The betting here in the White House is you have seen the last of the meetings on it."[18] It was a huge defeat for those of us who had fought so long and hard to get the government out of the business of deciding, based on race, who would be hired or receive federal contracts.

The episode left me further demoralized in a job I had begun to hate. Even when I broke through the barriers in place in the West Wing, I often felt like an outsider. I was a policy advocate in a world dominated by process and politics. I was a conservative on a White House staff less ideologically driven than it had been in the president's first term. I was a woman in a place dominated not only by men but by men of a generation not entirely comfortable working with women.

Don Regan had gotten himself in to hot water on several occasions because of his perceived insensitivity to women. In November, as the White House was preparing for a U.S.-Soviet summit in Geneva, Regan had offended feminists by suggesting that women weren't interested in foreign affairs. Worse, he'd made the remarks in reference to Nancy Reagan and Raisa Gorbachev, Soviet leader Mikhail Gorbachev's wife, who also happened to be a Ph.D. and a professor at Moscow University. In a story about the news coverage of the upcoming summit, Regan told *Washington Post* Style reporter Donnie Radcliffe that "he expects the coverage of [Nancy Reagan's] and Mrs. Gorbachev's activities to have high appeal, especially to women. 'They're not . . . going to understand throw-weights or what is happening in Afghanistan or what is happening in human rights,' he said. 'Some women will, but most women—believe me, your readers for the most part if you took a poll—would rather read the human-interest stuff of what happened.'"[19]

Regan was excoriated for the remark—which, if impolitic, also happened to be true. When asked my opinion by the *Wall Street Journal*, I teased, "I'm going to throw my weight around and knit him an afghan for Christmas." Regan later apologized for the comment but never lived it down. Despite getting off on the wrong foot with him, I actually grew to like Regan, who was always civil to me, something that couldn't be said of his dealings with others. Over time, I think he grew to respect me, though it was clear he was never all that comfortable with me—but then neither were most of the men in the White House, except for Pat Buchanan, who fought hard to make sure I was included in meetings and discussions.[20] Pat didn't see me as a woman but as a fellow conservative, and he needed all the allies he could muster in the treacherous political environment of the West Wing.

Others, including Jim Baker, who was thought of as one of the more "progressive" types in the administration, sometimes found my presence awkward. Baker once upbraided Regan for spoiling the masculine atmosphere of the legislative strategy group meeting by including me.

Regan was complaining that the president was traveling too much. "He's working his balls off," Regan said, which brought the meeting to a dead halt as all eyes turned to me see if I had fainted away at the salty language. Finally, everyone started giggling—like a bunch of schoolboys, I thought—when Baker looked at Regan.

"Don't blame me, you invited her," he said.

Even the president sometimes found my presence awkward. "Cover your ears for this one, Linda," he'd say when he walked to the back of Air Force One to joke with the staff. I actually found it refreshing. Here was a group of men who stood up when I entered the room, held doors for me, and wouldn't think of using foul language or telling an off-color story in my presence. They meant it as a sign of respect, and I took it in that spirit. But they were also of an older generation who had never worked side by side with women as peers, much less as superiors, and they had a hard time adjusting to someone like me. And some of them, I think, mistook my femininity for weakness and then were shocked when I showed toughness.

By mid-December, barely eight months into the job, I was anxious to leave the public liaison position, when my husband suggested that I should run for the U.S. Senate seat being vacated by Maryland Senator Charles McC. Mathias, a liberal Republican who had been senator for eighteen years. We had only recently moved to Maryland, having bought a home in Bethesda in

1984, and I had been a Republican for less than a year and knew next to nothing about local politics. It was a crazy idea—but what did I have to lose? And if I won, I would be in an enormously powerful position to influence the issues I cared most about.

Chris talked to his contacts at the National Republican Senatorial Committee, who came to meet with me to discuss my interest. No one believed I had much of a shot. I was a political novice, a carpetbagger, and a recent Republican convert. Democrats outnumbered Republicans in the state by more than three to one, and even the very liberal "Mac" Mathias had faced some tough elections in his three Senate runs. Maryland also had the largest black population of any state outside the Deep South—almost 20 percent in 1986—and my positions on affirmative action would mean I'd be lucky to do as well among black voters in Maryland as President Reagan, who had won less than 10 percent of the black vote in 1984 . However, the Republican Party was desperate to field a respectable candidate and hoped that I might establish some name recognition, make a credible showing in 1986, and then take on Senator Paul Sarbanes, who was up for re-election in 1988. If I was willing to do it, my visitors assured me, the party would help clear the field of other candidates.

The stories leaked to the press almost immediately. "Linda Chavez Considers Trying to Save Mathias Seat for GOP," the Baltimore Sun reported, "Republicans Woo Chavez to Run for Mathias' Seat," the Washington Times said, and "Chavez Lifts Maryland GOP's Hopes," joined the Washington Post. Suddenly Regan's aides were cozying up to me, passing me notes in the senior staff meeting. Regan's deputy, Dennis Thomas, offered, "As a 'future' constituent and someone who has been involved in Maryland politics for eighteen years, I would be delighted to do anything I can should you decide to do it."

Even Regan himself appeared eager to help. He agreed to call Jack Mosley, one of the leading businessmen in the state and chairman of U.S. Fidelity and Guarantee, a large insurance company headquartered in Baltimore, on my behalf. "He'll meet with you," Regan reported back in a handwritten note after his conversation. "He will keep an open mind. Thinks even tho' Md. is not a Rep[ublican] State the race is 'winnable.'" I wasn't sure whether everyone was being so nice because they genuinely wanted to help or whether they just wanted to get rid of me, but it didn't really matter. I had made up my mind: I was leaving.

8

On the Campaign Trail

In politics, if you want anything said, ask a man. If you want anything done, ask a woman.

—Margaret Thatcher

ON FEBRUARY 3, 1986, I met with President Reagan for my goodbye photo. It was a bittersweet moment. I was used to ushering in groups of visitors to meet with the president for a quick handshake and picture taking, but I wasn't accustomed to being on the receiving end. The president, as always, was standing when I entered the room, a smile on his face. He invited me to sit down for a few minutes to discuss my impending Senate race, but it was awkward since he couldn't formally endorse me until the Republican primary was over. Nonetheless, he gave me a few words of wisdom.

"Don't ever let anybody give you any grief about becoming a Republican late in life. I recall another fellow who did that, too, and he did okay," he joked, referring to his own history as a former Democrat. It was what I loved most about working for Ronald Reagan, his kindness and humility. He presented me with a lovely glass platter etched with a depiction of the south view of the White House and a long letter of appreciation for my services—which, in time-honored White House tradition, I helped draft.

I left the West Wing compound for the last time as an employee, holding back tears, but I had little time for nostalgia. With the help of my assistant, Nancy Watson, who had been with me since the Civil Rights Commission, I opened shop in a temporary office near my home in Bethesda and started trying to raise money for my Senate campaign. Despite the initial encouragement of my candidacy from the NRSC staff, the Republican Party wasn't about to commit itself before the primary election—one of the latest in the country on September 9, a full seven months away, so I was suddenly on my own. Worse, the Republican field, which was supposed to be wide open for me, quickly became crowded, first with a wealthy Baltimore businessman, Richard Sullivan, then with a prominent black Republican, George Haley—who happened to be the brother of Alex Haley, the author of *Roots*, an epic based in part on the family's history from slavery to the early twentieth century. Sullivan was going to be a particularly tough opponent. A silver-haired Irishman who had lived in Maryland for two decades, he had recently retired with a hefty golden parachute as CEO of Easco, a Fortune 500 tool-and-die company, hoping to land in the U.S. Senate.

Sullivan hired President Reagan's pollster, Richard Wirthlin, started making the rounds of Republican Lincoln Day Dinners across the state, and attracted a fair number of early endorsements from party officials. Most importantly, he put up $200,000 of his own money for the race—an amount I couldn't hope to match in the early months. But Chris turned out to be my secret weapon. A terrific fundraiser from his days working first for the Operating Engineers Union and then for the American Israel Public Affairs Committee and now as executive director of the National Jewish Coalition, he helped raise $100,000 during the first several months of the campaign.

Much of that money went to pay for my own consultants with Reagan ties: the firm of Russo, Watts, and Rollins, each of whom had worked for Ronald Reagan since his days as governor of California. Of the three, it was Edward J. Rollins, who had been political director in the White House when I first joined the staff, who was the big draw. Rollins ran the 1984 Reagan re-election campaign and I considered him a friend. He had encouraged me to run—though he cautioned that I had only about a 40 percent chance of winning. His price was steep: $5000 a month during the initial stages, increasing to $10,000 a month once we started raising real money. As I soon learned, even that hefty price tag didn't buy much, at least not much of Rollins's personal involvement. Within weeks of hiring Rollins, I was getting back reports that he was telling potential donors that I didn't have a shot at winning, which didn't exactly help my chances of raising the money to pay his fees, much less win the Republican nomination. And he was nowhere to be found near the campaign.

Through most of the spring and early summer, I crisscrossed the state meeting local officials, learning about local issues and trying to build name recognition on a shoestring. On weekends, I usually took one of my boys with me. Pablo, who was ten, always insisted on wearing his Los Angeles Dodgers jacket and cap, telling anyone who asked why he wasn't sporting Orioles gear instead: "Because they suck." Thankfully, none of the reporters covering the race ever thought it fit to quote him, which would surely have cost me votes in Baltimore. David, a freshman at the University of Maryland and an active College Republican, was my best volunteer, organizing meetings, making press calls, and stuffing envelopes. And seven-year-old Rudy provided some of my best laugh lines, especially before medical audiences. I loved to repeat the answer he'd given me when I'd asked him what he wanted to be when he grew up.

"A doctor, of course," he told me.

"Why?" I foolishly asked.

"Because they make a lot of money and get to see naked ladies," he said. The line always brought down the house.

Maryland was considered very unfriendly territory for Republicans generally, with only one county in the state—Garrett County in the far western part of Maryland—boasting more Republicans than Democrats. And the media was an even more difficult challenge for a Republican candidate. The media weren't necessarily hostile, just indifferent, rarely giving Republican candidates any coverage at all. I hoped to change that. Without money for paid advertising I had little choice but to try to raise my profile through "free media" news coverage. When University of Maryland basketball star Len Bias died in a well-publicized cocaine overdose, I scheduled a press conference to announce my anti-drug platform on the basketball court in front of the Murphy Homes, Baltimore's toughest housing project. The promise of a white, female, Republican candidate holding a press conference in Baltimore's most dangerous neighborhood, with broken glass and abandoned syringes littering the playground, was enough to bring the television cameras and newspapers out in force.

I knew how to get attention by piggybacking on important news stories with my own angle. When three Annapolis residents were killed in a terrorist bombing of a Trans World Airlines flight over Greece in April, I hired an ex–Secret Service agent, Dario Marquez, to test security at Baltimore-Washington International Airport. When the security system failed to detect two bomb-like devices placed in carry-on luggage, missing only the actual explosive materials, I issued a stinging critique of airport security in the BWI terminal, which infuriated airport authorities but brought needed attention to the risk of potential domestic terrorism, and I used the occasion to outline my own platform for dealing with terrorism.

"Chavez Urges Kidnap of Terrorist; Maryland Senate Hopeful Unveils BWI Security Study," the *Washington Post* headline screamed. I recommended that the United States follow Israel's example and capture terrorists overseas in order bring them to trial—which has finally become official policy in the wake of the attacks on the World Trade Center in 2001. The *Post* outlined my program:

> In defending her proposal of "capturing terrorists overseas and trying
> them in the U.S.," Chavez said that the Italian government's failure to
> extradite terrorists who hijacked the *Achille Lauro* cruise ship in

October and killed an American on board showed that "we cannot rely on the legal processes of other states to protect our citizens as fully as they deserve." . . . Other recommendations offered by Chavez included increasing the number of federal sky marshals, imposing an airport security fee, using onboard cameras to relay photos of hijackers to ground terminals, and boycotting overseas airports where security continually fails to meet State Department standards. She also said the news media should be asked to limit coverage of terrorists and "apologists for terrorist organizations."[1]

I also called for increasing security personnel by 50 percent, improving training, and eliminating the cumbersome overlap in jurisdiction for airport security among state police, private security firms, and the federal government, something Congress finally did in 2001 after September 11.

My efforts to attract attention were paying off, but I was still far from a household name in the state—certainly not as well known as any of the Democratic primary contenders, the retiring Governor Harry Hughes, Democratic Congressman Michael Barnes, a chief critic of the Reagan policy in Central America, and Congresswoman Barbara Mikulski, a feisty five-term House member from working-class Baltimore. My primary opponents Dick Sullivan and George Haley were making inroads, too. Then something happened that brought me instant name recognition and credibility.

WJZ, the Baltimore ABC affiliate at the time, decided to administer a current affairs quiz to all the candidates running for U.S. Senate. Reporter Don Williams showed up in my office with a camera crew for what I thought was going to be a routine interview, when he pulled out a piece of paper.

"I've got a few questions here I want you to answer," he said, suddenly turning very serious.

"Are there right and wrong answers?" I kidded.

"As a matter of fact, there are," Williams said. My heart raced. The cameras were rolling, and I was about to be given a test, a real test, which I hadn't prepared for.

"What was the specific terrorist incident that sparked the reprisal against Libya by President Reagan?" Williams read from his sheet.

"The bombing of a disco in Berlin; I think the name was La Belle Discothèque. It was popular with American GI's," I answered nervously. Two American soldiers were killed in the April 1986 incident, which prompted the U.S. to retaliate against the Libyan government of Mu'ammar Gadhafi, who was believed to be behind the terrorist attack.

"That's very good," Williams responded. "Let's see how you do on this one. Who is the Israeli prime minister now, and who will be the prime minister in November?"

Another easy one, I thought. "Shimon Peres is prime minister now, and under a power-sharing agreement between the Labor and Likud parties, Yitzhak Shamir will be the next prime minister later this year." This was hardly a difficult question for me. I had met privately with Shamir on a visit to Israel the previous January and remembered the visit fondly.

"What are Stinger missiles? Did the Saudis get any from the United States?" Williams went on.

This was tougher. "I remember debates on the sale of Stingers to the Saudis. I'm pretty sure the sale went through."

"Can you define Stinger?" Williams prodded.

"It's shoulder-held; it's a surface-to-air missile, I think," I said, hoping I remembered correctly. Williams smiled.

"So far so good. Who is the head of the African National Congress?" he asked next, referring to the anti-apartheid forces in South Africa.

"Nelson Mandela is officially the head. But he's in prison in South Africa," I offered a little tentatively. I wasn't sure if it was a trick question. "Oliver Tambo is the acting head."

"Either one will do," Williams said. "Now, how did Maryland rank in federal grants to state and local governments in 1985?"

I remembered reading a small article on the ranking in the *Baltimore Sun* earlier in the week, but I didn't have a clue where Maryland ranked. "Twenty-seventh?" I offered, lamely.

"No. It was ranked thirty-fifth. But you've done amazingly well," Williams said, signaling to the camera crew to stop rolling. "I'll let you in on a secret. You've done a whole lot better than your Democratic competitors. We'll air this segment sometime next week. You should be very pleased."

The series aired over three nights on Baltimore's top-ranked news program, and then the networks picked up the story. By the time it was over, it was news across the world. Vice President Bush later told me that he'd seen it on Jordanian television on a visit there. Although my success answering the questions was featured prominently in all the stories, it was my better-known opponents' failure that was newsworthy. "Among the worst scores posed were those of three major Democratic candidates: Rep. Michael D. Barnes, a subcommittee chairman on the House Foreign Affairs Committee who has promoted himself as a leader on foreign policy," wrote the *Washington Post*, "Rep. Barbara A. Mikulski, a five-term House member from Baltimore, and Gov.

Harry Hughes, who has occupied the State House for eight years. Neither Barnes nor Mikulski, for example, could name both the Israeli prime minister and his designated successor."[2] Nor could either one name the ANC head, even though, as the *Post* reported, Barnes's support for sanctions against the South African government was a cornerstone of his campaign. At one point in the interview, Mikulski asked plaintively, "Can we turn this thing off?" But the most embarrassing moment came when my fellow Republican, George Haley, mistook Oliver Tambo for "Sambo" and defined Stingers, oddly, as "missiles that come forth into the nation."

My poll numbers soared. It was the kind of story that people remembered. Shaking hands at a subway stop in the Maryland suburbs the morning after the *Post* story ran, people were suddenly happy to meet. "You're the smart one, aren't you?" was the common refrain.

Within weeks, Dick Sullivan, who had scored better than Barnes and Mikulski but still an embarrassing 2.5 correct answers, decided to drop out of the campaign. He had already spent nearly a quarter of a million dollars of his own money and figured he needed at least $300,000 more to have any chance of defeating me for the nomination. It wasn't worth it, especially since everyone knew that victory in November was a very long shot for whoever became the Republican nominee. With Sullivan out of the race, I easily won the nomination on September 9, with more than 70 percent of the vote. And Barbara Mikulski captured the Democratic nomination.

Flush with victory, I took the podium at the Belvedere Hotel in downtown Baltimore to launch my campaign against Mikulski and promptly stuck my foot in my mouth—or at least that was the way the story got reported over and over again.

"Mikulski's victory set the stage for a bitter general election battle with Republican Senate nominee Linda Chavez, marking only the second time in U.S. history that two women from major parties have squared off in a Senate contest," the *Post* reported. "Chavez, 39, said last night that the central issue of the campaign will be the 'differences' between her and Mikulski. 'We are as different as two people can be,' said Chavez. 'Barbara Mikulski is a San Francisco–style Democrat—people are going to reject her brand of liberalism.'"[3] The *Post* story conveniently left out the full phrase I had used: "a San Francisco–style, George McGovern, liberal Democrat."[4] The San Francisco Democrat reference was a familiar, if borrowed, theme. U.N. Ambassador Jeane Kirkpatrick had made it famous two years earlier in 1984 in her speech to the Republican convention in Dallas, when she attacked her fellow Democrats, whose convention had been held in San Francisco.

"This is the first Republican convention I have ever attended," Kirkpatrick told the Republicans gathered in Dallas. Kirkpatrick had been, up to that time, a life-long Democrat. She went on to excoriate her fellow Democrats, whom she referred to five times in the speech as "San Francisco Democrats." "When the San Francisco Democrats treat foreign affairs as an afterthought, as they did, they behaved less like a dove or a hawk than like an ostrich . . . ," she said. "When the Soviet Union walked out of arms control negotiations and refused even to discuss the issues, the San Francisco Democrats didn't blame Soviet intransigence. They blamed the United States. But then they always blame America first."[5]

My words were not nearly so elegant, but the point was the same. Mikulski represented the left wing of the Democratic Party, the San Francisco Democrats, out of step with the working men and women—most of them patriotic, pro-defense Democrats—of Maryland. If Michael Barnes had been the nominee, I would have used the same phrase to describe him, but the media assumed the phrase was subtle innuendo used to smear the unmarried Mikulski. The press wanted a catfight between Mikulski and me, and they were going to get it, even if they had to help start it themselves. Over the next eight weeks I followed the pattern I had during the primaries, issuing white papers on everything from tax reform to the dredging of Baltimore harbor to Mikulski's record on national defense, but the press coverage—which now included national as well as local media—concentrated almost exclusively on the novelty of two women duking it out to see which one would join the near-ly all-male U.S. Senate and on our very different personal styles.

Mikulski, who grew up solidly middle class, the daughter of a second-gener-ation Polish American grocer, was the homegrown, blue-collar candidate. I was depicted as an outsider—Mexican American in a state where less than 1 percent of the population was Hispanic—and as privileged, patrician even, despite my roots. "It was a far cry from her Bethesda home to the VFW's Star-Spangled Banner Post," noted one profile in the *Post* on my efforts to woo blue-collar voters, as if I rarely rubbed shoulders with anyone outside a country club. In one characterization in the *Baltimore Sun*, I was Cruella De Vil, the evil, dark-haired villainess from the Disney film *101 Dalmatians*. In television commentator Morton Kondracke's words, I was "the Ice Queen"—cold, aloof, out of touch. My negative poll numbers began to rise, from 15 percent nega-tive to 50 percent just before Election Day. Then things got really ugly.

Someone decided to tip off the media about my conversion to Judaism some twenty years earlier. Although it was never possible to prove who it was, I believe it was a Mikulski supporter, if not someone actually in her campaign. Despite signing papers that allowed me to marry my Jewish husband in a synagogue ceremony, I never practiced Judaism and didn't consider myself Jewish. Normally, this is the kind of issue the press would avoid, since it had virtually no relevance to the campaign. I wasn't campaigning as "the Catholic candidate." I didn't list my religious affiliation in my campaign literature and hadn't made an attempt to have myself photographed going to church, for example, as so many candidates have taken to doing in recent years. I hadn't raised my religion in any way during the campaign, though when asked about it directly, I described myself as a Roman Catholic who attended church irregularly. But perhaps because I had switched parties recently or maybe just because it made good copy, the media had a field day with the issue. The first stories appeared in the Jewish press but were quickly picked up by the mainstream media. ABC's *Good Morning America* even tracked down the Denver rabbi who had performed the conversion, Earl Stone, and he—shockingly—appeared on the show to discuss the matter. It is hard to remember a political campaign since President John F. Kennedy's when a candidate's religion was made more of an issue than mine was during my Senate race—while all the groups usually quick to condemn such tactics remained noticeably silent.

I was devastated. I was deeply ashamed of what I had done—not because there is anything wrong in converting from one religion to another but because I had done so out of convenience, not conviction. I felt exposed and alone in a fight I could not win. My children were confused and hurt. One of the younger boys broke down crying when he heard one local news channel ask, "Is Linda Chavez a religious chameleon, first a Catholic, then a Jew, then a Catholic again? Just what does Chavez believe?" It was the only time in the campaign that I cried, too. But, unlike a job that makes you miserable, you can't just quit a campaign. People are counting on you; the volunteers, donors, and voters look up to you. So I decided to take the gloves off for the rest of the campaign.

A few years earlier, Barbara Mikulski had been involved in a mini-scandal involving her decision to hire a self-described Marxist-feminist, Teresa Mary Brennan, in her congressional office—a subject I considered fair game. And despite the furor the issue raised for Mikulski in 1981, five years later she was still on the board of an organization that Brennan directed, which made the issue clearly relevant. With only two weeks to go before the election, I began airing a television commercial about the incident. "The Chavez campaign reminds voters that Mikulski hired Australian Teresa Mary Brennan and endorsed Brennan's philosophy, which was described at the time by other staff members as 'fascist feminism,' 'Marxist,' and 'anti-male,'" the *Washington Post* accurately reported.[6] Indeed Mikulski's staff staged a revolt over the issue in 1981, and about a third of the employees quit when Mikulski announced that she wanted the staff to read Brennan's dissertation and figure out ways to incorporate her theories into the work of the congressional office. The brouhaha became a major story in the Baltimore press that year, and my campaign commercial did nothing more than air clips from *Baltimore Sun* news articles and editorials describing the event, with the tag line, "That's kind of scary, but you can do something about it. Vote Linda Chavez for U.S. Senate." There was no question that the commercial was negative—but it was hardly a personal attack, as Mikulski and others tried to characterize it.

In the final weeks of the campaign, with my own polls predicting I'd barely win 30 percent of the votes, it was tough to remain enthusiastic. The one happy day in the general election campaign was when President Reagan flew to Baltimore to attend a five-hundred-dollar-a-plate fund-raiser for me at the Inner Harbor there. He landed at Fort McHenry, the sight of the battle in the War of 1812 that inspired Francis Scott Key's "Star-Spangled Banner." Chris and I stood on the grass as the president's "Marine One" helicopter touched down and then rode with him in the limousine through the streets of South Baltimore to the Inner Harbor convention center. As a Secret Service agent opened the door, the president pointed out how thick the glass was—it looked about two inches thick—a reminder of the near-fatal attack on his life in 1981. As we drove along, large crowds lined the sidewalks. Reagan never stopped waving to the men and women who had come out to see him, even as he carried on a conversation with Chris and me.

"Watch this," the president said as he caught the eye of a plump, middle-aged woman standing on the side of the road. She leaped off her feet, as light as a gazelle, as the car approached. "It doesn't matter how old they are or how much they weigh, the women always leave the ground if you look right at them," he said, smiling. "It's not me they're seeing. It's the president of the United States. It means a lot to them. They'll be telling their grandchildren about the day they saw the president. I feel I owe it to them. I remember [then Tennessee governor] Lamar Alexander told me he rode with Jimmy Carter in a motorcade when he was president and Carter never looked out the window once, the whole ride. Just ignored all those good people who'd come out to see their president," he said, wistfully.

President Reagan raised more than $400,000 for me with just that one visit, enough to keep my commercials on the air until Election Day, if sparingly aired. All told, I raised nearly $2 million dollars—an unheard of sum in Maryland politics. But Mikulski raised more, some $3 million, making the race the most expensive in Maryland history at that time. When the returns came in, I received a larger share of the votes than the polls predicted, by 10 percent, but it was still only 39 percent of the vote. Mikulski termed her victory a "slam dunk," which it surely was. I had made a respectable showing, winning more votes than any Republican in a statewide race except the liberal Mathias in some sixteen years. But I was a loser, nonetheless—and there's nothing lower in politics. Friends evaporate, phone calls don't get returned, job offers don't materialize. There were exceptions. Senator Orrin Hatch, who had been a stalwart supporter since my days at the Civil Rights Commission, helped me get some consulting work with a firm run by his former administrative assistant, Tom Parry, and a Democrat, Romano Romani, who had worked for Senator Dennis DiConcini from Arizona. But by and large, I was on my own.

The next several months were the nadir of my professional career. The Reagan administration, which under normal circumstances might have proved a refuge for a losing Senate candidate, was preoccupied with its own problems. Shortly after the election, all hell broke loose when it was discovered that my old colleague Ollie North had been involved in a clandestine scheme to raise money for the Contra rebels fighting in Nicaragua, as well as a separate project to sell arms to the Iranian government in order to help free American hostages being held by Iranian-supported terrorists—including a CIA station chief who was tortured and ultimately killed. With no likelihood of finding a suitable appointment in the administration, few options were available, save lobbying, which I had no interest in doing again, no matter how lucrative. National Public Radio hired me to do occasional commentaries, but at $125 apiece, they weren't likely to pay my mortgage, nor was the weekly column I began writing for the *Chicago Sun-Times*, which paid even less. By the spring of 1987, I was desperately looking for work when an old acquaintance gave me a call.

I had known Gerda Bikales for a few years. An immigrant who fled the Holocaust as a young girl, she had helped found an organization called U.S. English, whose cochairman, former Senator S. I. Hayakawa, was a charismatic and colorful figure. The goal of U.S. English was to establish English as the official language of the United States through a constitutional amendment. The group had already succeeded that November in passing a state initiative declaring English the official language of California and was contemplating running initiatives in other states as well. Gerda had decided to leave her post as executive director and wondered if I'd be interested in taking over. I was intrigued and thought the issue was an important one. I'd often spoken and written about the dangers of bilingual education and believed that it was crucial to immigrants that they learn English. However, I knew that as a Hispanic, the role could prove very controversial. I was about to find out just how controversial.

9

How I Became the Most Hated Hispanic in America

I love Spanish traditions, I love the people and the ancestors I hail from, and no one is prouder of his background, but I am prouder still of the ideals and traditions symbolized by the Stars and Stripes, so without apologizing for the past, I insist that in New Mexico the teaching of English should be stressed.

—New Mexico Senator Dennis Chavez

THE IDEA OF PASSING a constitutional amendment to make English the official language of the United States was not something I'd ever given much thought to. In general, I was skeptical of constitutional amendments and had even opposed a popular balanced budget amendment during my Senate campaign because I thought it would unnecessarily clutter the Constitution. I wasn't sure that amending the Constitution to declare English the official language would ever be more than a symbolic act, but I was very concerned about the semi-official status Spanish was acquiring in many parts of the country. As Miami's former mayor Maurice Ferre was fond of saying of his city, "Where else in America can you go from birth to death in Spanish?"[1] In fact, in many places across the country it was possible to attend public school, vote in federal elections, obtain a driver's license, even take a pilot's exam, all in Spanish.

I was especially concerned about the effects of bilingual education on young Hispanics—an issue I'd been involved in since my days at the AFT. In California and elsewhere, Hispanic youngsters were learning to read and write in Spanish instead of English when they entered first grade. Once enrolled in bilingual programs, they could be stuck there for years, sometimes for their entire school lives. Although many of these kids were recent immigrants or the children of immigrants, others were Americans by birth, often third generation or more. A Spanish surname was often enough to trigger placement in a bilingual classroom, something I knew firsthand. My middle son, Pablo Chavez Gersten, was almost placed in a bilingual program in first grade, simply on the basis of his Spanish-sounding name. The letter notifying me that he needed bilingual education—even though he didn't speak a word of Spanish—was written in Spanish as well, and I needed my babysitter, Margarita, to translate it for me.

These kinds of abuses were commonplace, something I'd learned a good deal about when I worked in the Carter administration. A 1977 study of all federally funded Spanish bilingual programs, released when I was working at the Department of Health, Education, and Welfare, showed that about two-thirds of the Hispanic students in bilingual programs could already speak English but were kept in the programs anyway, and the programs themselves were failing to improve the students' performance in math and other basic subjects.[2] Despite such research, the bilingual lobby had become a powerful force in Washington. No one dared take them on for fear of being labeled anti-Hispanic, xenophobic, or even racist. I knew that if I agreed to take the U.S. English job, I would become the most hated Hispanic in America—at least among the organizations that purported to represent the Hispanic community. But I also knew that learning English was the most important thing non-English-speaking Hispanics could do if they wanted to succeed in the United States—and those who were discouraging and, in some cases, preventing them from doing so were the real enemies of Hispanics. I hoped that by becoming president of U.S. English I might elevate the level of debate and give reassurance that there was nothing racist or anti-Hispanic about promoting a common language in this nation of immigrants, where most people had at least one grandparent or great-grandparent for whom English was not the mother tongue.

The U.S. English job seemed the perfect platform from which to wage this fight, but I wanted to make sure there were no hidden problems with the organization itself. I knew Gerda Bikales only slightly and the cochairman of the organization, S. I. Hayakawa, by reputation only. He was a renowned linguistics professor, whose 1941 book, *Language in Thought and Action*, not only was required reading for every English major in the 1950s and 1960s but became a national best-seller. However, he was perhaps best known for his stint as president of San Francisco State College in the late 1960s, where he took on black radicals who occupied college buildings and shut down the campus. Hayakawa became an instant hero in conservative circles when he climbed aboard a sound truck broadcasting protestors' speeches outside the college administration building and, literally, pulled the plug.

I once saw Hayakawa speak while I was still an undergraduate in Boulder. The protesters were able to turn the tables on the diminutive Hayakawa, who sported his trademark plaid tam-o'-shanter when he stepped on stage at Mackey Auditorium. When he tried to speak, dozens of students drowned him out and began throwing the folding chairs from the auditorium floor toward the stage, which drove me—and most of the others who'd come to hear Hayakawa speak—from the room. Like Ronald Reagan, Hayakawa's willingness to take on the radical Left helped propel him into national politics, and in 1976 he was elected U.S. senator from California, retiring after one term. In 1981, Hayakawa introduced a simple constitutional amendment, cosponsored by ten additional senators, declaring: "The English language shall be the official language of the United States. The Congress shall have the power to enforce this article by appropriate legislation."

I didn't know any of the other players at U.S. English, including the founder of the group, John Tanton, an ophthalmologist from Petoskey, on the northern tip of the lower Michigan peninsula. I did, however, learn that Tanton and Bikales were both active in the immigration restriction movement, which gave me some pause. Tanton, who had been the national president of Zero Population Growth in the mid-1970s, had also founded another public policy group, the Federation for American Immigration Reform (FAIR) in 1978, which advocated rigid restriction of legal immigration. Bikales had worked for FAIR before setting up U.S. English in 1983. I wanted to make sure that the board knew that I favored generous immigration, and I wanted to satisfy myself that U.S. English's mission was solely to promote a common language.

In my interview with the board, I found nothing to raise any suspicion and found the board members charming, certainly not nativists. Half of them were immigrants themselves: Hayakawa, though of Japanese ancestry, was Canadian-born; Bikales, a Jew, was born in Germany and came to the United States at sixteen, after fleeing Nazi-occupied Europe; and Leo Sorenson, a business man from Oakland, California, was a Danish immigrant. I accepted the job on condition that I be named president of the organization and given wide latitude on policy matters, and especially that FAIR's interests and U.S. English's be kept entirely separate. I also insisted that I be allowed to continue writing my weekly newspaper column and doing NPR commentaries, without any interference from the board.

U.S. English was just coming off a huge victory in California, having won a vote to amend the state constitution to make English the official language of government by 73 percent, the largest majority ever recorded for a statewide initiative, despite a bitter campaign in which the initiative was denounced as racist by practically every politician in the state, including the Republican governor George Deukmejian. Opponents warned that making English the official language of state government would cause Hispanics to be "disadvantaged, denigrated, and demeaned," in the words of author Norman Cousins, who publicly opposed the measure. They warned that "language police" would try to prevent immigrants from speaking their language in private, deny emergency services to non-English speakers, and force cities like Los Angeles to change their names (L.A. city councilmen Richard Alatorre and Michael Woo introduced a formal resolution to rename the city The Angels to draw attention to their opposition to the initiative). But the public rightly knew these were merely scare tactics and enthusiastically endorsed the initiative, which had required more than a million voters to sign petitions to place the referendum on the ballot. The plan was to build on the California victory by introducing referenda in as many states as possible. By the time I took over, plans were already underway for initiatives in Arizona, Colorado, and Florida, as well as a nonbinding vote on the Republican primary ballot in Texas.

In addition to running an organization whose primary funding came from direct mail solicitations, my main function was to be a public spokesman for the group, which entailed traveling around the country giving speeches, doing television and radio interviews, and engaging in frequent public debates. I soon found that the latter assignment could be hazardous. When I traveled to El Paso to debate Willie Velasquez, the founder of the Southwest Voter Education Project, the sponsors had to provide police escorts throughout my stay. The crowds were large and unruly, with many participants carrying picket signs to protest "English Only," the catchy—but inaccurate—phrase opponents coined to describe U.S. English. I was surprised at the level of animosity I encountered. Even at the height of my opposition to racial quotas, I never encountered anything quite like the visceral hatred I saw on these protestors' faces. It was clear that they viewed me not just as an opponent but as heretic, a traitor. The only time I had ever seen quite that level of hatred manifested was when my UCLA students trashed my car. And though Texas was tough, things got even more out of hand when I was invited to the University of Colorado, my alma mater, to debate the Colorado attorney general, Duane Woodard.

Charles King, a retired Spanish professor on campus and U.S. English supporter, warned me in advance that there could be trouble, so I hired an off-duty policeman to act as a bodyguard. We arrived in the parking lot outside the law school on the lovely campus set up against the Boulder Flatirons, a sandstone outcropping in the Rockies foothills overlooking the city. Students were already gathering to protest my presence, but I slipped by easily, unrecognized.

Woodard was cocky and patronizing. The standing-room-only crowd was certainly on his side, and with TV cameras rolling and newspaper photographers' bulbs flashing, it was a politician's dream. But he didn't know the issue well and was stuck repeating platitudes about tolerance and making outrageous claims about the ambulances that wouldn't show up for injured Spanish-speaking patients, the houses that would burn down for lack of Spanish-speaking fire department dispatchers, and other catastrophes that would befall Hispanics if the initiative passed—none of which were possible since the initiative explicitly allowed exceptions for emergency government services in Spanish to protect safety or health.

When I stood up to speak, the front row of protestors raised their placards so that the TV cameras would catch their images. Their eyes boring into me as I walked to the podium, they looked as if they would tear me to shreds if given the opportunity. Their signs, in Spanish and English, not only attacked "English Only" but me personally. "Tia Taco," one read—a Spanish knock-off of "Uncle Tom" but with the feminine "tia" for aunt. "Malinche," another said, a reference to the Indian woman who betrayed the Aztec emperor Montezuma to Cortez, thus aiding the Spanish conquest of Mexico. I never failed to be amused by the ironies in this little jab, which was frequently invoked in my honor. Malinche was a traitor for helping introduce *Spanish* to Mexico, the same tongue my antagonists now wanted to make a quasi-official language in the United States. I also wondered how many of the protestors even knew the real history of Cortez's conquest. The Spaniard was able to defeat the Aztecs because other Indians in the region joined forces with the foreign conquerors to oppose the cruel reign of the Aztecs, which included ritual human sacrifice, torture, and total subjugation of other tribes.

If they hoped to intimidate me with their tactics, it didn't work, and that seemed to infuriate them all the more. The angrier they got, the cooler I became—setting up a contrast I knew worked to my advantage. But it also struck me as ludicrous that anyone could consider it racist to expect Hispanics to learn English—just as every other group of immigrants in the history of the country had. It wasn't easy for Italians or Germans or Jews or Swedes to learn English either—but they did, or at least their children did once they entered public school. And everyone was better off for it.

"Duane Woodard and I couldn't even be having this debate if we were still speaking the languages of our ancestors," I told the crowd, to boos and hisses, which sounded oddly out of place in the moot-court room where we were debating. "The reason the United States has worked so well as an immigrant-gathering nation is that, once here, immigrants have adopted the common language, embraced the laws and customs of this nation, and become Americans. We could have gone the path of Belgium, or Canada, or Sri Lanka, or dozens of other places around the world where governments literally rise and fall on the issues of language and culture, where the prospect that the country itself might split apart on these issues is very real, where these conflicts can lead to bloodshed and civil war," I said. But my arguments fell on deaf ears in the auditorium. And I'd yet to raise the most contentious issue of all, which was bilingual education. Many of those in the audience weren't university students but bilingual teachers out to defend the program that provided their livelihood. They saw me and U.S. English as a threat to their paychecks.

"If you want to be angry about an organization working to keep Hispanics down," I taunted, "forget about U.S. English. The organization that has done more to harm Hispanics than any other is the National Association for Bilingual Education. Hispanic youngsters enter school in first grade and are shunted into bilingual education programs where they languish, not for a few months, or even a year or two, but year after year. They don't learn English well, and they don't learn much else either. But their teachers still earn an extra $5,000 stipend in some states."[3]

I was deliberately provoking the audience, and I knew it. However, the people I was trying to reach were in their homes watching the debate, not in this room of radical Latinos. Polls showed that almost 90 percent of Americans favored a constitutional amendment to make English the official language of government—in fact, most people presumed it already was. And polls in Colorado, where the initiative was struggling to get on the ballot, showed that if we could gather the signatures and survive a predictable court challenge, we'd win overwhelmingly. The Mexican American protestors, with their rude behavior and insulting signs, were helping win voters to my side and hurting the image of Latinos everywhere by giving the impression that they didn't believe Latinos could or should learn English. By the time the debate was over, the demonstrators were at a fever pitch and my six-foot-six Mexican American bodyguard had to whisk me from the room to his waiting car. "You know, I agreed with every word you said in there," he told me as he drove me back to my hotel. "These radical Chicanos don't speak for our community."

If the effort to make English the official language was controversial in Colorado, it became really ugly in Arizona. Not only were the opponents well organized, enlisting the help of Republican Senator John McCain as well as Democrat Dennis DiConcini, but they raised the money to mount an effective media campaign against the referendum. And their tactics were unscrupulous at best. One television ad featured pictures showing "Official English" signs and a voice warning, "It always begins like this. . . ." Slowly the images on the screen transmogrified, first into pictures of Senator Joseph McCarthy, then Adolf Hitler, and finally into concentration camp victims being led into the gas chambers. How could anyone suggest that requiring government to operate in English was equivalent to the slaughter of six million Jews? I could barely believe my eyes when I saw the ad the first time, but the tactic was effective, eroding support for the initiative so that it barely won on Election Day with 51 percent of the vote.[4]

The Colorado initiative won by a much healthier 61 percent, and the Florida initiative won by a whopping 83 percent of the vote, despite a last minute court challenge that tried to invalidate the petitions that put the measure on the ballot because they hadn't been circulated in *Spanish*. However, by the time ballots were cast, I had resigned as president of U.S. English, as had most of the high-profile members of the advisory board, including Walter Cronkite, Alistair Cooke, and Jacques Barzun, in what became a true crisis for the organization.

The rift began when I received a phone call from a reporter, James Crawford, who had previously worked for *Education Week*, a respected Washington-based journal, but who had recently been doing freelance writing, much of it in support of bilingual education. I didn't trust Crawford—he'd always seemed more of an advocate than a straight journalist.

"Have you seen a memo from John Tanton to something called the Witan Group?" Crawford asked me when he reached me at my Bethesda home.

"I don't know. What does it say?" I asked. I was vaguely familiar with Tanton's "Witan Group," named for some ancient Scandinavian council of wise elders. It was vintage Tanton, who was a very bright and committed man but also naive in the ways of the political world. Living in a small town in northern Michigan, Tanton always seemed to me physically isolated and socially aloof. I'd been a guest in his home once soon after I joined U.S. English and had long conversations with him as he walked me around his property showing me his apiary, which produced the honey he often gave as gifts. It was almost as if he were trying to get into my brain: What books did I read? Did I believe that one's views on one set of issues, say foreign policy, affected how one viewed other issues? Had I ever read Jean-Jacques Rousseau? What did I think of the idea of the "social contract"? What did I think of Thomas Sowell's book *A Conflict of Visions*? Did I have a "constrained" or an "unconstrained" vision in Sowell's terms? I felt he was testing my knowledge as well as my views.

His pale blue eyes never registered any expression as I patiently answered each question. He seemed emotionally flat—there was an almost total lack of affect, which made me somewhat uncomfortable. Still, I never sensed any prejudice in him, or much passion either, despite his obvious commitment to the issues he had spent a lifetime working on: preserving the environment and controlling population.

I was stunned when Crawford started reading from Tanton's memo.

"'Will Latin American migrants bring with them the tradition of the *mordi-da* (bribe), the lack of involvement in public affairs, etc.?'" Crawford read, savoring every word of the clearly damning document.

"It gets better," he said. "'Can *homo contraceptivus* compete with *homo prog-enitiva* if borders aren't controlled? Or is advice to limit one's family simply advice to move over and let someone else with greater reproductive powers occupy the space?'"

The arrogance of it was stunning, made almost ridiculous by Tanton's Latinate phrases. Then Crawford delivered the final blow.

"'[T]his is the first instance in which those with their pants up are going to get caught by those with their pants down!'" Crawford read. "So what do you think?"

"It's pretty disgusting," I said. "And I certainly never saw the document or heard any reference to it in the organization. When did you say it was written?" I asked, trying to compose myself. I regarded Crawford as a snake in the grass, so I wanted to be careful not to say too much yet, at least until I checked it out.

"The date on it says October 10, 1986," Crawford replied.

"That's almost a year before I was hired," I said. "I don't want to comment any further. I want to think about this and decide what to do."

By the time I hung up the phone, however, I knew there was only one choice. I had to resign. My own reputation was on the line. For months I had been battling wild-eyed protestors who claimed I was a sellout, a traitor to "my" people, a self-hating Hispanic who wanted to hurt my own community. I knew their allegations were untrue—I had absolutely no qualms about the policies I was promoting. I firmly believed that learning English was the only way to succeed in America—that it was the key to opportunity. My conscience was clear. But how could I continue to represent an organization whose founder and cochairman harbored such unsavory views and was so foolish as to commit them to paper? His statements were not only anti-Hispanic but anti-Catholic. He seemed obsessed by higher birthrates among Catholic immigrants, perhaps from his days as head of Planned Parenthood.

I called for an emergency board meeting in Washington to discuss the organization's future, but in the interim I learned even more disturbing news about the umbrella organization, U.S. Inc., controlled by Tanton, through which

U.S. English funds flowed. I discovered that U.S. Inc. had received donations from a foundation that had contributed to eugenics research and advocated forced sterilizations—views I considered beyond the pale. I also learned that Tanton's group had reprinted a book called *Camp of the Saints*, written by French author Jean Raspail, with which I was very familiar, having written a review of the book years earlier for *New America*. I considered the book one of the most foul, racist diatribes I had ever read, a paranoid fantasy about brown hordes from India and elsewhere who were taking over the world.

I quit my job a couple of days later, having no idea what I would do next. Rather than praising my decision, most of the Hispanic leaders I'd been debating over the previous months managed to use it to attack me further. "Here she was, the consummate planner," *Los Angeles Times* reporter Lee May wrote of my decision, "who in an uncharacteristically hasty move had resigned as president of U.S. English, a group Latinos deplore, and the best thing her Latino critics had to say about her was that she may have made the right move for the wrong reasons and that she'd waited too long to make it anyway."[5] "It's interesting that it took her 14 months to find out what we've told her all along," Marta Jimenez, a young attorney for the Mexican American Legal Defense and Education Fund, told May.

Jimenez and company were angry because I would not back down from my support for the initiatives or for the importance of maintaining English as the nation's common, unifying language. "It would be incorrect to assume that because I've stepped down from the organization that I have changed my views about a common language," I told May. Tanton resigned as chairman of U.S. English as well, realizing that his memo had greatly damaged the organization. I don't believe he ever understood how hurtful his words were, however. Although he claimed that the memo was merely an intellectual exercise "to work out the impact" of immigration on the future of the country, it stung me deeply.

Back at home full-time for the first time since the end of my Senate campaign, I took stock of what I really wanted to do with my life, perhaps for the first time ever. I had made many of my career decisions because opportunities fell into my lap—or because other people thought a particular job suited me— and they hadn't all turned out as I would have liked. Now it was time for me to think about what I wanted to do, what was important to me, what would give me satisfaction, as well as allow me to make a contribution. As a little girl, I'd always told people that I wanted to be a writer someday. Although writing had been an important part of many of the jobs I'd held, I'd never really tried to make a living at it. I decided I would write a book—if I could find a publisher and a way to support myself in the process. It struck me that my experience the previous year as I traveled around the country arguing that Hispanics should follow the same model as other immigrant groups had—learn English, stay in school, move into the social and political mainstream—was a message that wasn't being delivered, at least not by many Hispanic leaders, who were much more interested in portraying Hispanics as permanently disadvantaged victims of a racist society. "Each decade offered us hope, but our hopes evaporated," moaned my old boss Raul Yzaguirre, now president of the National Council of La Raza, one of the country's leading Hispanic civil rights groups. "We became the poorest of the poor, the most segregated minority in schools, the lowest paid group in America, and the least educated minority in the nation."[6] It was a common refrain, but one that simply didn't jibe with what I'd been seeing around the country. One incident in particular stuck out.

A few months earlier, while I was still at U.S. English, I'd been invited to Stanford University to debate Arnold Torres, the former executive director of the League of United Latin American Citizens (LULAC), the nation's oldest Hispanic civil rights group. Torres, whom I'd known for years and who had recently taken to calling himself "Arnoldo," took the podium first. Slamming his fist down, he shouted to approving applause of the mostly Mexican American students gathered in the auditorium: "We cannot assimilate—and we won't!" It was a preposterous statement on its face. Here we were, two Mexican Americans, both highly educated and affluent, debating—in English—at one of the premier universities in the world before an audience made up almost entirely of young Latinos. Sitting on the stage with us were four other Latinos: a Pulitzer Prize–winning *Los Angeles Times* reporter, a tenured member of the Stanford faculty, an assistant to the Republican governor, and an assistant to the Democratic leadership in the state legislature. Who was kidding whom? We were about as assimilated as it gets, and the kids that were cheering Torres on were well on their way to becoming investment bankers, engineers, college professors, and lawyers with fancy homes in the suburbs.

I decided that this was a story that had to be told and began research for my book, *Out of the Barrio: Toward a New Politics of Hispanic Assimilation.* I sold the idea to a small, free-market think tank in New York, the Manhattan Institute, and spent the next two years researching and writing the book, which was finally published by Basic Books in the fall of 1991. I worked on the book full-time at my home in Bethesda, which proved to be a real luxury. My two younger boys, Pablo and Rudy, were twelve and ten, respectively, when I started the project, and in their teens when I finished, allowing me to spend important time with them each day when they came home from school. My sons would get off the school bus in our cul de sac and head for my office on the first floor, where they'd plop their book bags down and join the family dogs—two standard poodles and a shih tzu—on the couch in my office. Our house became the gathering point for kids in the neighborhood. It was a part of mothering I'd missed out on with my oldest son David, who was already a student at the University of Maryland. For practically the first time in my married life, I could cook dinner and have it ready to serve when Chris got home. My time was now my own—and my family's.

Life didn't remain peaceful for long, however. I had expected a strong reaction when *Out of the Barrio* came out—after all I was challenging the reigning orthodoxy about Hispanics in the United States—but it was even more critical than I had anticipated. I had culled existing research and hired two old colleagues from my Civil Rights Commission days, economists Finis Welch and Nabeel Alsalam, to analyze Current Population Survey data. I'd found that, contrary to popular opinion, Hispanics, especially Mexican Americans, were following in the footsteps of virtually every immigrant group. They were learning English; most third-generation Mexican Americans, for example, could no longer speak Spanish. Like Greeks, Germans, and Italians before them, they had abandoned their mother tongue within two generations of coming to America. Young Mexican Americans were graduating from high school at only slightly lower rates than non-Hispanic whites. Their earnings were about 80 percent of those of non-Hispanic whites, and if adjusted for years of schooling and experience, hours worked, and region of residence, the difference was even less. On virtually every indicator, Hispanics who were born in the United States were doing well, with one exception: Among Puerto Ricans, especially those living in the Northeast, there was a large and growing underclass of unemployed men and women, characterized by single female-headed households, children born out of wedlock, and heavy welfare dependence. Immigrants, too, were on the lower rungs of the economic ladder, but there was substantial evidence to suggest that they wouldn't stay there long. Mexican men were even more likely than non-Hispanic whites to be in the labor force, for example, and though their education levels were abysmally low—six years on average—their earnings caught up with those of their American-born co-ethnics in about fifteen to twenty years and eventually surpassed them.

The Mexican American groups that might have found something to cheer about in my findings largely ignored them, preferring to stick with their laments about how downtrodden Mexican Americans were and how much government assistance they needed. Many Puerto Ricans, on the other hand, responded with outrage to what I'd written in my chapter on "The Puerto Rican Exception." Although I'd made it clear that the Puerto Rican population was by no means monolithic and that there was a large Puerto Rican middle class, made up primarily of married couples and their children, I also drew attention to an uncomfortable fact that many Hispanic advocates wanted to ignore. The large portion of unmarried Puerto Rican women who were giving birth, almost 53 percent in 1987, had become more or less permanently dependent on welfare and threatened to create a permanently disadvantaged underclass. Some 41 percent of Puerto Rican women on welfare were second-generation participants, and the average stay on welfare exceeded seven and a half years. "So long as significant numbers of young Puerto Rican men remain alienated from the work force, living by means of crime or charity, fathering children toward whom they feel no responsibility, the prospects of Puerto Ricans in the United States will dim," I wrote. "So long as so many Puerto Rican women allow the men who father their babies to avoid the duties of marriage and parenthood, they will deny their children the promise of a better life. The solution to these problems will not be found in more government programs. Indeed, government has been an accomplice in enabling fathers to abandon their responsibility. Only the Puerto Rican community can save itself, but the healing cannot begin until the community recognizes that many of its deadliest wounds are self-inflicted."[7]

These were strong words, and they sometimes provoked violent responses. When Angelo Falcon, executive director of the Institute for Puerto Rican Policy, invited me to participate in a panel discussion on my book with several Puerto Rican commentators, a large group of protestors gathered on the Manhattan streets below the group's offices. Even several stories up, I could hear their chants throughout my presentation, and if Falcon had not stationed guards at the door of the meeting, they no doubt would have stormed the premises. A few weeks later, a group of Puerto Rican professors from a small community college in the South Bronx invited me to speak to faculty and selected students, but when word spread that I was coming, things got ugly. I arrived with my host at the Hostos Community College campus to see New York Police Department barricades and what seemed like a crowd of about a hundred or more very angry protestors. As I walked toward the building where I was to speak, some picketers tried to hit me with their large cardboard signs, many of them the same ones I'd seen earlier at my visit to Falcon's group. The placards bore ugly caricatures of me in the guise of what at first appeared to be a bee or spider. Only later did I realize that they were supposed to be wasps, or more accurately, that I was being depicted as a WASP.

When I arrived in the holding room outside the auditorium, the president of Hostos College confronted me angrily.

"If you insist on speaking, I can't guarantee your safety," he said.

I was dumbfounded. "But *you* invited *me*—or at least members of your faculty did," I said. "Now you're acting as if I'm some kind of interloper." I could hear the noise from the auditorium, students shouting, chanting, hooting. It sounded more like a raucous pep rally before the big game with a hated rival school than students waiting to hear a guest speaker. The president went back into the auditorium and returned a few minutes later.

"The guards say some of the students have eggs and tomatoes. They might throw them," he said. Again I was incredulous. If they saw them, why didn't they confiscate them? I looked at my host, a very nice professor in the business department. "What should I do?" I asked.

"I think we should reschedule when things calm down," he advised. We left the room, hoping to get out of the building before the crowd found out, but by the time we emerged from the elevator, a mob had already gathered. The police didn't seem willing to step into the fray, so my host and I made our way toward his parked car, accompanied only by a couple of other teachers. Suddenly, a man of about forty stepped out of the crowd. I could see his fist coming toward me out of the periphery of my eye, but I kept moving. Luckily it landed on my shoulder, not my jaw where it was probably aimed. Not knowing what to do, I just kept walking, hoping I'd make it to the waiting car in one piece. When I got back to my hotel room, shaken and angry, I discovered a large bruise forming on my upper arm. I felt lucky it was only a bruise. I called home to speak to Chris, almost in tears. I couldn't keep taking risks like this, I told him. It wasn't fair to him or the kids. But I didn't want to back down either. If I didn't write and speak the truth on these issues, who would? I had an obligation not to be intimidated.

Bill Hammett, president of the Manhattan Institute, had a different reaction when I told him what happened. "You're crazy, Linda. You're like one of those test pilots. I think you've got an extra chromosome somewhere," he said. "You thrive on the excitement." And maybe I did. I was, after all, my father's daughter.

Over the years, I had several similar incidents, never so violent, but disruptive nonetheless. The University of Northern Colorado invited me to be a commencement speaker, but when Latino and black students on campus staged sit-ins in the president's office, he rescinded the invitation and apologized for inviting me in the first place, calling the invitation "uninformed" and "grossly insensitive."[8] The brouhaha resulted in front-page coverage in the

Denver newspapers and on television and a major debate in the state legislature, with Republican lawmakers threatening to cut the school's funding over the incident. I showed up at the commencement anyway and handed out copies of the Constitution to the graduating class.

Meanwhile, the National Association of Scholars, a group of college professors who were fighting to maintain academic standards and oppose the kind of censorship I'd encountered, invited me to speak at CU in Boulder when UNC shut me out. Feeling the heat from left-wing professors and students on campus, the Boulder administration turned over the university quadrangle the day of the event to protestors so they could harangue my appearance to their hearts' content. The publicity turned out a standing-room-only crowd, which filled the Old Main auditorium to the rafters, giving me far more of an audience than I ever would have had without a protest. It was the same pattern everywhere I appeared.

The more fuss my critics raised, the bigger my audience. But there were hazards as well. I sometimes faced truly nasty crowds. At the University of Illinois, Urbana-Champagne, where I debated affirmative action with syndicated columnist Clarence Page, a group of protestors, some in full gang regalia with red bandanas and baggy pants, looked as if they'd been bused in from Chicago, miles away. "During the debate, her detractors marched in carrying signs, banners and a Mexican flag," *U.S. News and World Report* columnist John Leo wrote. "Earlier at a campus bookstore, according to the *Daily Illini*, an egg and copies of her book *Out of the Barrio* were thrown and coconuts were placed on a table where she was signing books. This was to indicate that she offends Latinos by being 'brown on the outside, white on the inside,'" he wrote.[9] But what always surprised me was how little any of the protesting students seemed to know about me, except what they'd been told. Before I began my lectures or debates, I took to asking students to raise their hands if they had actually read anything I'd written. Few had—but they were absolutely convinced that I was dangerous anyway. "We see her as a sellout. She only uses her surname for self-advantage. She doesn't believe in Hispanics or her heritage," one student complained.

And it wasn't just uninformed students who saw me as the enemy. In a 1992 cover story, *Hispanic* magazine asked, "Who Is Linda Chavez and Why Does She Make People Furious?" Although the article—"a close-up look at the woman everyone loves to hate"—was generally fair, it questioned whether I was an "opportunistic politician? Affirmative action traitor? English only heretic? A racist? A token? She's been called all these things and more," the article went on, "and to some, just the mention of her name causes the blood to boil."[10] The article was replete with quotes from my critics, who called me everything from "the most hated U.S. Hispanic," to a "neo-conservative who is having an inner conflict with herself." My old boss Raul Yzaguirre had the most positive comments, and even they were a left-handed compliment: "I think Linda is very smart and very photogenic, but she doesn't have the typical Hispanic background and she has made a career of being different."

The Manhattan Institute proved to be a very comfortable base from which I could continue to write and speak on issues I cared about. Although I worked in an office in my Bethesda home for the entire time I was with the institute, being affiliated with a "think tank" meant that I could bounce ideas off of other Manhattan Institute fellows and participate in seminars or attend book luncheons in New York for authors of serious public policy books, an activity Manhattan Institute specialized in, providing the kind of intellectual stimulation and camaraderie one might hope to find at a university.

But after six years, I was anxious to run my own shop. I missed not only doing my own research and writing but also directing the research and writing of others, as I had at the Civil Rights Commission. I began exploring whether I could raise the funds to open my own small think tank—one devoted exclusively to issues of race, ethnicity, language, and assimilation. There was nothing like it on the Right, although the Joint Center for Political Studies and a few others existed on the Left. The late William Simon, former Secretary of the Treasury under President Nixon and the chairman of the John M. Olin Foundation, and Olin's executive director, Jim Piereson, encouraged me to strike out on my own, as did others. I told Manhattan Institute chairman Roger Hertog what I was planning on doing, and he generously allowed me to stay on the Manhattan Institute payroll for a few months while I put the pieces together to open my own offices and hire staff. John J. Miller, a talented young writer who had been my assistant at the Manhattan Institute since 1992, agreed to come with me as the new vice president of the Center for Equal Opportunity, as we dubbed the new organization. On January 1, 1995, we were in business on our own.

Ever since my Civil Rights Commission days, I had been interested in learning what effect affirmative action programs had on academic standards at colleges and universities. The commission had authorized a study of the issue on my recommendation in 1984 but abandoned it after I left. Now that I headed my own research group, I turned to the topic once again. Having spent several years debating affirmative action on college campuses, I knew that the topic was one on which opinions were firmly held—on both sides—but also one on which empirical evidence to back up those opinions was paltry at best.

Proponents of affirmative action argued that the minority students who were admitted to colleges and universities through affirmative action programs were fully qualified to be there and that their presence enhanced the educational experience for everyone. Opponents argued that affirmative action admittees were substantially less qualified than other students and that the universities' double standards harmed everyone, nonminority and minority students alike. I agreed with the latter camp's views, but I wanted to see if the evidence justified my position.

Almost as soon as we opened our door for business, CEO began collecting the data to test these hypotheses. Using freedom of information laws in the various states, we worked through a network of contacts with individuals and other organizations—usually local chapters of the National Association of Scholars—to solicit admissions data from public colleges and universities. Over the course of the next six years, we gathered, analyzed—with the help of two outside social scientists, Robert Lerner and Althea Nagai—and published our findings on forty-seven public colleges and universities, six medical schools, and three law schools in a total of eleven states.

Our studies were the most extensive and comprehensive ever done on this subject. As I suspected, not only were colleges and universities across the board applying double standards in admitting blacks and, to a lesser extent, Hispanics, but in the most prestigious institutions, the disparities were very large. At the University of California at Berkeley, black students had combined SAT scores that were 330 points lower than whites or Asians, and a similar pattern emerged at the University of Michigan at Ann Arbor, the University of Virginia, the University of North Carolina, and dozens of others. And for the most part, black and Hispanic students also had lower grade point averages than whites or Asians as well.

Not surprisingly, black and Hispanic students who were admitted with lower grades and test scores also graduated at much lower rates than whites or Asians. I was all too familiar with the problems these students encountered, having taught in affirmative action programs at UCLA and the University of Colorado. Although the law didn't allow us to collect data to enable us to see whether students admitted through affirmative action programs performed less well in school or concentrated on less challenging fields of study, we challenged the colleges and universities we studied to undertake such studies themselves. None took us up on the suggestion, I suspect because they didn't want to know the answers to the questions. Furthermore, disparities continued in postgraduate education, with wide differences in the average qualifications of black medical and law students and their white and Asian counterparts, and—as with undergraduate admissions—somewhat smaller discrepancies between Latino students and their white and Asian counterparts.

My interest in affirmative action programs had always been more than academic, however. I believed that affirmative action in higher education had actually helped sweep under the rug the evidence of wide disparities in educational opportunities available between white and black students, especially among the poor. Black students, on average, read at about an eighth-grade level when they graduate from high school, according to studies by the National Assessment of Education Progress.[11] To pretend that such students can compete with those who are much better prepared is unfair to everyone, not least to the black and Hispanic students who are the intended beneficiaries of affirmative action. There are no easy answers in how best to close the enormous skills gap that exists between whites and Asians, on one hand, and blacks and Hispanics, on the other. Providing vouchers to poor students or tax credits to their parents to help defray the cost of private or parochial schools would certainly help some students escape from poorly performing public schools. And improving the quality of public education by insisting on tougher academic standards would help, too. But there is little evidence that instituting double standards so that minority students can get into college will have any positive effect on closing the gap.

CEO also took on the issue of bilingual education, another issue dear to my heart. As with affirmative action, bilingual programs intended to help Hispanic students were clearly harming them. For more than thirty years, bilingual education experts argued that the best way to teach children English was to teach them to speak, read, and write Spanish first. The most radical proponents argued that children needed to spend anywhere from six to eight years in Spanish bilingual programs before they were ready to learn English—a notion that defies not only common sense but decades of experience with other immigrant groups, who quickly learned English once they came to the United States. The result of bilingual education had been years of failure, with Hispanic children falling farther and farther behind in school. I was committed to help change the bilingual education system through every means I could.

CEO staff began analyzing bilingual programs around the country and writing op-eds and magazine articles to publicize our findings. We published a *Parents' Guide*, in both Spanish and English, which gave parents of children in bilingual programs in several states practical information on how to remove their children from failing programs. We also published a *Teachers' Guide to English Immersion*, which provided specific information on how to set up an alternative program using English as the language of instruction for immigrant and non-English-speaking kids. This effort was especially important after voters in both California and Arizona adopted state constitutional amendments in 1998 and 2000, respectively, that eliminated bilingual education programs in favor of English immersion programs that would teach children English as soon as they entered school.

The English immersion program has been an enormous success, with children rapidly increasing their standardized test scores by double digits in reading, writing, and other subjects after years of falling scores. CEO also worked with Capitol Hill and the executive branch to try to rein in the worst excesses of federal policy, which still treats Hispanic children differently from all others, assuming that they can't learn English unless they're taught in Spanish for several years. CEO also helped students stuck in bilingual programs file suit against school districts that kept them there, including one African American student in Oakland who was involuntarily kept in a Chinese bilingual program against his father's wishes and despite not speaking a word of Chinese.

Meanwhile, I continued to write on this issue extensively and to debate it whenever asked, though increasingly my antagonists seemed to have wised up and abandoned their noisy protests, preferring instead to block invitations or simply encourage students to stay away. At one school where I was invited to lecture on my book, organizers found to their dismay that the campus Latino student association scheduled a pizza party at the same time I was scheduled to speak. To add insult to injury, a group of Latino professors on campus made attendance at the party mandatory for their classes, which deprived me of most of my audience. It was a far more effective strategy than throwing books or coconuts.

I was very content at CEO. I could take on new issues whenever I chose, and my ability to influence public policy was limited only by how difficult it was to raise funds for such a controversial enterprise. Most of the money for the organization came from a handful of foundations and individuals—with most corporate donors avoiding us entirely. Fortune 500 companies were happy to buy off critics like Jesse Jackson, making huge donations to left-wing projects and organizations as a form of protection money, but they wouldn't consider donating to an organization that preached color-blind equal opportunity and wanted to help immigrant children learn English.

Despite perennial fund-raising woes, I enjoyed the collegial atmosphere of working with people who shared not only my views but my passion on the issues. John Miller left after a couple of years to return to journalism, as political reporter for *National Review* magazine. But over the years I had recruited a committed and talented group to work with me, including my general counsel Roger Clegg, who had served as a deputy assistant attorney general in both the Reagan and Bush administrations, and my oldest son David, now married with a child, who had quit a better-paying job in the computer industry to come to work for me when Miller left.

The freedom of running my own organization opened up other possibilities as well. In 1998, Chris and I decided to leave the Washington suburbs and move to the country—something we had often thought about doing but couldn't accomplish until our children were all out of the house. We bought a log cabin on nine acres in rural Loudoun County, Virginia, sixty miles west of Washington, and I commuted into the CEO office only one or two days a week, working from home the rest of the time, a luxury made possible by the telecommunications revolution and the Internet. Then on May 30, 2000, another miracle of the Internet changed my life forever.

I was sitting at my desk in my CEO office in downtown Washington, just a couple of blocks from the White House, when I opened an e-mail that had been forwarded to me internally by Jorge Amselle on the CEO staff. I often received fan mail—along with occasional hate mail—through CEO's web site, and Jorge went through it first, forwarding anything that required my personal attention. I read the note through once, without fully comprehending it.

"Dear Linda," it began. The familiarity wasn't unusual, even from total strangers, who felt as if they knew me because they'd seen me on television over the years.

"I am sorry to be writing to you at work, but my mother, Cecily Little Chavez (now Toet) is ill. It would mean a lot to her to hear from you. She moved back to Australia in 1970 and remarried in approximately 1972.

"About four years ago I moved to New Zealand with my husband—we are retired and enjoying life in New Zealand. Mum has been diagnosed with Alzheimer's—and she is in the early stages of the disease, but one never knows how long she will remain so."

Funny, I thought, this woman's mother has the same name as my father's first wife.

"This is not at all how I intended to communicate with you and if you would please send me your personal email address, I will direct further correspondence there," the note went on. "I would very much like to be in contact with you. I can be reached at the address listed below." It was signed simply, "Fond regards from your sister Pamela."

I started shaking uncontrollably. It hit me that this was no mere anonymous woman asking me to write her ailing mother, but my own sister, whom I had not seen or heard from in forty-seven years. I reached for the phone and called Chris, sobbing. "You won't believe what's just happened," I said, and then quickly added, "It's a good thing, nothing bad," realizing that I sounded almost hysterical.

"I've found my sister. I've found Pamela. Or, rather, she's found me."

In fact, she had found out where I was in 1994 but had hesitated to contact me. She had discovered what had happened to me when she went to her adoptive mother's funeral, her adoptive father having died a few years earlier. As chance would have it, Cecily was back in the States visiting Pamela, and both of them flew to Clovis to attend the funeral. Afterward, Pamela was talking to family friends when she commented casually, "I wonder if anyone knows how to find my sister Linda."

"Find her?" the family friend seemed puzzled. "She's in the newspaper all the time—and on television," he said. They told her about my career, which everyone in their small circle of friends had followed over the years. When she and Cecily got back to their hotel room that evening, they turned on CNN.

"There you were. We couldn't believe it. We laughed, we cried. It was a miracle. I think I was just looking for this regular girl who was my sister, and it was a shock to find you a little less than regular—you're famous!" she wrote. But it was also a little intimidating, she said, so instead of immediately reaching out, she followed me from afar, searching Nexis for stories by and about me, surfing the cable news shows hoping to see me. It was Cecily's diagnosis that finally prompted her to write me.

Over the next several weeks, Pamela and I e-mailed back and forth everyday, sometimes more than once a day. And together we tried to piece together what we could of our mysterious childhoods. It was a process that raised as many questions as it answered. I learned that Pamela was my younger sister by only seven and a half months, even though she was my father's daughter from his first marriage. I learned that my father's sister Irene had tried to adopt Pamela, but that Cecily wouldn't allow it, and that Irene had stayed in contact with Pamela for a few years, until her adoptive parents cut it off. I learned that Pamela's life had eerily mirrored my own in ways that seemed to go way beyond coincidence.

She was raised in Clovis, New Mexico, by a successful attorney and his schoolteacher wife, but she continued to see Cecily each summer as she was growing up, until Cecily returned to Australia. She went to college and graduate school in Denver, while I was at school in Boulder, and then became a probation officer for the city. For a time, she lived only a few blocks from my parents' house. Pamela even knew where my parents lived—but was terrified of meeting our father, whom she had almost no memory of and about whom she had heard only terrible things. She had no idea how much he loved her or how painful it was for him to give her up. I described to her how I would sometimes find him crying alone at night, clutching her photograph, and I remembered that he kept her pictures and a newspaper article about her in a trunk in the bedroom.

When my father died, my mother had told me that Pamela was married to a man who knew nothing about her mixed ethnic background and that she had several children, but I learned that none of it was true. Pamela had remained childless. She had married an orthodox Jew in Denver and converted to Judaism, studying for a while with a rabbi at Temple Emmanuel, where Chris and I were married. She had kept a kosher home for several years, but when she and her husband divorced, she gave up Judaism. She married again, this time to a divorced Catholic, and they have remained married ever since. Pamela, like me, left Colorado and moved to Los Angeles—and ended up at UCLA, where I had also been a student, missing her by a couple of years. Both of us ended up with careers tangentially related to law, she working for a law firm and I working on civil rights law in various capacities over the years. We were both active in politics as well. Pamela had worked on former Colorado Congresswoman Pat Schroeder's first congressional campaign, while I had become one of Schroeder's chief critics and a frequent television sparring partner.

Pamela sent me photographs of herself, her mother Cecily, and our father, taken when he was stationed in Sydney during World War II. The childhood pictures of Pamela looked just as I remembered her—beautiful, blond, and blue-eyed. It was always a sore point with my mother that Pamela resembled her more than I did. She has told me over and over of the time she came to pick us up from the babysitter when we were still infants. "They had Pamela all decked out, and there you were, filthy, in dirty diapers, like they thought you were the maid's daughter or something. I guess they thought she belonged to me," she said, the anger fresh each time she told the story. "I grabbed you and walked out of there and never took you back to that place again." My mother was far more sensitive to the ethnic prejudice and slights of others toward my father and me than we were ourselves, and she seemed to resent Pamela for not having to put up with such bigotry. In the pictures of Pamela with her husband, Gil Guard, the family resemblance is clear; we even have the same haircut. As she put it in one e-mail, "we look very alike; I am the fair version, you are the dark version of the same person."

In August, Pamela came to visit from New Zealand, along with Gil. It was as if we had been apart for only a few years, like any adult sisters. There was an instant familiarity built on shared memories as well as blood. With my half-brother Michael's death in 1997 from liver disease and the deaths decades earlier of my half-brother Dickie and my sister Wendy, Pamela was now my only sibling, and I hers. Suddenly, we were family again.

10

Caught in the Media Crosshairs

People love it when you lose
They love dirty laundry

—Don Henley

FAMILY WAS MUCH ON MY MIND when I arrived back in Washington on January 2, 2001, fresh from the announcement of my nomination earlier that day to be secretary of labor. I flew back to Dulles Airport on a private jet with Vice President-elect Dick Cheney and my fellow nominees Norm Mineta and Spence Abraham. Chris, my son Pablo, his wife Bella, and daughter Abby were waiting for me on the tarmac with two dozen roses. When we got home, the house was filled with bouquets of flowers and telegrams sent by family, friends, and well-wishers. I was overwhelmed. It didn't seem quite real. Everything had happened so fast, and I had the feeling that my life would never be the same. It was what I had always wanted, I told myself—to be in the cabinet—but it meant a tremendous upheaval in my life. I would lose my cherished privacy. I'd have no free time. No longer would I be my own boss. When I spoke, my words would carry far more weight—but added responsibility. My words would now represent the president's views, not just my own. And I would have to move back into Washington. Although I'd have a car and driver, I couldn't very well commute the hour and a half each way every day, not with the kind of hours I'd be keeping. I would also have difficulty supporting two households on my new government salary, so I might have to give up my precious log cabin and land. But I had very little time to think about any of this because I knew the next few weeks would be critical. I was about to face the fight of my life—one that would make my Senate campaign seem like a cakewalk.

"I can't believe you're doing this," my old assistant and friend Nancy told me as she helped fill out the financial disclosure forms needed for my nomination to move forward, the following day in my office. "You know they're going to go after you."

Who "they" were was unspecified—but I had enough enemies that it could be almost anyone. I expected that the civil rights groups would be my most ardent antagonists, and I prepared to counter their attacks. They had a real stake in the Labor Department because it administered the program for federal contractors, the single biggest affirmative action program in the country. Hispanic groups would probably be more circumspect. Though they, too, were wedded to affirmative action programs, their commitment wasn't as deep in part because a smaller proportion of Hispanic workers benefited from affirmative action. Many Hispanic leaders still deeply resented my role in U.S. English and some disliked me personally, but others would likely not want to antagonize one of the new administration's most powerful Hispanics. I expected them to determine which way the wind was blowing. If it looked as if I'd be confirmed with only nominal opposition, they'd hold their fire. If it looked like I might go down, they would pile on. I hadn't heard much from the feminists, but of all the groups, the feminists disliked me most viscerally. And then there was the labor movement. John Sweeney was not cut out from the same mold as George Meany, much less Al Shanker. Unlike the old guard, Sweeney had made common cause with the Left within the labor movement, embracing affirmative action, comparable worth, and gay rights, which surely must have caused Meany to roll over in his grave. Given my affinity for the old leadership of the labor unions, Sweeney would have viewed me suspiciously even if I'd still been working for the AFT, which had opposed his election as AFL-CIO president. In any case, I'd left the union movement almost twenty years earlier, and he no doubt regarded me as a traitor for working for Republicans. I expected Sweeney and his cohorts to be genuinely worried about my becoming secretary of labor and to oppose my nomination with as much force as they could muster.

It didn't take long for my opponents to begin their offensive. Sweeney called Bush's decision to nominate me "an insult to working men and women to put an avowed opponent of the most basic workers' rights" in charge of enforcing labor laws. Sweeney also claimed that I was an "aggressive opponent" of minimum wage laws and affirmative action.[1] The AFL-CIO put together a team of researchers to begin culling my weekly newspaper columns—nearly a decade and a half's worth—pulling out any that might be used as ammunition to defeat my nomination. The major news organizations did the same, with the *New York Times* alone assigning three reporters to read everything I'd written over the years. Reporters even went back to the AFT to look at the magazine and newspapers I'd edited there, hoping to find something newsworthy— which, almost by definition, meant something negative. But it was the

Associated Press that struck hardest, and judging from the content of the story, it looked like it came straight from the AFL-CIO pressroom.

"Linda Chavez has scoffed at raising the minimum wage and cheered proposals to trim Social Security benefits," wrote Laura Meckler. "She has dismissed the notion that women face a 'glass ceiling' in the workplace and suggested that the rising number of sexual harassment lawsuits has made American 'a nation of crybabies,'" she said, and then went on to list my offenses, among them that I "ridiculed the Americans with Disabilities Act as 'special treatment in the name of accommodating the disabled.'" Meckler quoted one critic to whom she'd read my purported comments, saying, in horror: "Oh my God, I thought I knew how bad she was."[2] But Meckler's rendition of my words—which were then distributed and picked up by newspapers across the country—were taken entirely out of context. As my former colleague John J. Miller, now at *National Review*, wrote, "Meckler performs a selective review of Chavez's various writings and then invites feminist critics to say she 'has no business in the U.S. government.' It is a hit job, dressed up as objective journalism."[3]

I hadn't ridiculed the Americans with Disabilities Act. My actual words consisted of the following: "No one doubts that thousands of worthy disabled workers have benefited from a law that protects access to jobs for which they are fully qualified."[4] But Meckler conveniently left that sentence out of her story.[5] I did say that "The ADA is only the latest in a series of well-intentioned laws that have gone far beyond their original purpose of outlawing irrational and invidious discrimination," and went on to note that "the ADA has been used successfully by everyone from infertile cops to drunken airline pilots to force employers to offer special treatment in the name of accommodating the disabled." In fact, my examples were taken from high-profile cases where individuals had abused an important and necessary law, facts that Meckler, again, ignored. And Meckler's description of my views on sexual harassment were no more accurate than her distortions of what I'd written on disability laws.

In 1996, I wrote a column about a male federal employee who filed a sexual harassment complaint against a female colleague for telling an allegedly sexist joke at a conference. "According to the *Washington Post*," which covered the incident, I wrote in my column, "the joke involved a mermaid and a fisherman whose wish was to become five times smarter. The mermaid granted the fisherman's wish by turning him into a woman. Not exactly a knee-slapper as jokes go, but it elicited enough laughs from the mostly female listeners to send audience member John Boyer into quite a snit."[6] Boyer, a federal employee, then filed a formal complaint with the Social Security Administration, for whom both he and the woman who told the joke worked, alleging that the agency was dominated by women and rife with anti-male prejudice and demanding that the woman be demoted from her job and that the agency issue a formal apology. I noted that this man-bites-dog (or woman-bites-man) story was the exception in the sexual harassment arena, "But ever since the courts started interpreting a 'hostile working environment' to constitute sexual harassment, bad taste has become a federal offense. With men so often the targets of such witch hunts, it's no surprise that a few strike back," I wrote. But Meckler said only that I "suggested the increase in sexual harassment lawsuits is making the United States a 'nation of crybabies.' She [Chavez] added: 'With men so often the targets of such witch hunts, it's no surprise that a few strike back.'" As John Miller noted, Meckler's incomplete rendition not only made it appear that I didn't believe sexual harassment laws were necessary but made my comments about men striking back "sound like a defense of wife beating, or at least a rationalization of it."

Under the arcane, informal rules that govern presidential nominations, I was not allowed to answer directly any of the attacks being leveled against me but had to rely on the Bush transition office and surrogates to respond. I couldn't answer reporters' questions or write anything before my nomination was taken up by the Senate Labor Committee, which meant that any charges made against me went, by and large, unanswered, no matter how unfair or egregiously wrong. I had been in this position before, when I was nominated to be staff director of the Civil Rights Commission, and I knew the dangers. By the time you got to face your accusers, the die was already cast. I was being caricatured as anti-female, anti-disabled, anti-worker, not to mention anti–civil rights, and those characterizations would then be used to rally a grassroots effort to oppose my nomination. It was a no-win situation. Rather than wait for that to happen, I began organizing my own little rapid response team, made up of several former coworkers and friends, who were busily going through my voluminous writings and drawing up their own fact sheets. The Bush people were too busy to spend much time on any one nominee's problems, and most of the people assigned to me as "handlers" were young and relatively inexperienced on the issues that had made my reputation. Besides, my nomination was not nearly as critical to the incoming administration as the nomination of Attorney General–designate John Ashcroft, and most of their energy was directed there, since Ashcroft was generally regarded as the most vulnerable of the nominees.

Over the course of the week, I shuttled back and forth between the transition office on G Street and various appointments, meeting with labor union presidents, Hill staff, and key supporters to plan for my upcoming hearings.

On Thursday morning, I met briefly with an FBI agent, Mary Dolan, who went over my security questionnaire with me. We spent less than an hour together, since I had to be at the transition office for another meeting immediately afterward, and much of that time was occupied by my running out to the front desk to check a missing address or phone number. I also spent hours each day on the phone, making courtesy calls to senators and fielding well-wishers and advice-givers, who became more numerous as the week went on. Senator Edward Kennedy called back to tell me that he was looking forward to my hearing.

"It's been awhile, Linda, " Kennedy offered in a jovial tone.

"Yes, Senator, we go way back," I said. In fact, I had worked closely with Kennedy's staff when I was at the Democratic National Committee and as a lobbyist.

"You wrote some of my campaign literature, didn't you? And I recall it was pretty good," he said.

"Yes I did, Senator. You should have seen me trying to explain that one to Jesse Helms," I joked, which made Kennedy roar in appreciation.

This was typical Washington. You could be bitter enemies on the podium or when the television lights were glaring, but the chummiest of friends one-on-one. I knew Kennedy's friendliness meant nothing. He'd be fiercely attacking me in a few weeks when I was before his committee for my confirmation hearings. I got similar calls from Democratic senators Tom Daschle, Barbara Mikulski, and Patrick Leahy, none quite so warm and fuzzy, but cordial just the same. They'd be raking me over the coals soon, and in fact their staffs and allies were stoking those coals as we spoke.

By Saturday, I was exhausted. Having spent the week in town at some friends' house in my old Bethesda neighborhood, I came home to be with my family Friday night in a snowstorm. I decided to take a few hours off and go shopping. I needed a gown for the Inaugural Ball, so I headed off, alone, to Tyson's Corner, almost all the way back to Washington. I worked the phone in my pickup along the way, answering calls I hadn't been able to get to during the week. I was feeling pretty much on top of the world—not exactly carefree, knowing that my confirmation hearing would be tough, but confident that I could handle whatever they'd throw at me. I finished my shopping quickly and stopped to get a bite to eat, luxuriating in a little time to myself. When I finally got back to my truck and turned the key in the ignition, the phone rang instantly.

"Where have you been?" Chris yelled, anxiously. "The transition office has been trying to track you down all afternoon. You've got to call Clay Johnson immediately," he said.

It didn't sound good, but I tried not to worry as I dialed Johnson's number. His assistant, Brooke, put me right through.

"It seems we've got a 'nanny' problem. There's a *Wall Street Journal* reporter sniffing around," Johnson said. "Are you on a land phone?" he asked.

"No, I'm in my truck," I said, confused. My youngest son had just graduated from college, and we hadn't had regular baby-sitters since I had started working at home full time in 1988. As far as I knew, my baby-sitters had been legal residents, besides which the law making it illegal to hire undocumented workers didn't even go into effect until November 1986.

"I want you to call Fred Fielding when you get home," Johnson instructed. "He'll explain what's going on." It was the way the transition office operated: Compartmentalize problems. If there was going to be a scandal, they would distance themselves immediately. Fred Fielding got to handle the dirty work.

I hung up. Then it hit me. It must be Marta, I thought. Someone has told them about Marta, an illegal alien who lived in my home nearly a decade earlier. It didn't even occur to me at first that it was my neighbor Peggy Zwisler who'd leaked the story. I had no reason to suspect that she was anything but a friend, or that it would be in her interest to go public with the information, because Marta had worked for her at the time, which might raise potential legal problems for her.

"People can be really ugly," Fred Fielding said when I finally reached him, his voice heavy with disappointment. "Tell me about this Guatemalan woman."

I told him what I remembered, which wasn't as much as I would have liked. I couldn't remember what years Marta had lived with us, or even for exactly how long. I knew I'd given her money, but I couldn't remember how much.

"I gave her money periodically. A few hundred dollars at a time, I think. I know I helped pay for her plane fare back to Guatemala. I gave her money for books for school and money to send back home to her children. I gave her clothes. She was in very desperate shape when she came to my house," I explained. "I helped Marta enroll in English classes, and once, when she got beat up by someone, I called the police for her and later helped get her in a therapy group for battered women."

"Who knew that she lived with you?" Fielding asked.

"Well, certainly Peter Skerry, who asked me initially if I could take her in.[7] She was living with his housekeeper, and the situation was very bad, and she needed a place immediately. He knew I had a big house and that I'd taken other people in over the years."

"Other illegal aliens?"

"No. I had a couple of Vietnamese refugees live with me sometime in the late 1970s. Two brothers who were 'boat people.' They lived in my basement for a few weeks when they first arrived in the States. I also take in a couple of Puerto Rican kids every summer from New York. I met them through the Fresh Air Fund," I said, referring to a *New York Times*–sponsored charity that sends underprivileged children from New York City to live with families in rural and suburban areas. "And I pay for their Catholic school tuition," I added. "I know it sounds funny, but I really don't know how much money I've spent on this kind of thing. I suppose I've spent more than $10,000 on the kids and at least a few thousand on Marta. I just didn't keep track."

In my family, my better-off relatives helped out when we needed it, and I tried to do the same for others when I was able. But I felt strangely embarrassed telling Fielding about all this. I had never even told Chris how much money I'd given away over the years. It wasn't something I had ever shared publicly, and I didn't like having to talk about it now.

"So who else knew about the Guatemalan?" Fielding asked.

"My neighbor, Peggy Zwisler. Marta worked for Zwisler," I said.

"She's a big Democratic lawyer?" he asked.

Now, *that* I didn't know, though I should have assumed she was a Democrat, since most everyone in our Bethesda neighborhood was.

"Does this woman have something against you?" he queried.

"Not that I know of," I said. "Look, I don't want to cause problems for the president-elect. I would never do anything to hurt him. I'll step down right away, if you want," I offered.

"Don't do anything yet," Fielding counseled. "The FBI will want to re-interview you tomorrow."

Shortly after I spoke with Fielding, Clay Johnson called back. He had Tucker Eskew, a transition spokesman, on the line as well. Johnson's voice was much warmer than it had been when I spoke with him in my truck. Apparently he'd talked to Fielding and was feeling better about my circumstances.

"Andy Card talked to the president-elect," Johnson told me. "He wants you to know that he was proud of you when he nominated you, and he's even prouder of you now," he said, in obvious reference to my charitable acts.

"This might be a blessing in disguise," Eskew chimed in. "This presents us with an opportunity to tell a whole different story about who Linda Chavez is. I think people could end up seeing you in a totally different light," he said.

"That's true," I agreed, eagerly. "I'm sure that the people I've helped over the years would come forward. I can give you their names. You can steer reporters to talk to them. If Marta's situation is put in some context, maybe it will actually help me," I said. And at least while I was on the phone with Johnson and Eskew, I even believed it.

"Now when did you learn that this woman was illegal?" Eskew asked. "Could it have been when she went back to Guatemala?"

I didn't remember any specific conversation Marta and I ever had on the subject, which would have been difficult, at least in her first months in my home since she spoke no English when she moved in and I spoke little Spanish. Surely I must have known her situation from the very beginning of our relationship, and I told Johnson and Eskew that. "I think I always knew," I said.

"But you don't remember exactly when she told you?" he pushed. I could see him trying to spin this in the best possible light. If I didn't employ Marta and didn't know she was an illegal alien when I let her move in, then the story became much ado about nothing.

"No, I don't remember exactly when I learned. I think I knew it all along. I knew she had kids back in Guatemala and she missed them terribly, and I encouraged her to go back home. I'm pretty sure I gave her the money to buy the ticket."

"Let's just see how this plays out on the Sunday shows tomorrow. ABC has the story, and they'll probably lead with it on *Sunday Morning*," Eskew suggested. By the time I got off the phone, I was feeling better.

A short while later, Marta called. I hadn't spoken with her in several years, and she'd had difficulty finding me, finally driving to my old house in Bethesda where the current residents gave her my phone number. She was clearly distraught, worried that reporters kept calling her to ask about me.

"I was tormented by this," Marta later told a *New York Times* reporter. "Ms. Chavez told her to cooperate with the F.B.I., Mrs. Mercado said, but left it up to her to decide whether to talk to the reporters," the *Times* reported. "One of the things I was scared about," Marta said, "was that I had to say how I got into this country, and I know that it's not pleasant for Americans to hear about that, to hear that people have entered the country like I did."[8]

Although we spoke only a few minutes, I did finally learn the dates of Marta's stay with me, which I hadn't been able to recollect precisely. I was surprised at how long she'd stayed, slightly more than two years—from late 1991 to late 1993. It had seemed a much shorter time to me, but I knew her memory on this matter was bound to be more accurate than mine. The information prompted a memory of my own. John Miller, who had been my assistant at the Manhattan Institute, had worked out of my Bethesda home at the very time Marta had lived with me. I called him later that evening.

"Do you remember Marta?" I asked him, after explaining my conversation with transition officials.

As Miller later explained at length in a piece for *National Review*, where he is currently national political reporter:

> When Chavez asked me on January 6 whether I remembered Marta
> Mercado, my answer was yes. I had started working for Chavez in
> December 1992. She was a senior fellow at the Manhattan Institute,
> and took me on as an assistant. Although the New York-based think tank
> then maintained an office in downtown Washington, Chavez worked
> primarily out of her home in Bethesda, Md. For the first six to eight
> weeks of my employment, I took the bus to her house every day and
> worked there from roughly 9 to 5. I got to know her husband, her kids,
> her pets, and Mercado.
>
> Actually, I didn't get to know Mercado very well. But I did recall her,
> and Chavez wanted my observations. I remembered Mercado as a
> houseguest, someone who lived with the family for reasons I never fully
> understood and, frankly, never thought about. Sometimes she was in the
> home the whole day, and sometimes she wasn't there at all. Chavez
> wanted to know if I had thought she was an employee, such as a live-in
> maid, and I said no. If that had been true, I would have seen her vacu-
> uming the carpets, mopping the floor, and dusting the office. I didn't
> recall her doing any of these things. I did remember her doing the odd
> chore, such as washing the dishes. What I saw was someone pitching in
> to help around the house, just as any family member or guest would do.
> And Mercado certainly wasn't a nanny—the youngest of Chavez's three
> children was 13 or 14 years old and didn't require that kind of attention.
> No, my impression of Mercado was that she definitely wasn't an
> employee.[9]

I didn't watch Cokie Roberts and Sam Donaldson the next morning. It was a habit I had gotten into during my Senate campaign. I avoided watching painful stories about myself that would just end up angering and demoralizing me, let-ting my staff keep tabs instead. But I didn't have to turn on the television set to know what the press was up to. By morning, crews were camped out at my home, thankfully at my property line a hundred yards away from my front doorstep. Nonetheless, an assistant producer at ABC, Jon Garcia, knocked on my door and asked if he could interview me. ABC seemed to be the lead net-work on this story, which it had been the first to break that morning.

I knew it was against the rules to talk to him, but I decided that I had nothing to lose going on "background," which meant that he could use the information he obtained and credit it to a "source close to the Chavez family." It was all such a big scam—insiders know the rules, and the viewing public is left in the dark. I gave him Ada Iturrino's name, the mother of the kids I'd helped in New York, Josh Reyes and Celenia Ruiz. I gave him Benson Bui's name, one of the two Vietnamese refugees who'd lived with me in the late 1970s. And I told them what I could remember about Marta. In a note sent to me after the interview, Garcia said, "I felt like our off-camera conversation was very compelling—far more compelling than listening to the Bush campaign trying to tell your story. My editors, who reviewed my account of our interview, thought it was very human and powerful. I would be most appreciative if you granted us a follow-up, on-camera interview."[10] I knew the transition office would flip out if I agreed to be interviewed, so I refused. For most of the day, I avoided press calls, letting Chris or one of my kids, who came over to keep me company, answer the phone.

The FBI agents showed up a short time later. This time Agent Mary Dolan was accompanied by an older, more experienced agent, Jerry Campane.

"Our job is to get you confirmed," Campane said reassuringly when we sat down in my basement rec room, away from the kids and the noise of the football game everyone was watching upstairs.

"I suppose you know why we're here," he said. And then more cryptically, "Is there anything you left out in your discussion with Agent Dolan that you might want to add now?"

I began at the beginning, describing how I met Marta through a friend and colleague and how her relationship with me and the family developed. I described helping her find work—including recommending her to my neighbor Peggy Zwisler, who hired her part-time—teaching her how to use the bus line, helping her enroll in school, and calling the police on her behalf when she came home one day with her lip split open and her eyes blackened after a man attacked her at a party. I described speaking to a counselor on her behalf and how she joined a women's support group and slowly began to emerge from her shell, having spent her early months living with me mostly hidden away in her bedroom, sleeping much of the day, and taking all her meals there and barely interacting with anyone. I also told Campane that Marta had called me the previous night, after reporters began calling her, and that I had subsequently called John Miller, who had worked for me in my home when Marta was living with me.

I gave Campane phone numbers for Peter Skerry, John Miller, and others. I also offered him copies of immigration forms—"I-9s," which are required to be filled out by every employer proving employees' eligibility to work in the United States, and "W-2s" that I'd kept on housekeepers that I had hired since 1995. I explained that I had thrown away older forms for previous employees when I moved in 1998, since the law required that they be kept for only five years. I told him that I would ask my accountant to try to obtain all previous records, which I would turn over to them as soon as I got them. Over the years I'd hired perhaps a dozen people to do work in my home, off and on, depending on my own finances and the demands on my schedule. But I had not had regular, daily help since I had taken up working full-time out of my home in 1988. I joked that anyone who had ever been in my often messy house could attest that I didn't have a full-time maid.

Campane listened attentively, revealing no emotion. It was impossible to detect what he was thinking.

"Now I want you to listen carefully to this question," he said, suddenly sounding ominous. "Be very careful on this one." I sensed he was signaling me in some way, but I couldn't figure out exactly what he was trying to convey.

"After you were nominated, or maybe when you were filling out your security forms, did you talk to anyone about Marta? Maybe call someone to refresh your memory?"

"No," I said.

"After your nomination, you never talked to any of your ex-neighbors about Marta?"

I froze. Of course I had talked to Peggy Zwisler, but weeks earlier, not since my nomination, as Campane phrased the question. He told me to be careful on this one. Was he being careful? Was he restricting the time frame on this question on purpose?

"I didn't talk to anyone after I was nominated," I repeated.

It was a terrible mistake. I knew my answer was misleading even if technically correct. I regretted immediately that I didn't tell Campane about my conversation with Zwisler, although I knew that it would raise questions about why I hadn't told Fred Fielding in our first meeting, before I was offered the cabinet position, that I'd had an illegal alien living in my home a decade earlier. In retrospect, I certainly should have. I'd been in Washington long enough to know that there are no secrets. I was digging myself deeper and deeper into a hole, and I had to extricate myself one way or another.

By Monday morning I was feeling under siege. Reporters were still camped out at my house in the cold, damp rural Virginia countryside. Pablo and Bella felt so sorry for them that they went out and bought a pizza and gave it to the hungry camera crew. As I left my property, I told the crew not to bother sticking around, that I wasn't returning there that evening. But other camera crews were waiting at my downtown office when I drove into town. I was scheduled to meet with Chris Hicks, an old colleague from my Reagan White House days who had come into town to help me work with the transition office in picking my political appointees for the Labor Department. Hicks had also worked for a time for Fred Fielding, when Fielding was White House counsel in the Reagan administration.

"You need a lawyer before you talk to anyone else," Hicks asserted, almost before he said hello. "Unless you have someone else who you'd rather have represent you, I'd be happy to do it." I hadn't even thought about hiring a lawyer, though I probably should have, so I agreed, and we spent the next hour going through everything I could remember about Marta and about my dealings with Fielding and the FBI on the matter, including my failure to tell the agents about my discussion with Zwisler. He advised me that I should call the agent back immediately and tell him about the Zwisler conversation, which I did. But once on the phone, the agent raised an entirely new issue. The *Washington Post* that morning carried an article that said it was illegal to "harbor any person who is in the country without proper documentation."[11] Had I "harbored an illegal alien?" Campane wanted to know.

The allegation was ridiculous, I said. Harboring an illegal alien is a criminal offense, applying only to individuals who "receive and conceal" illegal aliens as part of alien smuggling or other organized crime activities.[12]

"I didn't try to hide the fact that Marta was living with me," I told Campane. "As I told you yesterday, I called the Montgomery County Police when she was assaulted. They probably have a record of it, since they interviewed her in my home, and I told them that she was an illegal alien, which was one of the reasons she hesitated to prosecute the man who attacked her." I felt like I was becoming a character in a Kafka novel.

There was another problem with the *Post* piece, I realized as I re-read it when I got off the phone with Campane. "Chavez was not aware of the woman's illegal status in the 1992–93 period, said Bush spokesman Tucker Eskew," the article reported. But that was not what I had told Eskew on Saturday evening. I had made it clear that I knew from the time Marta moved into my house, or very soon after, that she wasn't in the country legally. Maybe the *Post* had got it wrong. I'd have to call Eskew and make sure he corrected what he was telling reporters. Hicks and I went over to Fred Fielding's office instead of going to the transition office, at Fielding's suggestion.

"You don't want to go to the transition office, Linda," Fielding said. "Think how uncomfortable you'll feel," he offered, as if he were watching out for my interests. But I knew his real—and proper—concern was to protect the president-elect, and I certainly had no interest in causing more problems than I already had.

Throughout the day, I was getting reports from my staff and family about the news coverage. "I think we've turned the corner," Chris told me cheerfully when I called home. Some of the cable networks had aired interviews with Benson Bui, who talked about how I had taken him and his brother in when they arrived in the United States with only the clothes on their backs. "Everything I have I owe to her," Benson tearfully told reporters. Benson, whose Vietnamese name was Le Nghia, and his brother Than Nanh had lived with us only a short time in the late 1970s. When we met them at Dulles Airport they were wearing cotton shirts and rubber thongs on their feet. We took them to K-Mart and bought them winter jackets and boots and gave them a place to live in our large house on Geranium Street. After a couple of weeks, the Catholic Church, which sponsored the two men, located relatives in the Maryland suburbs, and the brothers went to live with them. I hadn't heard anything from them for several years afterward, when one day Nghia—now with his adopted American name, Benson—showed up at my door in Bethesda. He had been trying to locate me for years, he told me in English, a language he couldn't speak when he lived with me. He and his brother had gone to college in the States and had good jobs. Benson had married a wonderful Vietnamese woman, Marie, and they had two young children, Carolyn and Felix. It was a great immigrant success story, one repeated millions of time in America. I was always humbled by Benson's gratitude for what was such a small, almost insignificant role my family had played in his life.

The news media was also interviewing Marta at length, and she, too, had spoken kindly of her time living in my home. Although repeatedly pressed by reporters to describe her relationship as that of an employee, she said time and again, "I did some things in the house, but, you know, it was not like it was a job." She even explained to one reporter, "She was trying to help me find a job," which, indeed, I had done—with my neighbor Peggy Zwisler.[13] She also told reporters that I encouraged her to talk to the FBI. Maybe the worst was over, Chris consoled me.

Nevertheless, I had a terrible sinking feeling. I knew that the transition office had to be in fits over this. It was exactly the kind of "surprise" they didn't want. Everyone knew that I was going to be difficult to confirm because the interest groups had lined up aggressively against me. Even the AFT had now condemned my nomination—in a patently dishonest statement. Sandy Feldman smelled blood in the water and had decided to join the sharks:

"Linda Chavez is distorting the facts when she suggests that the late Al Shanker and the AFT share her extreme views. Al Shanker was a teacher unionist through and through, a human and civil rights advocate and an opponent of vouchers. Linda Chavez's contempt for policies such as the minimum wage, affirmative action and bilingual education is an outrage and an anathema to everything the AFT believes in. Any effort to suggest that Al or the AFT would share her views on these matters is irresponsible and false."[14] Of course, I had never suggested that Shanker shared my views on vouchers or the minimum wage, but Shanker's views on both affirmative action and bilingual education were identical to mine—as anyone who read his *New York Times* column over the years could attest. Furthermore, he had also been a member of the board of advisors of my two organizations, the Center for the New American Community at the Manhattan Institute and the Center for Equal Opportunity, until his death in 1997.

I was feeling under siege. When Hicks and I went to Fielding's office, I sensed a real change in atmosphere. The usually jovial Fielding was sober, even adversarial. At one point, he brought up the name of Henry Cisneros— the former secretary of the Department of Housing and Urban Development in the Clinton administration, who was prosecuted for lying to the FBI about payments he'd made to his former mistress. The implication was clear: By failing to tell the FBI about my conversation with Peggy Zwisler, I had put myself into serious legal jeopardy.

"That's bullshit," I said, slamming my fist down on the table in Fielding's office. I had never used such language with anyone in a position of authority in my life, but I was furious. "Don't insult my intelligence, Fred. This isn't the same at all, and you know it." I had always believed that Cisneros had been treated very unfairly, and I couldn't believe that Fielding was trying to scare me by bringing up his name. But it was a clear sign that, no matter what Fielding said to the contrary or what Bush spokesmen were saying publicly, they wanted me gone.

I had clearly caused many of my own problems by not telling Fielding about Marta in our first conversation when he asked me the catch-all question posed to all potential nominees, "Is there anything in your past life which can be used against you, fairly or unfairly?" I had hoped, naively, that an act I considered a kindness to a woman in need—albeit one who was in the country illegally—would not become an issue. And I don't believe it would have mushroomed into the cause célèbre it had become in the previous forty-eight hours had I been a moderate Republican with noncontroversial views. Indeed, Christine Todd Whitman was expected to sail through her confirmation as

Environmental Protection Agency administrator, despite having hired two illegal aliens in the early 1990s, a matter that she disclosed in 1993 when she was running for governor of New Jersey. But I was who I was, with many enemies, some of whom considered me—worse than a political adversary—a traitor

I had hoped for a little more empathy from the Bush staff, since they had had to deal with a similar "surprise" in the president-elect's past, an arrest and conviction for driving while under the influence of alcohol in 1976, which the press uncovered just four days before the election. Bush had assiduously avoided revealing the incident throughout his public career, going so far as to have Al Gonzales, the man designated to become the White House counselor, get him out of serving on a jury in 1996 where he might be asked under oath to reveal his DUI conviction.[15] But I had no deep or long-standing ties to this president-elect or to any of his top lieutenants. I had become a political liability to them, and they, quite properly, wanted the hemorrhaging to stop. My problems had already dominated the news for two days, crowding out other stories they wanted the country to focus on. I couldn't blame them. I had become a real political liability. By the time I left Fielding's office, I had pretty much made up my mind to withdraw my nomination.

Chris joined me at the home of our friends Alan and Suzanne Peyser in Bethesda, where I'd been sleeping the previous week in order to avoid the long commute home to Loudoun County, Virginia. We turned on the television to catch the evening news, hoping that the tide had indeed turned. However, the networks were now reporting that a "source" close to the FBI investigation had reported that I'd spoken with my neighbor Peggy Zwisler and that the agency was investigating whether I had tried to influence her testimony. This was more than I could bear. The FBI appeared to be leaking information directly to the networks.

I bitterly complained about it to Fielding when I reached him by phone. And once again, I told him, news organizations were incorrectly reporting that I had told transition officials I didn't know that Marta was an illegal alien when I let her move in with me. Worse, they were suggesting that I'd changed my story over the course of the last few days. This was simply untrue. I told Fielding, Clay Johnson, and Tucker Eskew on Saturday night when the issue first arose that I had taken in a woman whom I knew was an illegal alien. Yet, it appeared that someone in the campaign had repeatedly misstated what I'd said. I called and left a harsh message on Tucker Eskew's cell phone demanding that he correct the mistake. I wasn't sure whether Eskew had initially tried to spin the story in a way he thought would be more favorable to me and then been unable to back down from his original assertion or whether something more sinister was going on. However the misinformation had been spread, it had the effect of making me look like I'd lied directly to the transition team.

I was feeling totally alone, twisting in the wind, undone by my own mistakes and by my lack of support within the Bush camp. I went to sleep with a heavy heart. But when I woke up early the next morning, I felt as if a deep burden had been lifted. The anxiety of indecision suddenly disappeared. Chris was still sleeping soundly by my side.

"Wake up. I need your help," I said, gently shaking him.

His eyes opened, startled.

"What's wrong?" he asked.

"Look, I need you to make some phone calls. I want to hold a press conference this afternoon. I don't care what the transition office thinks. I am going to tell my story on my terms. I am not pulling out with my tail between my legs, like some thief in the night. What I did for Marta was not wrong. And I have helped a lot of other people in my life, and I think they will come out and say so. I want you to call Benson, and Ada, and Margarita. And I want to get ahold of that Florida orthodontist whose Mexican wife I helped get back into the United States when I was in the White House, the one who wrote me a few months ago thanking me for my help when everybody else turned a deaf ear to his plight. See if they'll come to a press conference this afternoon."

"What are you going to say at the press conference?" he asked.

"Take this job and shove it?" I joked. "I don't know. I'll deal with that later. Just see if you can pull everybody together. See if Ada will bring the kids down from New York with her. See if Benson and Margarita can take off work, and have someone in my office call Dr. David Bowden. He's a long shot, but he did say he wished there was a way he could repay my kindness. Well, this is the way."

Bowden had written me a few months earlier, out of the blue. In 1985, when I was in the White House, Bowden had written President Reagan pleading for him to intervene because his fiancée had inadvertently jeopardized her immigration status by returning to Mexico to visit her family for a few weeks while she was awaiting permanent resident alien status. Because she left the country while her permanent status was still pending, she was not being allowed to return to the United States, and the couple could not marry and live together. The letter landed on my desk, and instead of passing it on or ignoring it altogether, I made a few phone calls and straightened out the mess, and the two were reunited. They had recently celebrated their fifteenth wedding anniversary, and Dr. Bowden had found my address on the Internet and written to thank me in August.

I quickly dressed, choosing a black suit, which I thought would fit the occasion, and headed downtown for an early morning meeting with AFL-CIO president John Sweeney. The meeting had been set up the previous Friday, before any of the current crisis had developed. It seemed pointless now, but I decided to honor the commitment anyway. It had been years since I'd been in the AFL-CIO building on 16th Street, across from Lafayette Square and the White House, and it felt truly odd going into the building under these circumstances. Sweeney was brusque but warmed up after the first few minutes, while Richard Trumka, the secretary-treasurer and former Mine Workers Union president, was downright cordial. I reminded Trumka that I'd once invited him to breakfast in the White House executive dining room when I was director of public liaison. We talked for about half an hour, and I gave no hint that I was considering pulling out later that day. When it was time to leave, Sweeney invited in Linda Chavez-Thompson, my namesake who was an AFL-CIO vice president. Chavez-Thompson was curt, despite my attempts to make light of the fact that several news organizations had run her picture with stories about my nomination. Trumka insisted on having his driver take me the two blocks to my office, a kindness that touched me under the circumstances, and I bid the three top AFL-CIO officers goodbye.

Chris was waiting for me back at my office, along with Chris Hicks, now acting as my lawyer. I called Clay Johnson to tell him about my meeting with Sweeney. He seemed more annoyed than interested, another sign that the Bush people just wanted me to go away. I had a meeting scheduled later in the afternoon with Trent Lott, but his office called to cancel. Something had "come up," the scheduler said. Meanwhile, everyone, including Dr. Bowden, had agreed to be available for an afternoon press conference. Around noon, Chris, Hicks, and I headed for Fielding's office by taxi. Fielding came into the small conference room he'd set aside for us in a better mood than the day before. He'd just returned from the FBI.

"It's good you called the agent back and told him about your phone call to your neighbor," Fielding announced. "I don't think they're going to make any problems over your failure to tell them on Sunday," he said.

"I've decided to withdraw my nomination," I said without warning. The words came out of my mouth without my even stopping to consider what I was saying. Chris started to interrupt. "No, I've made up my mind. I've already reserved a room for a press conference, and I've asked some of the people I've helped over the years to be with me. Now, we can either hold this press conference at the hotel or at the transition office. I think it would be better for the transition team if I did it in their offices, but it's obviously their call."

"I'll call Andy Card," Fielding said, looking very relieved. Card was the president-elect's chief of staff–designate.

Fielding returned a few minutes later. "You've made the right decision, Linda," he said gently. "Everybody appreciates what you've done. Andy will be in touch with you about the press conference. I'm just so sorry things turned out this way." He added, "You'll get a call from the president-elect or vice president-elect within forty-eight hours."

We shook hands and the three of us left. By the time we got back to my office, camera crews were camped outside again, asking questions about what I intended to say at my press conference later that afternoon, which my office had just announced. Upstairs, my guests had arrived, except for Dr. Bowden, who was on a plane from Florida and wasn't due to arrive until right before the news conference. I hugged everyone and commented on how handsome Josh Reyes looked, the young man who'd been a guest at my house every summer for ten years starting when he was just six years old. I told the group that I was going to withdraw my name from consideration, prompting tears and protests from several of the participants, and I made a few other phone calls to give family and friends a heads-up, including Marta, who sounded near tears as well.

Card called a few minutes after I arrived back at my office. "Everything is set for you to come to the transition office," he informed me. "Clay Johnson will be with you when you go out to meet the press. We'll send a car to pick you up and bring you and your guests," he said, and then asked me to give him their names and the proper spelling so the press office could provide the information. At about 3:00 P.M., we went downstairs, where two vehicles waited to pick us up. Chris, my oldest son David, and I got into a black SUV, just like the one that had picked me up in happier times in late December to whisk me to the Madison Hotel to meet with President-elect Bush. The others went by government van to the transition office, where we entered through the garage and went upstairs to a holding room. The whole place seemed deserted, as if everyone had fled our arrival. What few cabinet nominees and their staffs were around remained in their offices, the doors closed, blinds drawn. I felt like we were in a funeral home or hospital, with everyone talking in hushed tones as if death hung in the air.

Tucker Eskew came to greet me. "You'll go out, make your statement, and let the others make their statements, and then leave. Don't take any questions," he admonished.

"Who'll introduce me?" I asked, "Clay?"

"No, you'll just go out by yourself. We'll be in the wings, giving you moral support," he said, without irony.

"I thought Clay Johnson was going to be with me. That's what Andy Card told me. I think it looks really bad for me to be out there alone," I said. As we were talking, Donald Rumsfeld walked up and introduced himself.

"This is just such a shame," he said, grasping my hand. I was deeply appreciative. I had never even met him before, but he was the only one who had come by to express his regrets. It was as if we had some communicable disease that everyone wanted to avoid contracting.

"Who's going to be with you?" he asked.

"Good question," I said. "Andy Card told me that Clay Johnson would go out on stage with me, but apparently not." Eskew had taken the opportunity of Rumsfeld's arrival to disappear.

"That's not right," Rumsfeld said definitively. "Let me see what I can do," he said and disappeared down the hall.

When he returned, he said, "Cheney says the decision has been made that you should do this alone. I did my best. I am very sorry."

"I really appreciate it, " I said. I was surprised at how thoughtful this man was. I later learned that Cheney was worried about what I might say at the press conference and what questions might be asked. Given the unpredictable quality of the event, it was Cheney's view that the farther away they stayed, the better. Cheney was doing what many politicians would do under the circumstances, but it still felt like a slap in the face.[16]

I walked into the briefing room with Chris, David, Ada Iturrino, and her two children, Josh Reyes and Celenia Ruiz, Benson Bui, and Margarita Valladares at my side.[17] I introduced myself and the others, who each stepped to the microphone to say a few words about what I had meant to their lives, some of it in halting English, but heartfelt nonetheless. Margarita, at four-feet-eleven, could barely be seen over the podium. She had known me the longest and had taken care of my children when they were young. "She encouraged me to go to school. She encouraged me also to become a citizen. She also helped me to get my first job in the federal government. Thanks to her, today I have a good life. My kids are in college. . . . I will always be . . . grateful to Linda and Chris, both of them," she said.

None of the participants had ever spoken in front of a group of people before, but now they stood before a crowded room of aggressive reporters. Each told of the role I'd played in their lives, helping them get schooling, helping them get jobs. But it was Josh and Celenia whose words seared my soul: "I call her my mother sometimes because [of] the things that she done," Josh said, and Celenia added, simply, "I love Linda very much. . . . She's like a second mother for me."[18] I'd watched them grow into such a fine young man and young lady and was so proud of their grace and composure in what must have been an intimidating setting, with dozens of television cameras and microphones and a hundred zealous journalists, screaming out questions.

"I've not led a perfect life. I don't think anybody has. I'm not Mother Teresa," I said when I stepped to the podium. "However, I have tried to do right by people who have been in need," I offered. I wasn't reading a script and hadn't even thought out clearly what I would say. I looked around the room at the reporters' faces, many of them familiar to me from my years in the spotlight. Most were hardened, skeptical, even cynical, but I went on anyway.

"In order to try to put perspective on some of the stories that have been out there over the last several days involving a Guatemalan woman whom I took into my home in the early 1990s, who came from a very abusive relationship, who fled Guatemala at a time of turmoil in that country, who landed in the United States knowing no one and having no friends and having no place to live and no way to support herself," I listed all the circumstances that had affected my decision. "I was asked by a friend if I would, in fact, provide her a room in my home and try to help her so that she could get back on her feet and eventually return to her family in Guatemala. And I did that," I said, without apology.

"And I did that even at the time knowing that there was some risk to me in doing it. And I have to say to you today that knowing everything that has happened over the last week, that if that woman showed up at my door, if I was asked by a friend to do that again, I would do it in an instant, without hesitation."

"Defiant," "impenitent," the *Washington Post* and other news organizations described me. In fact, I was unrepentant about having taken Marta into my home. It seemed the right thing to do at the time, and nothing has changed my view, even the loss of a cabinet position. But I was not unmindful of my own complicity in my undoing.

"Did I make a mistake? Absolutely," I answered a reporter's question. "I made the mistake of not thinking through that this might be misinterpreted and coming forward with it at the first available opportunity," I said.

But whatever the merits of my defense, I knew that I had become a terrible distraction to the president-elect's transition. He needed to be able to get on with putting together the new government, and I needed to get on with my life. I left the pressroom knowing that I had made the right decision for us both.

In the days and weeks that followed, much was written about my decision, some of it quite vicious. The *New York Times* dismissed my press conference. "No doubt Ms. Chavez has helped immigrants and young people over the years. But the testimonials felt rehearsed and exploitive," the editors wrote. The

Times editorial went on to accuse me of violating a criminal statute: "Harboring an illegal alien is a felony," the *Times* opined in an arguably libelous accusation.[19] "The narcissism and duplicity of Chavez's press conference announcing her withdrawal . . . was simply staggering," the *New Republic* wrote. "She trotted out a gaggle of immigrant admirers to offer staged testimonials about her history of assisting those in need," they said, and then went on to attack me for my religious conversion, which they falsely claimed I had "categorically denied" during my Senate campaign. The entry in the magazine's unsigned "Notebook" section was distinguished by containing not a single completely accurate statement in the entire piece.[20]

In fact, several of the articles attacking me made points that were untrue, including two that continue to rankle me: first, that I lied to Bush press aide Tucker Eskew about when I discovered that Marta was an illegal alien—a small but egregious accusation; and second, that I attacked Zoe Baird, President Clinton's first nominee for attorney general, for hiring illegal aliens. Why Eskew continued to insist that I had misled him about when I knew Marta was an illegal alien remains a mystery to me to this day, particularly after I lodged complaints about his misrepresentation at the time not only to him but to Fielding, Clay Johnson, and reporters, beginning on the Monday when I first learned what Eskew was telling the press.

The second accusation caught me by surprise. I didn't think that I had criticized Baird over her hiring of illegal aliens when she was nominated, but the networks kept playing a tape of me talking about the nomination that certainly sounded like criticism. It took a few weeks before the real story came out, long after most people were paying attention or cared.

Reporter Stuart Taylor was the first to write about the press's misrepresentation in an article in *National Journal*, titled "Smearing Linda Chavez: The Poison of Partisan Thinking." "[T]he assertions by the *New Republic* and others that Chavez hypocritically 'trashed' Zoe Baird in 1993 for employing an illegal immigrant couple as a nanny and driver are bogus," Taylor reported. "These claims stem from a misinterpretation of a passing reference Chavez made to Baird's illegal-alien problem during a December 1993 television interview focusing on Bobby Ray Inman's nomination to be Defense Secretary." As it happened, the interview on the *MacNeil-Lehrer Newshour* on PBS took place almost one year *after* the Baird nomination—a fact not a single news organization thought worthy of mention when they showed the tape throughout my labor nomination ordeal. "But Chavez said nothing that could be fairly called an attack on Baird for hiring (let alone housing) illegal immigrants," Taylor noted.[21]

A week after the Taylor article appeared, Jeff Jacoby, a syndicated columnist, went further to explain what had happened, quoting my original remarks in their proper chronological context. "The topic that day wasn't Baird, it was Bobby Ray Inman—Clinton's choice for defense secretary after Les Aspin resigned. Inman, it turned out, had also failed to pay Social Security taxes for a housekeeper [as Baird had been accused of doing], but the revelation set off no sparks. Jim Lehrer pointed this out, then asked Chavez why Inman wasn't being treated the way Baird had been," Jacoby explained. "'There are some real important differences here,'" Jacoby accurately quoted me. "'I think most of the American people were upset during the Zoe Baird nomination that she had hired an illegal alien. That was what upset them more than the fact that she did not pay Social Security taxes. . . .' What a difference a little context makes," Jacoby noted. "Chavez didn't attack Baird—not then, not ever." I was engaged in political analysis on the *Newshour*, not giving a personal opinion about Baird, which the context made clear.

Other facts came out as well. Robert Novak reported that my chief accuser, Peggy Zwisler, "is no simple housewife. She is a member of the high-powered Democratic law firm of Howrey and Simon. Her associate is W. Neil Eggleston, a former Clinton White House associate counsel and later President Clinton's personal lawyer who was a principal figure in the administration's protection of the corrupt Laborers' union."[22] Novak also noted that Eggleston was representing Zwisler in the "allegations about the illegal immigrant (though it is not clear why she needed a lawyer)." Months later, when I received a copy of my FBI file under a freedom of information request, I discovered that Zwisler had initially raised the issue of my nomination with her law partners in what she described as a "Socratic dialogue."[23] Though Zwisler also told the FBI that "she would never go to the *Washington Post*" with the information about Marta, she didn't say anything about going to ABC News, which was the first news organization to break the story. I've since learned that Terry Moran, the White House correspondent for ABC, is Zwisler's brother, a relevant fact the network never reported in its many stories on my troubles.

For all the unpleasantness surrounding my failed nomination, I quickly discovered there were blessings as well. For every unkind word I heard or read, there were hundreds of phone calls and letters from family, friends, colleagues, and strangers. Neither Bush nor Cheney ever called, as Fielding had promised, but senators and governors, congressmen, former cabinet members and cabinet-designees did, including the woman chosen to succeed me, Elaine Chao, an old friend whom I greatly respect, and her husband, Senator Mitch McConnell. But it was the ordinary people whom I'd never met before whose kindness most touched me. Coat-check ladies, janitors, airplane mechanics, waiters, and parking lot attendants—many of them immigrants themselves—stopped me wherever I went to pass on words of encouragement. They told me their own stories, relating the difficulties they'd encountered when they arrived in a strange land with little money and no friends. They talked about the people who'd helped them along the way and then proudly described their success in the United States—the home they'd recently purchased, the children in college, the small business they'd been able to open. They usually ended their conversation with "Thank you for what you did," which left me feeling both grateful and humble.

Throughout my life, I've encountered obstacles, even tragedy. And this latest episode was no different, except that it took place on a larger stage and under the media spotlight. I hope I've learned from my mistakes, but I've always tried to move forward, not dwelling on the past. "Whenever the Lord shuts one door, He opens another," one woman reminded me as I rushed through Dulles Airport on the way to make a speech. It was a theme I heard repeated time and again in the months that followed my cabinet nomination. I wasn't sure what new doors would open next, but I knew I was ready to walk through.

Epilogue: Thorn in Their Side

Very little is needed to make a happy life.

—Marcus Aurelius

AFTER A FLURRY OF MEDIA ATTENTION and speech requests in the months following my decision to withdraw as labor secretary nominee, my life returned to normal—more or less. I signed an exclusive contract with Fox News Channel to provide regular commentary on the cable network and returned to writing my syndicated newspaper column. I also took up my post as president of the Center for Equal Opportunity, once again devoting myself to the issues I'd been involved with throughout my career: promoting color-blind equal opportunity, immigrant assimilation, and English acquisition.

Even with Republicans in control of both the White House and the House of Representatives, there was little indication that the federal government would change its policies on racial preferences or bilingual education. Indeed, the Bush administration early on gave every indication that it would retain the status quo on both. In August 2001, a case that challenged a federal program giving special preferences to minority contractors was about to be heard by the Supreme Court, and the Bush Justice Department chose to defend the program. The administration took this position despite both candidate George W. Bush's repeated assertions that he opposed preferences and Attorney General John Ashcroft's previous vote against the specific program at issue when he was in the U.S. Senate. Nor did the Bush administration show any interest in rescinding a last-minute executive order signed by outgoing President Bill Clinton that mandated that all federal contractors provide services to non-English speakers in their own languages. Clearly, there was much work ahead for CEO—and for me—even with Republicans in power.

Another issue continued to nag at me as well. The labor secretary job had interested me not only for the obvious reasons of prestige and honor but because

I believed that in that position I might be able to do something to rein in the enormous—and growing—political power of the labor unions. Unions represent only about 12 percent of the American workforce, but they virtually control the Democratic Party and play an enormous role in American politics.

Funded by mandatory dues from workers who, in many instances, must join a union under the terms of their employment, unions are the single largest source of political contributions in the nation—much of it hidden. In the 2000 elections, unions raised and spent $75 million in direct contributions, but they are estimated to have spent as much as $800 million, if one factors in the amount spent on publications endorsing candidates or legislation, staff time "volunteered" to campaigns, get-out-the-vote drives, and other expenditures that are largely hidden from public scrutiny and reporting. And some of these activities are illegal.

When I was editor of the American Federation of Teachers publications, it was routine for the AFT to publish campaign literature on behalf of candidates. Although it was legal to distribute such material to union members, we often printed hundreds of thousands of extra copies and gave it to candidates to distribute to the general public, which was not legal. I once personally delivered several boxes of union-printed campaign leaflets to Ted Kennedy's presidential campaign headquarters in 1980. And I witnessed phone banks set up in union headquarters, staffed by paid employees acting as "volunteers," making calls to the general public on behalf of candidates—which constituted a substantial contribution outside the legal limits of campaign finance law.

What the AFT did was nothing out of the ordinary. Many unions engage in similar activity. And in return for huge union contributions in staff, time, and money, the unions often call the shots in the Democratic Party. The Associated Press reported that "in exchange for extensive financial support, Democratic Party officials let union leaders approve or veto election strategies in statewide campaigns" in 1996.[1] Yet, when a Federal Elections Commission investigation unearthed documents revealing the extent of ties between the unions and the Democratic Party, the unions sought a court injunction to conceal the information from the public, arguing that it constituted "proprietary information."

I have decided to try to do something about such abuses. Shortly after my failed labor secretary nomination, I began to explore the creation of a new organization that would tackle this problem head-on. In spring 2001, I formed Stop Union Political Abuse (SUPA), a grassroots effort to monitor political expenditures by trade unions—direct and indirect political contributions, as well as secret activities like the ones I'd witnessed at the AFT. In addition, the organization will monitor the federal government's own efforts to regulate union political activity through the Federal Elections Commission, the Internal Revenue Service, the National Labor Relations Board, and the Department of Labor.

A 1988 Supreme Court ruling known as the *Beck* decision gave workers the right to recoup that portion of mandatory union dues spent on activities unrelated to collective bargaining or union representation.[2] However, the decision has been widely ignored, and President Bush's efforts to enforce it are now tied up in the courts. In my view, the *Beck* decision—even if properly enforced—doesn't go far enough. Therefore, SUPA has drafted federal legislation that would prevent unions from collecting money for anything other than collective bargaining and contract administration—unless they do so entirely through voluntary donations. In January 2002, Congressman Tom Tancredo, a Republican from Colorado, introduced H.R. 3632, the Workers' Freedom of Choice Act. I believe that passage of this legislation would have more impact on cleaning up campaign abuses than any amount of "campaign finance reform," which restricts individual citizens' voluntary contributions while doing almost nothing to control unions' use of coerced union dues for political purposes with which members may not even agree.

When I was nominated by President Bush for secretary of labor, *Wall Street Journal* columnist Paul Gigot described me as the AFL-CIO's "worst nightmare."[3] In fact, I don't consider myself anti-union. I believe workers have the right to form unions to promote their own interests. But I am opposed to forcing anyone to pay to support political candidates or issues with which they disagree. Although about 40 percent of union members vote for Republican candidates for federal offices, nearly 98 percent of union contributions go to Democratic candidates or the Democratic Party directly, and much of this money comes out of union dues. Unions are the only institution that uses involuntary funds for political purposes with impunity—and on a scale that has a corrupting influence on American politics.

I think it's time for this practice to end, and I will work to see that it does. I may not have become the AFL-CIO's worst nightmare as secretary of labor—but I intend to remain a thorn in their side.

Notes

PROLOGUE: ON TOP OF THE WORLD

1. Stefan Gleason, "Laboring for a Solution," *Washington Times,* February 20, 2001, A17. Rutgers University professor Leo Troy testified that labor unions spent at least $500 million on in-kind and "soft money" donations in the 1996 elections as well. See statement of Professor Leo Troy, Committee on House Oversight, U.S. House of Representatives, March 21, 1996.
2. Hobart Rowan, "Mondale's Turn to Right Leaves Party Empty Handed," *Washington Post,* November 11, 1984.
3. See John Aloysius Farrell, "Baird's Nomination in Peril," *Boston Globe,* January 22, 1993. Senator Edward M. Kennedy noted at the time that Baird's admission "struck a very raw nerve" in America, which produced a deluge of phone calls and letters against the nominee. Baird withdrew her name when it was apparent that she could not be confirmed. Clinton's second nominee, Judge Kimba Woods, fared no better. Woods's babysitter had also been an illegal alien when Woods initially hired her, but by the time of Woods's nomination, the woman was in the process of becoming a legal resident. Nonetheless, Woods withdrew her name when the first stories about the babysitter appeared. After Baird and Woods, politicians became obsessed with ferreting out so-called nanny problems among political appointees.
4. Linda Chavez, "Immigration Politics 1996," *International Economy,* November/December 1993.
5. Whitman revealed her "nanny problem" during her race for governor of New Jersey in 1993, but since her opponent had also hired illegal aliens in the past, neither was penalized by the voters.

CHAPTER 1   SKELETONS IN THE CLOSET

1. Throughout this book I use the terms Mexican American, Hispanic, and Latino interchangeably. Although I grew up thinking of myself as Spanish, as did most of those persons of my generation whose ancestors came to New Mexico from Spain via Mexico in the seventeenth and early eighteenth century, I adopted the conventional "Mexican American" to describe myself as an adult. Although Hispanic and Latino both refer to any of the two dozen national origin groups from Latin America, the term Latino has become the more "politically correct" usage.
2. Zora Neale Hurston, *The World Tomorrow* (Library of America: New York, 1995), 829.
3. Lee May, "Linda Chavez Has Eye on White House," *Los Angeles Times,* October 28, 1988.

4. Nearly a decade after I graduated, however, Denver became the center of a major school desegregation case in 1973, *Keyes v. School District No. 1*, in which the Supreme Court accepted the novel theory of the lower court that school board decisions affecting only a handful of schools could actually *cause* segregated housing patterns to occur across the city. The courts ordered a citywide busing system, which contributed heavily to white flight from Denver, as forced busing did nearly everywhere it was tried.

5. Mexican American militants adopted the term "Chicano" to refer to themselves in the 1960s. I use the term where appropriate in that context.

6. Ernesto B. Vigil, *The Crusade for Justice: Chicano Militancy and the Government's War on Dissent* (Madison: University of Wisconsin Press, 1999), 18–21, from which this account is adapted.

CHAPTER 2   FROM TEENAGE BRIDE TO CAMPUS ACTIVIST

1. For ease of reading, I've adopted the phonetic Yipsel, for the acronym YPSL of the Young People's Socialist League.

2. Stephan Thernstrom and Abigail Thernstrom, *America in Black and White: One Nation, Indivisible* (New York: Simon and Schuster, 1997), 158–161.

3. See Vigil, *The Crusade for Justice*, 27.

CHAPTER 3   AFFIRMATIVE ACTION NIGHTMARE

1. Elaine Brown, *A Taste of Power: A Black Woman's Story* (New York: Pantheon Books, 1992), 165.

2. Helene D. Hutchison, ed., *Mixed Bag: Artifacts from the Contemporary Culture* (Glenview, Illinois: Scott Foresman, 1970).

3. Ibid., 150.

4. See Vigil, *The Crusade for Justice*, 133–183.

5. The acronym stands for Movimiento Estudiantil Chicano de Aztlan, founded in the late 1960s at the University of California.

6. Rodolfo Gonzales, "I Am Joaquin: An Epic Poem" (Washington, D.C.: Library of Congress, 1991).

CHAPTER 4   WATERGATE, NIXON, AND ME

1. Ronald Radosh, *Divided They Fell: The Demise of the Democratic Party, 1964–1996* (New York: Free Press, 1996), 135.

2. Ibid., 139.

3. See Thernstrom and Thernstrom, *America in Black and White*, 330–335.

4. See Tony Castro, *Chicano Power* (New York: E. P. Dutton, 1974), 198–214.

5. The committee was previously known as the Interagency Committee on Mexican American Affairs, but it had been elevated by Congress to "cabinet committee" status, which meant that cabinet secretaries or their designees sat on the committee, and its purview extended to other Hispanic groups, namely Puerto Ricans and Cubans.

6. See Hugh Davis Graham, *The Civil Rights Era: Origins and Development of National Policy* (New York: Oxford University Press, 1990), 136–139.

7. Betty Friedan, *The Feminine Mystique* (New York: Dell, 1984), 305.

8. Simone de Beauvoir, *The Second Sex* (New York: Alfred A. Knopf, 1993), 94.

9. Although Armendariz and I were political adversaries in the 1970s, over the next twenty years we became quite friendly. After I wrote *Out of the Barrio* in 1991, Armendariz called me and asked whether I might be interested in having his collection of books on Mexican American issues. He was moving and had no space for them, so I happily collected a box of now out-of-print books, some of which I consulted in preparing this memoir. Alex Armendariz died in 1992.

10. The best description of Nixon's Chicano strategy is contained in Castro, *Chicano Power*, 198–214.
11. Ibid., 294–295.
12. Thernstrom and Thernstrom, *America in Black and White*, 425.

CHAPTER 5   THE EVOLUTION OF A NEOCONSERVATIVE

1. See especially Max Green, *Epitaph for American Labor: How Union Leaders Lost Touch with America* (Washington, D.C.: AEI Press, 1996), 39.
2. See Chapter 1.
3. "Snobsville, not Nashville," *New America*, September 15, 1975, 10.
4. As it happened, the 1975–1976 fiscal crisis that nearly forced New York City into bankruptcy occupied a great deal of the AFT's political energy and my own time as an AFT lobbyist. And despite Shanker's disdain of my former boss, Don Edwards, my years on the subcommittee proved very useful to the AFT during the crisis. In 1975, the city was in dire economic straits, having basically binged for more than a decade on municipal spending to build housing, fund generous welfare programs, provide tuition-free education at City University, set cheap bus and subway fares, and keep the city's municipal unions—including Shanker's own UFT—happy. But it had done so all on borrowed money. By the time Abe Beame became mayor in 1974, the city faced a $1.5 billion deficit in a $10 billion budget. Finally, the banks and bond markets that had lent the city money over the years balked, nearly forcing the city to declare bankruptcy. The only thing that saved the city—as Shanker told it—was the UFT's decision to use its pension funds to make loans to the city. In fact, the New York City bailout included many other components, including loans from three other municipal unions, a $2.5 billion federal loan guarantee, and most importantly, the creation of the Municipal Assistance Corporation, headed by investment banker Felix G. Rohatyn, which sold bonds to raise money for the city.
5. Margarita was a legal U.S. resident, though in 1976 no one even asked such questions, since it was not against the law to hire illegal aliens at the time. The law changed with the passage of the Immigration Reform and Control Act of 1986, which went into effect one year after it was passed.
6. HEW was reorganized later in 1978, with the education functions going to a newly created Department of Education and the health and welfare responsibilities left in the renamed Department of Health and Human Services.
7. Adam Smith, *The Wealth of Nations* (New York: Random House, 1965), 423.
8. Albert Shanker, "Where We Stand," *New York Times*, September 25, 1977, as reprinted in *American Educator*, Vol. 21, Nos. 1 and 2 (Spring/Summer 1997): 41. Shanker wrote most of his own columns, pecking them out on an old manual typewriter every Thursday afternoon.
9. Ibid., 31.
10. Published by the liberal American Jewish Committee, *Commentary* magazine has been for several decades the leading journal of neoconservative thought on a variety of foreign policy and domestic issues. At the time Shanker made this statement, the magazine was edited by neoconservative author and intellectual Norman Podhoretz.
11. Bennett would later become chairman of the National Endowment of Humanities and Secretary of Education in the Reagan administration; Jeanne J. Kirkpatrick later became U.S. ambassador to the United Nations in the Reagan administration; and Robert Bork, a federal appeals court judge at the time he wrote for me, was later nominated by President Reagan to the U.S. Supreme Court but failed to be confirmed by the Senate in a highly contentious confirmation fight. Thomas Sowell, a fellow at the

Hoover Institution, remains one of the leading black conservative intellectuals in the country, while James Stockdale was the Reform Party vice presidential nominee in 1992, and Diane Ravitch, an education historian, became assistant secretary of education in the Bush administration.

12. William Bennett, "The Homosexual Teacher," *American Educator*, Vol. 2, No. 3 (Fall 1978): 21–24.

13. See Linda Chavez, "Teaching About Nuclear War," *American Educator*, Vol. 7, No. 3 (Fall 1983): 16–21.

14. "Children from One-Parent Families: The Schools' Newest Problem-Ridden Minority," *American Educator*, Vol. 4, No. 4 (Winter 1980): 12.

15. William J. Bennett, "Teaching the Young About Sex," *American Educator*, Vol. 4, No. 4 (Winter 1980): 22.

16. Robert G. Kaiser, "Carter's Campaign Stalls," *Washington Post*, October 8, 1980, A1.

17. David converted to Catholicism in 2002, along with his wife.

CHAPTER 6   BATTLING THE CIVIL RIGHTS ESTABLISHMENT

1. "Unionist Rebuffs Praise of China Schools," *Denver Post*, December 8, 1977, 38.

2. Neither Shanker nor I approved of President Reagan's controversial decision to reverse a decade-old decision on tax-exempt status for schools that practiced racial discrimination. In 1970, President Richard Nixon had directed the IRS to revoke the tax-exempt status of private schools that discriminated, but the new Reagan administration argued that the IRS lacked statutory authority to do so. Bob Jones University, a private college that prohibited interracial dating, sued the government, and the Reagan administration stance supported the university's position. The decision provoked a storm of protest, and the Reagan administration quickly proposed legislation to give the IRS the authority it said the agency lacked, but it was too late. The Reagan administration had earned the deep enmity of the civil rights community—and its position was eventually rejected by the U.S. Supreme Court, which upheld the IRS's authority by an eight-to-one decision.

3. See Howard Schuman, Charlotte Steeh, and Lawrence Bobo, *Racial Attitudes in America: Trends and Interpretations* (Cambridge: Harvard University Press, 1985), 75.

4. The quotes here come from several contemporary news sources, including Juan Williams, "Reagan's Civil Rights Commission Nominees Have Fiery Hearing," *Washington Post*, July 14, 1983, A3.

5. I never used the car to take me to or from home, except once, in my final week at the commission, and then only with the blessing of the solicitor of the agency. I became ill at work, and my assistant called the solicitor to inquire whether the car could be used to take me home since it was being used to transport my personal papers and books there that day anyway. He gave his okay, but I was later accused by the General Accounting Office, the investigative arm of Congress, of routinely using the car for personal use—a charge I flatly denied. When the GAO could find no evidence that I had improperly used the car and could offer no dates or anything else to corroborate its charge, it said: "Charges were made that the Commission's automobile was used for other than official purposes such as transporting the Staff Director between her home and work. . . . [The driver] stated that the automobile was used only for official purposes during that time. Without the missing trip logs, we could not verify that the Commission automobile was used only for official purposes while it was stationed at Commission headquarters or its warehouse." General Accounting Office, *The Operations of the United States Commission on Civil Rights*, (Washington, D.C.: Government Printing Office, 1986), 88–90.

6. United States Commission on Civil Rights, "Statute, Rules, and Regulations" (Washington, D.C.: Government Printing Office, 1980).

7. Robert Pear, "New U.S. Rights Aide Backs Whites for Jobs in Memphis," *New York Times*, September 11, 1983, A24.

8. Felicity Barringer, "Rights Panel Attacks U.S. Stand in Memphis Case," *Washington Post*, September 13, 1983, A17.

9. Pear, "New U.S. Rights Aide Backs Whites."

10. See Linda Greenhouse, "Seniority Held to Outweigh Race as Layoff Guide," *New York Times*, June 12, 1984, A1.

11. "Commissioners for Life?" *Washington Post*, August 8, 1983, A12.

12. "Transcript of Address by President on Lebanon and Grenada," *New York Times*, October 28, 1983, A10.

13. "An Interview with Mary Berry," *American Educator*, Vol. 1, No. 4 (December 1977): 23.

14. Mary Frances Berry and John W. Blassingame, *Long Memory: The Black Experience in America* (New York: Oxford University Press, 1962), 224.

15. William Raspberry, "Gutting the Civil Rights Commission," *Washington Post*, October 31, 1983, A13.

16. George Lardner Jr., "Compromise Apparently Reconstitutes Civil Rights Commission," *Washington Post*, November 11, 1983, A14.

17. Senator Hubert Humphrey, one of the original cosponsors of the Civil Rights Act of 1964, died in 1978.

18. Robert Pear, "Aides Doubt Reagan Is Planning to Rename Rights Panel Member," *New York Times*, December 2, 1983, A25.

19. See Harris Wofford, *Of Kennedys and Kings: Making Sense of the Sixties* (Pittsburgh: University of Pittsburgh Press, 1980), 134.

20. Robert Pear, "Two Appointees Fill U.S. Rights Panel," *New York Times*, December 16, A9.

21. Robert Pear, "New Director of U.S. Rights Panel Calls for Major Change of Course," *New York Times*, January 6, 1984, A1.

22. Juan Williams, "Rights Panel Urged to Change Emphasis," *Washington Post*, January 7, 1984, A1.

23. "The Civil Rights Commission as Parrot," *New York Times*, January 25, 1984, A24.

24. "The Civil Rights Dispute," *Washington Post*, January 20, 1984, A20.

25. Technically, the commission held a "consultation" on the comparable worth issue, not a formal hearing, which would have required that the commission issue subpoenas and swear in witnesses. Consultations were a slightly less formal mechanism, but both hearings and consultations led to the same kind of reports of findings and recommendations, which were then passed on to the president and Congress.

26. William Raspberry, "Linda Chavez Is Right," *Washington Post*, June 22, 1984, A19.

27. Peter Perl, "Rights Chief Derides 'Comparable Worth,'" *Washington Post*, November 17, 1984, A6.

28. *American Federation of State, County and Municipal Employees* v. *State of Washington*, 770 F.2d 1401 (9th Cir. 1985).

29. Watt resigned in October 1983, after making a series of gaffes, including once referring to the members of a federal advisory committee as a black, a woman, "two Jews and a cripple," and Burford resigned in March 1983 under fire for withholding documents from congressional investigators looking into how toxic waste cleanup funds were being used.

30. David Hoffman, "Rights Panel Director Eyed for Liaison Post: Staff Changes Seen at White House," *Washington Post*, January 31, 1985, A4.

31. U.S. Commission on Civil Rights, "Comparable Worth: An Analysis and Recommendations" (Washington, D.C.: Government Printing Office, June 1985), 70–72.

32. W. Dale Nelson, "Linda Chavez: Another Democrat in the White House," Associated Press, April 16, 1985.

CHAPTER 7   A WOMAN'S PLACE IN THE REAGAN WHITE HOUSE

1. David Hoffman, "Mistakes in Two Capitals Said to Have Led to Bitburg Outcry; Three Decisions Fused Political Bombshell," *Washington Post*, May 1, 1985, A13.

2. See "Reagan Tells of Respect for War Victims," *Los Angeles Times*, April 14, 1985, 1.

3. These and other recollections from my White House days come from contemporaneous notes I took while director of public liaison.

4. See Rudy Abramson, "Reagan Trip to Include Death Camp; Emotional Appeal to Cancel Visit to Cemetery Rejected," *Los Angeles Times*, April 20, 1985, 1.

5. Philip Shenon, "For Wiesel, the End of Two Long Days of a 'Nightmare and Disbelief,'" *New York Times*, April 20, 1985, 4.

6. Years later, Ward Connerly experienced a similar incident. Vice President Al Gore did the same thing to him when Connerly, I, and six others met with Gore and President Bill Clinton in the Oval Office in 1997, which Connerly wrote about in his memoir, *Creating Equal: My Fight Against Racial Preferences.*

7. Debate still rages about Demjanjuk's guilt, with the Department of Justice insisting that Demjanjuk was indeed a war criminal who participated in heinous acts while working as a death camp guard in World War II.

8. Joshua Muravchik, who has written the most thorough analysis of Buchanan's positions, quoted Buchanan as admitting that he had changed positions on Israel: "Buchanan allowed that 'yes, a change has taken place' in his attitude toward Israel as compared with the time 'from June of 1967 . . . until I went back into the White House in 1985 [when] I was an uncritical apologist for Israel.'" See Joshua Muravchik, "Patrick J. Buchanan and the Jews," *Commentary*, Vol. 91, No. 1 (January 1991): 29–37. But Muravchik said, "It is true that in earlier years Buchanan had produced columns friendly to Israel, but he was certainly never 'an uncritical apologist.'"

9. Bob Davis, "Protectionism Underlies 'Buchanomics': Patrick Buchanan Argues That History Shows High Tariffs and Bars on Immigration Are Keys to Economic Prosperity," *Portland Press Herald*, February 23, 1996, 2A.

10. Ibid.

11. Martin Pomerance, "How Much Access Do Jews Have to the White House, and Which Jews Have It? A Deaf Ear," *Palm Beach Jewish World*, August 23–29, 1985.

12. "U.S. Policies Assailed at Women's Parley," *Chicago Tribune*, July 18, 1985, 10.

13. "Reagan Aide Counters Charge of Imperialism," Associated Press, July 18, 1995. Of course, Vietnam's invasion of Cambodia in 1979 halted the horrendous genocidal policies of the Pol Pot regime, which killed an estimated 2 million people, a fact that the State Department officials who drafted my statement didn't mention. Instead of withdrawing once the situation became more stable and Pol Pot was ousted, the Vietnamese continued their occupation for some ten years.

14. Blaine Hardin, "U.S. Delegates in Nairobi Back Feminist Moves: U.N. Conference to Back 'Equal Value' of Work," *Washington Post*, July 20, 1985, A15.

15. See Graham, *The Civil Rights Era*, Chapter 7.

16. See Thernstrom and Thernstrom, *America in Black and White*, 428.

17. These quotations were derived from the official minutes of the Domestic Policy Council meeting of October 22, 1985, prepared by Staff Secretary David L. Chew.

18. "Reagan Expected to Retain Affirmative Action Order," *Los Angeles Times*, December 10, 1985, 1.
19. Donnie Radcliffe, "Nancy Reagan's Peak Role; Public Image-Building and Private Advice at Geneva," *Washington Post*, November 18, 1985, B1.
20. Pat Buchanan was proud of his record of putting women in positions of responsibility. When the *Washington Post* was doing a piece on the Regan flap, Pat wrote me a memo: "Lois Romano of the *Post*—following up on the very thoughtful observations of the Chief of Staff—is doing a Jane Mayer [a *Wall Street Journal* reporter who had earlier written a critical piece on sexism in the Reagan White House] type piece on women in the White House. Should be exciting. Can you get together with me briefly on this— as they will surely be calling you. Points to make. In Communications, four of the six 'shops' are headed by women.... Of the 12 Commissioned Officers in Communications—50 percent are women...."

Chapter 8   On the Campaign Trail

1. Sandra Sugawara, "Chavez Urges Kidnap of Terrorist; Maryland Senate Hopeful Unveils BWI Security Study," *Washington Post*, May 9, 1986, B3.
2. Michel McQueen and Sandra Sugawara, "Quiz Stumps Md. Candidates; Chavez Shines While 16 Rivals Blush," *Washington Post*, July 25, 1986, A1.
3. Tom Kenworthy and Michel McQueen, "Schaefer, Mikulski Win in Md.; GOP Nominates Chavez for Senate Race; Turnout Is Modest," *Washington Post*, September 10, 1986, A1.
4. I was speaking off-the-cuff, so there is no written text to confirm my memory; however, several news organizations covered the speech, including the Associated Press and E. J. Dionne for the *New York Times*, who quoted the longer phrase. See E. J. Dionne "Maryland Voters Choose Two Women," *New York Times*, September 10, 1986, A15; Terrence P. Hunt "Motherhood Becomes Issue in Woman-Vs-Woman Senate Race," Associated Press, September 10, 1986.
5. "Convention in Dallas; The Republicans; Text of Jeane J. Kirkpatrick's Remarks at Republican Convention in Dallas," *New York Times*, August 21, 1984, A22.
6. Michel McQueen, Tom Kenworthy, "Impolitic Politics? Chavez Tactic Upsets Some in Md. GOP," *Washington Post*, October 26, 1986, C1.

Chapter 9   How I Became the Most Hated Hispanic in America

1. Edward Cody, "With Latins in Miami, the Melting Pot Melts," *Washington Post*, May 14, 1983, A1.
2. See "Evaluation of the Impact of ESEA Title VII Spanish/English Bilingual Education Program" (Palo Alto, California: American Institutes for Research, 1978).
3. Not all teachers supported bilingual education. In August 1987, the United Teachers of Los Angeles, an affiliate of the AFT, voted 78 to 22 percent to replace bilingual education programs with English immersion. The vote had only symbolic impact, however. Not until 1998 did California abolish bilingual education, and then with an initiative measure put to the state voters.
4. The Arizona amendment, alone among twenty-seven amendments passed in other states, was declared unconstitutional by the state supreme court. In a separate federal case, a state employee sued to be able to use Spanish on the job, even though her supervisors were non-Spanish-speaking. The U.S. Supreme Court ultimately ruled that the case was moot since the plaintiff no longer worked for the state, allowing the court to avoid ruling on the merits of the First Amendment challenge to the Arizona amendment.

5. Lee May, "Linda Chavez Has Eye on White House," *Los Angeles Times*, October 28, 1988, View Section, 1.

6. Raul Yzaguirre, speech to the Leadership Conference on Civil Rights Fortieth Anniversary Dinner, May 8, 1990.

7. Linda Chavez, *Out of the Barrio: Toward a New Politics of Hispanic Assimilation* (New York: Basic Books, 1991), 159.

8. Carol Innerst, "Campus Climate: Chavez Encounters Big Chill," *Washington Times*, May 4, 1990, A1.

9. John Leo, "The Espresso Uprising," *U.S. News and World Report*, May 6, 1996, 23.

10. Anna Maria Arias, "Making People Mad," *Hispanic*, August 1992, 11–16.

11. For an excellent discussion of the skills gap, see Thernstrom and Thernstrom, *America in Black and White*, 348–360.

CHAPTER 10   CAUGHT IN THE MEDIA CROSSHAIRS

1. Paul West and Ellen Gamerman, "Bush Puts Final Touches on Cabinet," *Baltimore Sun*, January 3, 2001, 1A.

2. Laura Meckler, "Chavez's Writings Arming Critics," Associated Press, January 4, 2001.

3. John J. Miller and Ramesh Ponnuru, "Inapt AP: A Dishonest Attack on Linda Chavez," *National Review Online*, January 5, 2001.

4. "The ADA: A Law Gone Haywire," *Chicago Tribune*, February 18, 1998.

5. In a highly unusual move, the Associated Press eventually printed a modification of its original piece, "AP Clarifies Chavez Story," admitting that its earlier story "failed to give the full context of her position on the Americans with Disabilities Act when it quoted her as calling the law 'special treatment in the name of accommodating the disabled.'" Associated Press, January 11, 2001.

6. "Sexual Harassment Game Is Getting Out of Hand," *Milwaukee Journal Sentinel*, August 3, 1996.

7. Skerry was on a backpacking trip at the time the story about Marta broke. The *New York Times* later reported: "Peter Skerry, who worked at the American Enterprise Institute at the time, said his cleaning woman had asked him in 1991 about finding shelter for a friend, Ms. Mercado, who was being abused by an alcoholic husband. Mr. Skerry broached the issue with Ms. Chavez. 'We raised it with her because we knew she lived in a large house in the Maryland suburbs and had taken in people before,' Mr. Skerry said." Steven A. Holmes and Frank Bruni, "Chavez Cites Bush's Silence in Her Decision to Withdraw," *New York Times*, January 11, 2001.

8. Eric Schmitt, "One-Time Illegal Immigrant Chavez Sheltered Recalls Painful Past," *New York Times*, February 8, 2001.

9. John J. Miller, "The Chavez Debacle: A Personal Account," *National Review*, February 5, 2001.

10. Letter from Jon Garcia, January 8, 2001.

11. Thomas B. Edsall, "Chavez Is Under Fire over Illegal Immigrant; Guatemalan Lived in Designee's House," *Washington Post*, January 8, 2001, A1.

12. See Grover Joseph Rees, "Immigration Law Run Amok Claims Another Victim," *Wall Street Journal*, January 11, 2001.

13. In every statement Marta made to the press, and in her FBI interview, a copy of which I obtained under the Freedom of Information Act, she maintained—even when pressed to say otherwise—that she viewed me as a friend, not an employer, and that the financial and other assistance I gave her was not in return for work. See, for example, CBS News Transcripts, January 8, 2001; CNN Early Edition Transcript No. 01010902V08.

14. "Statement of AFT President Sandra Feldman Regarding Linda Chavez," January 8, 2001.

15. Like me, Bush chose not to volunteer the information. On a jury questionnaire given to him when he was called as a potential juror in 1996, he left the question about arrest records blank, and he had Gonzales argue on separate grounds that he should not serve. Bush was evasive about the issue throughout his public career. In 1998, *Dallas Morning News* reporter Wayne Slater asked Bush about his arrest record after information became public about another arrest in 1966 for disorderly conduct in a trivial incident while Bush was a student at Yale. "Asked whether he had been arrested on anything 'after 1968,'" Slater wrote, "the governor replied, 'No.'" Slater recalled that Bush seemed ready to change his response when Karen Hughes, his spokeswoman, stopped the conversation. See Carlos Gerra, "Dubya's DUI Raises Bigger Questions," *San Antonio Express News*, November 5, 2000, 1B.

16. The next morning, Clay Johnson called to apologize that I hadn't been told in advance that he wouldn't be there, as had been originally promised, citing a conflict on his schedule.

17. Margarita Valladares had been Margarita Mejia when I originally hired her in 1977, but she had married a few years later, taking the name Valladares.

18. Federal Document Clearing House, Inc., "Linda Chavez Holds News Conference," January 9, 2001.

19. "A Speedy Exit for Linda Chavez," *New York Times*, January 10, 2001.

20. "Notebook," *New Republic*, January 22, 2001, 8.

21. Stuart Taylor, "Smearing Linda Chavez," *National Journal*, January 20, 2001.

22. Robert D. Novak, "The Assault on Linda Chavez," *Washington Post*, January 11, 2001.

23. Although the FBI interview with Zwisler is heavily redacted, several statements survived the FBI's excisions.

EPILOGUE: THORN IN THEIR SIDE

1. John Solomon and Larry Margasak, "Documents That Democrats Want Kept Secret Detail Coordinated Political Work with Unions," Associated Press, July 20, 2001.

2. *Communication Workers of America* v. *Beck* (1988).

3. Paul Gigot, "Bush's Cabinet Has Mortgages and Agendas," *Wall Street Journal*, January 5, 2001.

Index